The Coming of the Mass Market

Other books by W. Hamish Fraser

Trade Unions and Society: The Struggle for Acceptance, 1850–1880 (1974)

Workers and Employers: Documents on Trade Unions and Industrial Relations in Britain Since the Eighteenth Century, co-edited with J. T. Ward (1980)

The Coming of the
Mass Market, 1850–1914

W. HAMISH FRASER

First published 1981 by
THE MACMILLAN PRESS LTD
London and Basingstoke
Companies and representatives
throughout the world

Photoset, printed and bound in Great Britain by
REDWOOD BURN LIMITED
Trowbridge & Esher

ISBN 0 333 31033 0 (hc)
ISBN 0 333 310349 (pbk)

Contents

List of Plates

Acknowledgements

For anyone working in a university the debt to one's colleagues and students, built up over many years, is incalculable. I would, however, like to make special mention of Professor John Butt, who first suggested this to me as a possible topic for a book, and of Dr Gordon Jackson, who lent books and provided information on a whole variety of topics. He kindly let me see his most useful manuscript on the Humber ports, which proved invaluable when I was writing about the fishing industry. Another colleague, Mr John Hume, was an unfailing source of information on Scottish industries. Particular thanks are due to Dr J. H. Treble. Not only did Dr Treble read a substantial part of the manuscript, but, as a result of his own studies on urban poverty, regularly provided an antidote to any over-optimistic interpretations of the standard of living of the working class.

Librarians, particularly at the National Library of Scotland, at the Universities of Glasgow and Strathclyde, and at the British Library have, on almost all occasions, provided a splendid service. My typist, Mrs Jean Fraser, not only produced an excellent manuscript, helped bring order into the footnotes and even corrected blatant errors, but she displayed an encouraging enthusiasm for what she was reading, for which I was very grateful. Special thanks are due to her. At Macmillan Sarah Mahaffy and Susan Dickinson have, as in the past, been considerate and helpful with the editing.

All of these and others have contributed to what is worthwhile in the book. Any remaining errors, infelicities and misunderstandings are entirely my own.

Finally, thanks are due to my wife Helen, who, although not a historian, has generally succeeded in maintaining an impression of interest and enthusiasm for the subject of the growth of the mass market over many years. The love and gratitude due to her can never be adequately expressed.

August, 1981   W. H. F.

For my daughter, Louisa Mairi

Introduction

This book examines how the mass of the British people spent their money in the decades after 1850, when a substantial majority of them had more to spend than ever before, and how commerce and industry adjusted to deal with the increased demand. In spite of problems and setbacks for many and the persistence of deep-seated poverty, for most people the late nineteenth century brought a real improvement in living standards. The British people were able to concern themselves with more than mere subsistence; they had a surplus to spend on more and better food, on a wider range of clothing, on more elaborate furnishing for their homes and on a greater variety of leisure pursuits. For the first time most people had a *choice* of how and where to spend their money. The first part of this book is concerned with the kinds of choices that were made.

Consumers were discontented with the lack of choice and the poor quality of goods generally available in existing shops, but it took time for the necessary adjustments in distribution to be accomplished. In Part Two the revolution in retailing that this brought about is examined. New kinds of retailing outlets were developed to meet a new kind of demand, and traditional shops had to learn from the multiples, the co-operatives and the department stores how to respond to the needs of new customers.

If this growing demand, stimulated by advertising and modern sales techniques, were to be satisfied, then changes had to take place in the manufacturing industries as well as in the service sector. Part Three is concerned with the transformation of particular industries: food processing, the production of clothing, furnishing and household goods and the whole range of industries which emerged to satisfy a growing desire to be entertained. To meet demand output was increased by changes in technology and organisation and by the introduction of a variety of new products. In other cases new industries were set up to grasp the new opportunities. Britain went through a second great phase of industrialisation, with the coming of factory production in those consumer industries whose techniques had been largely untouched by the classic industrial revolution. In addition a whole new leisure industry was created as more and more people found time and money for reading, going on holiday, taking exercise or just sitting enjoying themselves in music hall and cinema. More traditional pastimes, like drinking or going to the races, had to be modernised if they were to meet the challenge of this greater choice.

The developments examined here are only part of a massive transformation of the *world* economy which was taking place in these crucial decades. Foodstuffs, raw materials and many manufactured goods were being drawn from all corners of the globe. For this to happen there had to be an effective and cheap transport network and a sophisticated financial and commercial system. Major changes also had to be made in the production of basic products like coal, iron, steel, rubber and cement. Much of the expansion of output and many of the changes in industrial organisation were only made possible by the increased availability of gas and electrical power. While all of these are obviously related to the changes that are being examined in this book, they have to be beyond its compass. The intention is to focus on those aspects of economic change which most directly affected people as consumers and laid the foundations of the mass market.

Part I
The Growth of Demand

1. Numbers

The England of the past has been an England of reserved, silent men, dispersed in small towns, villages and country homes. The England of the future is an England packed tightly in such gigantic aggregations of population as the world has never seen before.
C. F. G. Masterman, *The Heart of the Empire* (1901).

Broadly, there are three ways in which demand for goods can increase: firstly through an increase in numbers; secondly through an increase in spending power; and thirdly through a change in fashion or taste, whereby what was formerly spent on one particular set of goods is now spent on some other set. For all three reasons demand for goods and services increased substantially in Britain in the years after the Great Exhibition. To meet this demand industry had to expand and to be restructured; distribution had to be accelerated and made more efficient; taste had to be guided, and demand for one particular product in preference to another had to be stimulated. The outcome was a striking alteration in the life style of the bulk of the British population, and a major transformation of the nation's industries.

Births and Deaths

When the fifth decennial census was taken in 1851 there were over 27 million persons in the United Kingdom: 18 million of them in England and Wales, under 3 million in Scotland and over 6 million in Ireland. Sixty years later the total number had increased to over 45 million and the populations of Scotland and Ireland were more or less equal at around 4·5 million each. In other words by 1911 there were 18 million more mouths to feed, bodies to house and clothe, tastes to satisfy and demands for fashion to pamper than there had been in 1851. To do this, industry and services had to go on growing and adjusting even more than they had been doing in the hundred years before 1851. It

3

was in the eighteenth century that the population began to grow with unprecedented rapidity. In part this resulted from that complexity of events which can so conveniently, if not necessarily illuminatingly, be covered by the terms 'agricultural revolution' and 'industrial revolution'; in part it was the cause of both.

At the first census in 1801 there had been almost 9 million people in England and Wales and almost 2 million in Scotland, and over the next century the population grew by anything from 12 to 18 per cent each decade. Even in the first decade of the twentieth century the increase was over one per cent per year. A myriad of factors – geographical, political, religious, psychological, social, with perhaps more than a fair share of luck – had come together in the right order and at the right time to prevent such a rate of population growth bringing in its wake the Malthusian checks of disease, pestilence and famine. Disasters were not avoided entirely, and a century of agricultural and industrial change did not prevent a million of the nation's people starving to death in Ireland in the five years between 1845 and 1850. Death rates of 30 per 1000 and more had been the price paid for the rapid concentration of population in the wynds, rookeries and closes of the cities. But, by the second half of the century, the struggle against being overwhelmed by sheer weight of numbers had been won and industrialism, having fended off starvation, now brought improved standards of living, not for all, but for most of the population.

By 1881 the crude death rate which had proved so difficult to cut was under 20 per 1000; twenty years later it was under 17 per 1000; and by 1914 it was around 14 per 1000. The work of Edwin Chadwick and John Simon, the devotion of overburdened Medical Officers of Health, the researches of medical men, the education in sanitation which the terror caused by four cholera epidemics in forty years had given, began to have their impact at last. Fewer young people died in their prime, more survived from middle age into old age. Only the very young were still overwhelmingly vulnerable. In the last fifteen years of the nineteenth century the national rate of infant mortality rose quite sharply to a peak of 163 per 1000 in 1899, concealing rates that ranged from a mere 73 per 1000 in Oxfordshire to a staggering 242 per 1000 in some of the central wards of Manchester. Ignorance of methods of child care, of the dangers of infection through want of cleanliness, of all but basic knowledge on diet, all linked with appalling poverty, had ensured that throughout the century enteric diseases had taken their toll of infants. Some sought to use the rise in infant death rate at the end of the century as a stick with which to beat the working mother, who, in her rush to take advantage of the new job opportunities for women, was abandoning breast feeding in favour of nutritionally inadequate condensed milk. It is doubtful if such criticisms were really justified. In surveys taken in the first decade of the twentieth century it was found that well over 80 per cent of working-class mothers breast-fed their babies for the first three months and well over 60 per cent for up to six months.[1] If breast-feeding was in decline it was among the middle class. Not until after 1906 did the government give backing to efforts to reduce the infant death rate. Ante-natal and post-natal clinics were established in a number of areas, with marked effect upon the local death rate. By 1914 the rate of infant mortality had been brought down to 105 per 1000, despite the persistence of levels more than twice that in Lancashire towns like Burnley, Wigan, Preston, Oldham and Blackburn.

Large as the increase of population was in the second half of the nineteenth century, it was not the 'explosion' that such a fall in the death rate by itself would have occasioned. In the 1860s and 1870s many neo-Malthusians, like John Stuart Mill and Charles Bradlaugh, believed that the battle against numbers was not yet won, and that Malthus's sombre prophecies of population overwhelming resources could still be fulfilled. For it was in the 1860s that the birth rate first passed 35 per 1000 and in the mid-1870s it was over 36 per 1000. But again disaster was avoided by the decisions of thousands of couples to have fewer children than their parents had had. The birth-rate curve peaked in 1876 at 36·3 births per 1000 and from then on the trend was sharply downwards: 34·2 in 1880, 30·2 in 1890, 28·7 in 1900, 23·8 in 1914.

Family Size

No social development of the last century has been so important for the welfare of the country's inhabitants as this phenomenon of the reduction in family size. Although more people were marrying than ever before, by a conscious decision they were having smaller families. The average couple of the 1860s and 1870s had between five and six children, but these children in their turn had under five and those couples marrying in the first decade of the present century were to have just over three children on average. In analysing this phenomenon, however, it is difficult to differentiate between cause and effect. It was a product of a better standard of living and contributed to a better standard of living. It was a product of the expansion of education and also allowed more children to have a better education. It was a product of greater independence for women and gave to women greater independence. It was a product of the desire for higher personal consumption and a cause of greater consumption. It was a product of a greater knowledge of contraceptives and caused the development of an adequate protective industry. The relationships were not simple.

It is not really possible to decide the relative importance of these factors, but Professor J. A. Banks, in his important work on the subject, *Prosperity and Parenthood*, has argued that the really significant decades are the 1850s and 1860s, when the living patterns of middle-class families in England began to alter. It was among the middle and upper classes that the trend towards smaller families developed initially. A rising standard of living among middle-class families in the third quarter of the nineteenth century was accompanied by a vastly more extravagant style of life. The concept of what was suitable and proper for the gentleman and his family perceptibly altered and involved what has been called the 'paraphernalia of gentility'. This meant larger houses, more servants, better furniture, more lavish dinner parties and more elaborate holidays. But, since the cost of such items rose faster than income, the middle-class couple, if they were to achieve and maintain the necessary standard, had to think in terms of smaller families.[2] Artifical means of birth control were available and were used. *Causes célèbres* like the Bradlaugh–Besant trial of 1877, when the two leading secularists of the age were charged with circulating an 'indecent, lewd, filthy, bawdy and obscene book' on birth control, helped to spread an awareness of the possibilities, and the Malthusian League continued their work by ever more extensive publicity over the following decades. But probably the most effective limit on families was late marriage. By the second half of the century most professional men were thirty before they felt it wise or regarded themselves as financially secure enough to set up a home of their own.

The reduction in family size was very much a phenomenon of the middle and upper classes. By 1900 the professional man's family was likely to be less than four in number, while the labourer's would still be around six. But even among working-class families the trend towards smaller numbers was beginning to show. Domestic servants picked up the ideas and habits of employers. The opportunities offered by higher earnings from a working wife in, say, the textile industry became clearer. If there were paraphernalia of gentility there were also paraphernalia of respectability. The trend towards smaller families among the working class came later because there were still, even in the twentieth century, many pressures encouraging large families. A working-class couple with a grown-up family could turn to them for aid and comfort in their old age, but without a family they could only look to the workhouse. In the mining areas, where large families persisted longer than elsewhere, the man with sons was economically more valuable than the man without. As Mrs Bosanquet observed in 1906,[3] among the Derbyshire miners 'a man with sons will get employment easier than a man without', and in Northumberland, where free houses were provided for miners but were scarce, 'the man with working sons always gets the first house vacant', and the pattern was similar in Cumberland and South Wales. Not until during and after the First World War did the fashion for smaller families spread to insulated communities of miners, dockers and farm labourers. But, by 1914, the possibilities of greater spending power, of more varied opportunity or freedom, which a smaller family gave to parents, was evident to all.

Urban Growth

The population was an urban one. The transformation from a rural to an urban society had taken place in the fifty years before the Great Exhibition. Only one in five of the population had lived in a town of over 10,000 inhabitants at the beginning of the nineteenth century. Half a century later the number had grown to more than one in three, and the census of 1851 described over 50 per cent of the population as 'urban'. The process of rapid urban growth continued, and by the turn of the century almost 77 per cent of the population were in urban areas. In 1851 only Belfast, Birmingham, Bradford, Bristol, Edinburgh, Glasgow, Leeds, Liverpool, London, Manchester and Sheffield had more than 100,000 inhabitants; by 1901 there were another twenty-three towns in that category. By 1911 Belfast, Bradford, Bristol, Edinburgh, Hull, Leeds, Newcastle, Nottingham, and Sheffield had a population of over 0·25 million and Birmingham, Glasgow, Liverpool, and Manchester topped 0·5 million.

London's growth was even more rapid than that of the nation as a whole. Since time immemorial it had been the 'Great Wen', pulling to it ever greater numbers of people. Even in 1801 it had had more than one million inhabitants. In forty years its population doubled, and the next forty to 1881 saw it double again. By 1914 numbers had swollen to 7·25 million. To cope with such expansion it had to swallow up the surrounding countryside.

The suburbs of London had been growing for many decades before Queen Victoria came to the throne. Those who could afford it travelled by carriage to and from the fashionable residences of Richmond or Putney, as early as 1815. Most of the metropolitan population, however, had to think in terms of walking to work, and lived as near as possible to their place of occupation. For the working class, home and work concentrated in traditional areas and this often divided between East End and West End. Tailors and dressmakers were to be found in the lanes and alleys behind the fine façades in Savile Row, Sackville Street and Conduit Street and in Westminster and St Marylebone, or in the East End in Stepney, along Middlesex Street and the Commercial Road. For centuries furniture- and cabinet-makers had congregated in Shoreditch and Bethnal Green, and the skilled watch tradesmen in Clerkenwell. In the mid-nineteenth- century they continued to do so in ever increasing numbers.

For the middle class the main consideration seems to have been to get away from the working class. They moved west. Stepney and Hackney ceased to be suitable areas for the genteel, who moved to the Georgian splendours of Eaton Square and Belgravia, to the elegant façades of Paddington, to developing Bloomsbury, which was bringing a handsome financial return to the Russell family, or to the perfection of Nash's Regent's Park terraces. Then in the 1840s came the railways, and the process of geographical division by class speeded up. Clerks, tradesmen and shopkeepers suddenly realised that their tastes lay with the middle class, and they joined the westward spread to Bayswater and Notting Hill, or north into Islington and Holloway, both of which developed rapidly in the 1840s and 1850s. With expansion went deterioration of standards, and Georgian grace declined into late-Victorian vulgarity. The new middle class required its villas to be large, but inexpensive, a difficult problem which, perhaps, the Victorian architect cannot be altogether blamed for solving as he did.

Transport had to be provided as the suburbs moved out. The London General Omnibus Company was formed in 1855 to carry the middle classes from the new estates to the West End at a leisurely pace – an hour from Islington to the West End – in 'a box lined with blue velvet', as Molly Hughes remembered, with straw on the floor to keep the travellers' feet warm.[4] Throughout the 1860s and 1870s suburban lines and stations were built, carrying the middle class even further out to Norwood and Croydon. Great new termini were built within walking distance of the business centres, ignoring the warning of the late Duke of Wellington that a French army might arrive at one of them before anyone knew they had landed.[5] In 1863 the first stretch of the underground was opened from Paddington to Farringdon Street. Transport was provided for new areas, but in many cases it was the development of transport that encouraged the growth of particular areas.

Like Attila the Hun, as *Punch* described it, the railway slashed through the working-class housing areas in the mid-century decades, forcing the inhabitants into ever-more crowded conditions. Only gradually with the development of cheap workmen's trains – at parliamentary, not commercial instigation – were areas far from the centre opened up to working-class people.

Availability of employment was still an important consideration for the working class, and dock-building between Bow Creek and Barking Creek was important in pulling people further east, as were the 10,000 jobs available at the Beckton Works of the Gas Light & Coke Company by 1900. But, as always, it was the railway that was the harbinger of change. The Eastern Counties Railway Company's works at Stratford employed 1500 workers in 1850 and 6800 in 1900, and the same company's railways opened up West Ham, East Ham and Barking for working-class commuters between 1840 and 1890, and Ilford, Wanstead, Woodford and Chingford for middle-class commuters. In a rash of jerry building, housing sought vainly to keep up with an explosion of population. West Ham's population rose from 19,000 in the mid-nineteenth century to 300,000 in 1911; Leyton's rose from 4000 to 125,000.

The middle classes saw working-class housing advancing on their spacious villas 'like some gigantic plasmodium' as Charles Masterman had it, with the 'abyss' of the working class being driven forward by pressure of numbers on to 'respectable streets'.[6] They tried to resist trams in Stanmore, Harrow and Hillingdon, and Ongar thrived because workmen's trains did not run there.[7]

A similar pattern of development can be found in most other cities. Clearance and improvement in the centre of the city, the need for cheap land, and the seemingly irresistible lure of a railway journey to work, all contributed to the growth of Birmingham. Working-class housing development pushed middle-class businessmen out of Sparkbrook and Handsworth by the 1860s and 1870s, forcing them to seek space for their red-brick villas in the more exclusive areas of Yardley and Moseley. Edgbaston, aware of the dangers, for a long time resisted the extension of the tram lines. By the twentieth century, however, the more affluent were moving yet further out to Knowle and Solihull, abandoning Acock's Green and Olton to the small tradesmen and respectable artisans. In Glasgow the city expanded in a kind of desperate game of leapfrog, with the middle classes moving west, then south, then west and ever westwards to Milngavie and Bearsden. In Manchester, Bristol, Newcastle or any great city numbers and class gave social and geographical shape to the environment.

Migration

The main reason for city population growth was the increasing number of births over deaths, but another major reason was migration from country areas. In London about a third of the population growth after 1841 was due to this migration.[8] The movement of population from rural areas was not new. The towns had always attracted the young and ambitious. People did not move very far, but agricultural areas around cities had always had to resist the pull of the city on many of their people. In the early decades of Victoria's reign the process accelerated as employment opportunities in rural areas declined. Increasingly farm machinery was substituted for labour, and in the forty years after 1861 the number of male agricultural labourers declined by more than 40 per cent.[9] Ever more cost-conscious farmers were less inclined to offer odd jobs to casual labourers in a village, and the growth of large-scale industry eroded the demand for the rural craftsman. Professor Saville has provided examples of this trend from the smallest of counties, Rutland. The 1851 census showed 63 millers in the county, the 1911 census only 22; 31 cabinet-makers had been reduced to 10, 116 blacksmiths to 83, 236 shoemakers to only 138.[10] Restrictions on the employment of children by the extension of education after 1870 meant some reduction in family earnings, and was probably another factor in encouraging migration from a rural area.

It was the young and fit who tended to migrate, and from some rural areas as many as 40 per cent of the men aged between twenty and thirty might emigrate, while a high proportion of young women also migrated to domestic service in the towns. Some districts, like the south-west and the Welsh rural counties were losing 66 per cent of their population in a generation.[11] A high rural birth rate hid the process for a time, but by 1851 Wiltshire and Montgomeryshire showed an absolute decline in population. By the 1880s and 1890s, there was an absolute decline in Cornwall, Dorset, Hereford, Shropshire, Westmorland, Cambridgeshire, Huntingdonshire, Rutland, most Welsh counties and the Highland and Border counties of Scotland. By this time, ironically because of earlier migrations, there were fewer potential migrants being born, and in fact the rate of migration slowed down.

The goal of most migrants was a town or city, though in the 1880s the flow to the cities was checked by overseas migration. In that decade more than 2·5 million people left these shores, principally for the United States. In the following decade the attractions of overseas emigration diminished and the flow to the cities resumed, but at a reduced level, and by the end of the century most urban growth was coming, not from migration, but from the natural increase of city populations. Indeed, by the end of the 1890s ever larger numbers of people were reversing the trend of decades and moving out from the cities into the surrounding villages and countryside in an effort to escape the overcrowding of the central areas.

The rate of growth in different areas varied. The womb of industrialisation, Lancashire, more than doubled its population between the censuses of 1851 and 1911. The transformation of South Wales, with the exploitation of its smokeless steam coal, was evident in the five-fold increase in the population of Glamorgan, from 232,000 in 1851 to 1,122,000 in 1911 – a rate of growth faster than that of the United States. In Scotland the population of industrial Lanarkshire trebled in the same period. The growth of individual towns was in some cases quite phenomenal. The small village of Blackpool, with a population of only 3000 in 1851 had leapt to almost five times that by 1880 and twenty times that by 1911. Similarly, elegant Bournemouth, catering for a different clientele, gained from people's desire for the health-giving qualities of the fresh sea breezes and increased its population thirteenfold. It was certainly not clean air that brought people to Middlesbrough, but Cleveland iron too had its attractions, and the population of 8000 of 1851 quadrupled in twenty years and had become 120,000 by 1911.

Such a rapid rate of growth posed massive problems of health, sanitation and housing. There were few less healthy places for the young child than a Glamorganshire mining village, with thirty-four more deaths per thousand births than the national average in 1908, and more than twice the infant death rate of arcadian Oxfordshire. It was not industry, population or politics which decided the death rate, but a complexity of factors which had resulted over the years in inadequate sanitary provisions. No single factor can adequately explain why 202 infants in every thousand born in Burnley died within their first year, while only 112 died in Huddersfield, or why it was much more dangerous, even in the twentieth century, to be a born in a small industrial town like Aberdare or Featherstone or Tunstall than in most parts (though by no means all) of the notorious cities of Liver-pool, Manchester or Leeds. If a child had to be born in a city, then it was wiser to choose to be born in the metropolis than any other.[12]

Some of the improvement in the quality of life that had helped to save the lives of infants had resulted from the reduction in overcrowd-ing which had been brought about by the turn of the century. 8·6 per cent of the population of England and Wales still lived more than two to a room in 1911, but this was just under 3 per cent better than twenty years before. Some towns had done remarkably well. Bradford had reduced its overcrowding from 20 per cent to 9 per cent, though its population had increased by 22,000. It was easier for Halifax to come to terms with its housing problems and to reduce overcrowding from 21 per cent to 12 per cent, when in the decade before 1911 it had shown a net loss of 3000 in its population. Further north in Newcastle and Sunderland almost one third of the population lived more than two to a room, but this was still a great deal better than in Scotland, where almost half the population in 1891 lived more than two in a room. Twenty years later some improvement had been made in Scot-land, but 45 per cent of the population still lived in such circum-stances. Of course economic factors alone did not explain this massive difference between the two countries. Rather it was the persistence of cultural differences, dating back for centuries. Even in 1914 there was a greater demand for the 'single end' in central Scotland than for a room and kitchen.[13] Such conditions were reflected in the levels of infant mortality. Since the start of comprehensive records in the 1850s, Scotland had had a substantially better rate of infant mortality than England and Wales. At the end of the century there were thirty per thousand deaths less in Scotland than the English peak of that year. Eight years later the position was fractionally better, but from then on the gap widened in England's favour.

The substantial demographic changes of the fifty years before the First World War irrevocably changed society, and undoubtedly influenced demand for goods and services. Firstly there were more people; secondly more and more of them lived in towns, thus increas-ing the demand for goods and services; thirdly more parents were having smaller families and so were spending more on themselves and on their families. Living conditions for many of the population improved greatly. There was less overcrowding. A higher proportion of the population had homes of their own, and therefore required the furnishings and fittings for these. As Professor Banks has argued, demand grew among the middle class because their expectations of what was a fitting standard for their social class increased. Although no one has done a similar exercise for other classes, there seems little doubt that, with a time lag, the ways of the bourgeoisie were emulated by the working class: at any rate, by that section of the working class who had persistently been influenced by the attitudes, opinions, and manners of the middle class. The sheer anonymity of urban life encouraged this tendency. Antecedents were less important than appearance and style of life. Emulation was possible because income rose, and it is to this factor that we must now turn.

Numbers are important in demand. But as the experience of the emerging nations of Asia and Latin America has taught, if the bulk of the population has a standard of living below subsistence level, then the effect on demand of anything but foodstuffs is likely to be fairly slight and certainly not sufficient to stimulate industrial growth. In Britain, however, the standard of living of seven in ten of the population was above subsistence level. There was income to be spent on more than the basic necessities, and in the second half of the nineteenth century this income was rising. With more to be spent, the nation's industries were transformed to meet the impact this had on demand.

2. Incomes

> The general conclusion from all the facts is, that what has happened to the working classes in the last fifty years is not so much what may properly be called an improvement, as a revolution of the most remarkable description. . . . From being a dependent class without future and hope, the masses of working men have in fact got into a position from which they may effectually advance to almost any degree of civilisation.
> Robert Giffen, *Essays in Finance* (1887), p. 473.

The pressure of population on limited land resources and shrinking employment opportunities in rural areas were certainly important in pushing people into the towns and cities. But 'pull' was probably always more important than 'push' in migration and undoubtedly the city had its attractions. The city meant 'life', excitement, thrills for the young. It could mean independence from the restraints of the family. Even in Engels's Manchester many single people were setting up homes with friends of their own age before they got married: asserting their independence from their parents. For the single girl the city offered a greater chance of marriage than she was ever likely to get in a village. But, most important of all, it offered higher earnings. The young male migrant to the city could expect to earn roughly 50 per cent more than he could as an agricultural labourer. This was true throughout the second half of the nineteenth century, and probably the gap between town and country widened fractionally in the first decade of the twentieth century.[1] Also, in the towns, there were many opportunities for jobs other than labouring. With some experience of rural crafts, a man could hope to move to a skilled position in the building trades or in engineering. Money could be made in the towns and earnings were rising.

Generalisations about money wages and real wages are never particularly satisfactory, especially in a country where regional variations persisted well into this century and even now have far from disappeared. However, some general indicators provide a starting point. Firstly money wages: taking 1850 as a base year at 100, G. H. Wood's index shows a rise to 180 by 1900. Nearly two-thirds of the rise took place between 1850 and 1874, when the index, allowing for unemployment, rose to 159. Over the next quarter of a century the increase was a further 13 per cent. The movement of money wages was very much in line with the trade cycle both in terms of timing and extent, though, as Phelps Brown and Browne have pointed out, there were limitations on how far wages would fall at times of deep depression. The first leap forward in wages occurred between 1853 and 1856, as demand for labour increased in line with the expansion of industry, which had been stimulated by gold discoveries in California and Australia and by the needs of a war economy. A further sharp rise, again much affected by developments in the American economy in the post-Civil War period, took place from the late 1860s up till 1874. From 1870 to 1874 average money wages rose by some 17 per cent. Not until 1889 did money wages again reach the level of 1874, as the rate of industrial growth slowed in the aftermath of the great boom of the early 1870s. A further sharp rise took place between 1893 and 1900, but as the country moved into the new century there was a down-turn between 1900 and 1904 and again in 1907 and 1908. After 1910, however, the trend was clearly upwards. By 1914, therefore, money wages had almost doubled from their level of 1851.

In the same period the various price indices reveal a more or less common pattern. Comparing the level of wholesale prices in 1873 with that in 1850 there had been a very clear rise: by about 48 per cent according to Phelps Brown's and Hopkins's index. Such a comparison is deceptive, however, since the rise in prices is largely confined to two periods in 1852–3 and 1872–3. Between these two booms prices remained fairly stable, and, if anything, there were signs from the mid-1860s of a downturn in some prices. A great expansion in world demand as other countries in Europe and North America embarked on a process of rapid industrialisation pushed up the prices of some key raw materials such as coal, iron, wool and tin, but foodstuffs such as wheat, potatoes, sugar and rice showed little change.

For the farmer and the capitalist the twenty-two years after 1874 were the years of the 'great depression'. Prices fell by some 40 per cent, with only the briefest of reversals in 1880 and from 1889 to 1891. In 1884 prices were back to the level of 1850 and the fall continued until 1896, when the index of prices was seventeen points below the level of 1884, a fall of around 23 per cent. The reasons for the fall in prices are far from being fully agreed. Increased foreign competition, over-expansion in many industries, a shortage of gold bullion and continued technological developments are among the main contributing factors. The opening up of vast new lands by means of railways, particularly in the United States and in the southern hemisphere, revolutionised food supplies. The price of commodities such as sugar, tea, wheat and wool fell by over 50 per cent in twenty years and that of almost all foodstuffs, including mutton and beef, fell by at least 25 per cent.

A revival of overseas demand at the end of the 1890s, which had been stimulated by gold discoveries this time in South Africa, when coupled with very buoyant home demand, began to pull up prices. Average price rises between 1896 and 1914 were about 39 per cent according to the Sauerbeck-*Statist* index, 45 per cent according to the Rousseaux index and 32 per cent according to the Board of Trade index. In 1912 prices were above the level of 1850 for the first time in almost thirty years.

Despite the undoubted inadequacies of all the indexes available to historians, some attempt to set wages against prices produces a picture of trends in real wages. There was little advance in the 1850s, as prices more than matched the money wage rise for most workers, but from the early 1860s onwards the trend in real wages was upwards and, although there was a sharp set back in 1866–8 largely brought about by a rise in food prices, the trend was upwards until 1900. Money wages in the early 1870s were clearly outpacing the rise in prices. Professor Bowley calculated that between 1850 and 1874 real wages rose by 32 per cent. There was a minor set-back from 1875 to 1879, but the substantial price fall ensured that, despite unemployment and wage cuts, for many the overall picture was one of improving living standards. Not until 1900 was this trend halted, when real wages began to fall and continued to until 1905. An upturn in 1906 and 1907 failed to halt the trend, and between 1900 and 1913 at no point did real wages again reach the level of the last two years of the nineteenth century.[2]

These general averages hide a great number of complexities. Detailed studies of particular areas and groups of workers are only gradually being undertaken for this period. Two studies of the Black Country have been published recently which present a very different picture from that of the general averages. The weakness of the general indexes is that the figures for unemployment are based on returns from only a few major unions – in other words from skilled workers – and they take no account of short-time working and irregular work, which the writings of Charles Booth, Seebohm Rowntree and all other social investigators at the end of the nineteenth century testify to being a major cause of destitution. In his study of Black Country living standards, Dr Barnsby found that in the eighty-five years after Waterloo there were only three periods that could be regarded as periods of sustained full employment, 1834–7, 1845–55 and 1870–4. He found no substantial rise in real wages among the groups of workers he examined until the 1890s. In his study of Stourbridge, Dr Hopkins confirmed this finding when he showed that the real wages of nailers and ironworkers *fell* in the late 1870s and 1880s, and that only an 'aristocratic' group like the glassmakers were able to maintain their standard of living, but even then it was at the expense of jobs.[3] Perhaps the Black Country is exceptional. The combined decline of the iron and mining industries in south Staffordshire after 1871 may have made the fall in real wages of iron workers there in the late 1870s and 1880s abnormal. Irregularity of employment had to be an accepted feature of life in the Black Country in a way that it was not, for example, in the Lancashire cotton towns. But Staffordshire's experience illustrates the need for caution in generalisation. Professor Pollard, in his studies of Sheffield, has also calculated a smaller degree of improvement, around 30 per cent, among the workers in that city between 1870 and 1900.[4]

A second caveat is that average real wages were considerably influenced by the shift of a substantial number of workers from low-paid to better-paid work: the agricultural worker becoming the urban labourer; the unskilled man becoming the semi-skilled machine minder. Undoubtedly a great deal of this went on. There were plenty of complaints from skilled men that their jobs were under pressure from country men. In addition, with the expansion of service industries, the opportunities for better-paid work for people without any skill increased. There was also, towards the end of the period, a greater chance of obtaining a white-collar job as government, the professions and commerce all expanded. The number of white-collar employees increased by 81 per cent in the period from 1851 to 1871, by 103 per cent from 1871 to 1891 and by 72 per cent between 1891 and 1911, from 2·5 per cent of the occupied male population in 1851 to 7·1 per cent in 1911. As at any period, the continuing process of industrialisation brought gains for some at the expense of others. The 1870s saw a rapid expansion of factory shoemaking, the 1880s of factory furniture-making, the 1890s of factory clothes-making. Home workers in all these crafts had to pay the price of a steady decline in their standard of living and – as important – in their social status. The general picture, none the less, is of a substantially improved standard of living for the mass of the population in the 1870s, 1880s and 1890s and a partial set-back to this in the first decade of the twentieth century.

In the 1860s a highly-skilled, time-served craftsman could earn between 28s and 35s a week. In some trades this would vary with the season. The building trades, for example, worked a 60-hour week in the summer and only 47 hours in winter, and payment was by the hour. At other times much depended upon the general state of trade which governed the amount of overtime available. A study of Barrow-in-Furness found examples of engineers working 72-, 93- and 95-hour weeks in 1896 and one example of a 110-hour week in 1914. Into this skilled category would fall the building trades' craftsmen, like masons, carpenters and bricklayers, the skilled turners and fitters of the engineering industry, cotton spinners and engine drivers. Twenty years later the range of earnings for this group would be from 29s to 39s and by 1914 from 38s to 47s. There were always those, of course, who did a great deal better than the average. As early as 1860, a Black Country glass-maker could expect to earn over £3 a week. By the turn of the century a compositor in a daily newspaper was in this position and the average steel worker was on over £4.

At a slightly lower earning level were the less skilled grades of machine minders, the putters and fitters in mining, the painters and slaters in building. Their earnings ranged between 21s and 25s in 1867. Twenty years later they ranged from about 21s to 29s, and by 1914 from 30s to 35s. An unskilled labourer working with a bricklayer or mason, or acting as a holder-up or general helper for a skilled superior, could expect to earn under 20s in the 1860s, from 18s to 22s in 1886, and from 21s to 30s in 1914. It seems probable that in the 1850s and 1860s the gap between the earnings of skilled man and labourer had widened. By the end of the 1860s a skilled engineer earned twice as much as his labourer. By the 1880s some narrowing of differentials had taken place, and the skilled engineer was earning only 50 per cent more than his labourer.

At the bottom of the earnings scale were the agricultural labourers, in some cases earning as little as 12s a week in the 1860s and few earning more than 17s. Thirty years later they ranged from 15s to 19s and many were still earning less than £1 in the first decade of the twentieth century. The variations in the wages of agricultural workers underline a major problem in dealing with wages in the nineteenth century, namely that there are such massive regional variations in wage rates that concepts of a typical wage are of limited value. The high wage areas of agriculture in the 1860s were Kent, Middlesex, Surrey and Sussex, that is the metropolitan counties; and Yorkshire,

Lancashire, Northumberland and Durham (in the last, wages had already reached £1 by 1867), that is the main industrial area, where farmers had long experienced the problem of competing with mines and textile factories. At the other end of the spectrum were the Highland counties of Scotland (9s a week was not uncommon in Argyll in 1867), the south-west of England and most of Wales. Fifty years later the gap between high and low wage counties had narrowed a little. Wages in the south-west had risen, so that a Devon labourer was earning little more than a shilling less than one in Kent. The rapid industrialisation of South Wales meant that the southern Welsh counties no longer lagged behind other areas. The Scottish Highland counties had improved by 5s or 6s a week. Oxfordshire, Suffolk and Norfolk now lay at the bottom of the earnings league, with weekly wages of less than 16s, and in parts of these counties wages were only half the level of parts of Northumberland and Lancashire.[5] Even generalisations in terms of counties have to be treated with caution, since on neighbouring farms earnings could differ by as much as 20 per cent.

A further complication is that payment in kind still formed part of some workers' wages. The farm labourer could expect a sack of potatoes or turnips from time to time, and had probably enough space around his cottage or access to an allotment on which to grow the family vegetables and keep a pig. Coal-miners had a supply of coal, and like farm labourers lived in tied housing at lower than average rents. The building craftsman could readily get an odd job in the evening and at week-ends in a way that factory workers could not. For many such extras probably meant the difference between mere subsistence and a little comfort, but it is impossible to quantify their importance in general terms.

Farm labourers were the lowest paid large group, but there were many people who earned considerably less than the average farm labourer. Every town had its floating population who 'lived mysteriously', like those in Worcester whom Mrs Bosanquet described in 1912 as doing 'a little pea-picking, a little strawberry picking, a little hop-picking, a little pocket-picking and a little oakum picking' according to the season.[6] In the first decade of the twentieth century, just as in the 1850s when Henry Mayhew had observed them, there was a countless variety of street-sellers, some earning a comfortable 30s or more per week, others scraping a bare subsistence selling a few flowers or matches. In Glasgow it was not uncommon for blankets to be pawned in the morning and the money used to buy a basket of fish or fruit, which was then sold at a profit which bought the day's food and left enough over for the blankets to be redeemed before the pawn-shop closed at 10 p.m. in the evening.[7]

Women workers were the most exploited of all. Mayhew in the 1850s and Charles Booth in the 1880s, as well as parliamentary enquiries and trade-union reports, revealed the fearsome conditions and pathetically low wages of the workers in the sweated trades of ready-made clothing, shoemaking, cabinet-making and box-making in London's East End. Much of the work was done by unskilled females working at home, like Mrs Perrott in Arthur Morrison's *A Child of the Jago*.

> She was a clumsy needlewoman: else she might hope to earn some ninepence or a shilling a day making shirts, by keeping well to the needle for sixteen hours out of the twenty-four; and from the whole sum there would be no deductions, except for needles and cotton, and what the frugal employer might choose to subtract for work to which he could devise an objection. But, as it was, she must do her best to get some sack-making. They paid one and sevenpence a hundred for sacks, and, with speed and long hours she could make a hundred in four days. . . . Then there was a more lucrative employ-ment still, but one to be looked for at intervals only: one not to be counted on at all, in fact, for it was a prize, and many sought after it. This was the making of match boxes. For making one hundred and forty-four outside cases with paper label and sand paper, and the same number of trays to slide into them – a gross of complete boxes, or two hundred and eighty-eight pieces in all – one got a farthing a gross more; and all the wood and the labels and the sandpaper were provided free: so that the fortunate operator lost nothing out of the twopence farthing but the cost of the paste, and the string for tying up the boxes into regularly numbered batches, and the time employed in fetching the work and taking it back again. And if seven gross were to be got, and could be done in a day – and it was really not very difficult for the skilful hand who kept at work long enough – the day's income was one and threepence three farthings, less expenses: still better that, than the shirts.[8]

Morrison was writing in the 1890s, when the position of such workers was probably getting worse. Twenty thousand Jewish immigrants, fleeing from the pogroms of Poland and Russia, crowded into the East End in the first half of the 1880s, adding to the already highly competi-tive position of hand workers. By the end of the century alternative work was available in the new jam, meat and lemonade factories, but they offered little improvement in either wages or conditions. As an inexperienced bottle-washer in an aerated water factory during the first decade of this century the indefatigable social investigator, Olive Malvery, earned 3s per week for a day that stretched from 8 a.m. to 7 p.m.[9] Along the road in a jam factory a princely 7s per week could be earned at the height of the fruit season; or there was the meat-packing factory, where a few earned 15s, but the average was 8s–11s a week.[10] Conditions in such places were deplorably bad. Basic sanitary arrangements were totally lacking and the workers were brutalised by their surroundings. It was easy for Miss Malvery to opine that 'a man must be low and degraded indeed to allow his wife to work in a factory', but in many areas there were not many alternatives. For the reasonably attractive the job of waitress, in one of the many tea-rooms that burgeoned in the later decades of the century, might certainly offer more pleasant surroundings and the elevating conversation of ladies at afternoon tea, but the wage was still only 10s a week.

Not all factories were as bad as those in the East End of London, but even in models like those of Huntley & Palmer in Reading wages for women were not high: in 1893–4 average wages ranged from 4s at the age of 14 to 10s at 21, less than half what was paid to men.[11] Only in Lancashire could the woman factory worker receive a substantial wage of more than 25s a week, which was comparable to what one of the increasing number of lady typists – or 'typewriters', as they were called – could expect to receive. For those women with a reasonable level of education there were an increasing number of opportunities, though earnings were still relatively low. A Post Office girl clerk, for example, could earn £35–£40 per annum, a district nurse £50–£80, a librarian £30–£100, a policewoman, usually appointed from the ranks of prison warders, £50–£65. But promotion opportunities in such jobs were very limited, and they came to an end on marriage.[12]

By 1871 agricultural labourers had been overtaken by domestic servants as the largest single occupational group. Over 1·5 million people were in domestic service in 1861 and numbers continued to rise until 1914, when there were more than 2 million in service. Wages were not high. In the mid-century a general maid might get something between £10 and £16 per year, a footman £20 to £40, depending on appearance and experience. A cook could earn £20 plus and a housekeeper £25 to £30, while a butler could make £50 or more. With these wages, however, went full board in small but probably quite reasonable surroundings, because good servants were hard to get and hard to keep. In addition there were many perquisites. The housekeeper could expect tips from the guests; the cook or the housekeeper could expect 5 per cent commission from shopkeepers on most food bills; the lady's maid could expect hand-me-down clothes, and even the kitchen staff could sell off left-over food. Of course, what was true of the 'big house' with its hierarchy of twenty or more servants, was not true of the small, suburban semi-detached, where a maid was none the less *de rigueur*, whether she could really be afforded or not. In the latter case financial stringency, coupled with social insecurity, often brought very nasty exploitation.

Levels of wages do not tell the whole story of working-class standards of living, since it was family earnings that decided the level of comfort that could be achieved. Minimum wages were generally based on some idea of what was regarded as necessary for a man to support a wife and three children. As Professor Bowley showed, however, in a study of working-class households in 12 towns in 1911, such a family occurred in only 56 households per 1000 among skilled workers, and in 52 households per 1000 among unskilled workers. 10 per cent of households consisted of a man and wife with no dependents, and the average number of dependent children under 14 was 1·32 among skilled workers and 1·40 among the unskilled. In the average working-class household 1·9 persons were occupied and 2·3 dependent. In calculating a household's standard of living, therefore, Bowley suggested that one has to think in terms of 1·4 times the earnings of a man.[13] The average family income of workers in the Ashworth cotton enterprise in the 1840s was 33s 4d per week, although adult male employees were paid 21s per week.[14] In a sample of working-class households used by Bowley, taken from Bristol, Newcastle, Bethnal Green, Shoreditch and Stepney, the average weekly earnings in 1911 were 38s 6d. It was not necessarily a question of a large number of married women going out to work. Elizabeth Roberts has shown in her study of Barrow and Lancaster that wives found many ways of making money at home, by taking in washing, dressmaking, baking pies for sale, baby-minding and some more ingenious methods. On the other hand, as Seebohm Rowntree pointed out, 50 per cent of married men had 'at one time or another in their lives' three or more children to support and the cyclical nature of poverty was well documented by many observers.[15] The working-class family passed from the relative comfort of the newly-weds to the hard years of bringing up a young family, to the brief lacuna when two or three children were adding to the family income and back to the poverty of middle and old age, when the family had gone and the man's earning capacity was much reduced.

Finally, in considering working-class earnings, one has to bear in mind that there were considerable variations in earning between different parts of the country, even for the same jobs. Trade-union pressure throughout the period had certainly done a great deal to create a trend towards uniformity, but it was not until the years of the First World War that national negotiations were common, and standards of pay agreed by trade unions tended to be on a regional basis. Throughout the period from 1850 to 1914 the areas of high earnings in almost all trades were London and the northern industrial counties of England. Despite the great extent of poverty, with one in three of the population living in extreme poverty as Booth found in the 1880s, for most people the best hope of earning high wages was in London. The building worker, craftsman or labourer, the engineer, the domestic servant and the shop assistant could expect to earn more at his job in London than anywhere else. The industrial areas of Lancashire and the Midlands were also areas of high earnings. For example, wages among building workers in Manchester, Preston and Bradford were between 6 per cent and 15 per cent above the national average. Northumberland and Durham too were high wage areas until the First World War, with wages in Newcastle very much on a par with those of Manchester. Industrialisation had its social costs, in the destruction of traditional hand crafts, in the overthrow of a traditional way of life, but it also clearly had its pecuniary compensations. In the second half of the nineteenth century the rise of wages followed the spread of industrialisation. By 1914 South Wales and central Scotland had both joined London and the north of England as high-wage regions.[16]

Middle-Class Incomes

Although working-class incomes are very well documented at this period, it is, as we have seen, extremely difficult to generalise about them. It is almost impossible to generalise about middle-class earnings. J. C. Stamp estimated that the number of income-tax payers in 1860, that is those in receipt of an income of over £160, was 280,000, and those just under the income-tax level, earning £100–£150, was 160,000. By 1880 there were 620,000 in the income-tax net and by 1913, there were 1,190,000.[17] At the beginning of the period the group caught by income tax ranged from doctors, solicitors and architects upwards; by the turn of the century it included some skilled mechanics, bank clerks, solicitors' clerks, board-school teachers, county council clerks, sanitary inspectors, police inspectors, curates, and commercial travellers, among others. The average earnings of income-tax payers were £855 in 1880 and £838 in 1913.[18]

The earnings of those in industry or commerce, 'something in the city', by their nature do not lend themselves to generalisation. What is clear, however, is that they could be in a highly risky business. Some made it and joined the ranks of the Strutts, the Brasseys or the Morleys. Many failed. Some fell from a great height, like Morton Peto or some of those who pinned their faith in the Gurney name. But even at a lesser level such disasters were all too frequent. One need only think of how this is reflected in fiction, in the large number of Victorian and Edwardian novels and melodramas that centre on father losing all. For some, like Mrs Webb's father, Richard Potter, losses in Welsh coal-mines could quickly be balanced by gains from the Barry Docks, or rash speculations, like a grand canal through Syria, could be more than compensated for by £60,000 profit from providing huts for the Crimean troops.[19] For others the way back from financial disaster was hard, if a way back was possible.

In spite of the gains made by the working classes, the distribution of the national income was generally in favour of non-wage earners. Only for a brief period between 1870 and 1873 did income from wages grow more rapidly than income from salaries: 72 per cent and 70 per cent respectively. From 1873 to 1899 the figures were 41 per cent and 120 per cent and between 1899 and 1914, 21 per cent and 81 per cent. Phelps Brown's and Browne's 'wage–income ratio', which is based on money wage earnings divided by income per occupied person in industry, shows a similar pattern. It averaged 67 per cent in the 1870s, 71 per cent in the 1880s, 66 per cent in the 1890s and 65 per cent between 1900 and 1910.[20] While income from employment rose from 47 per cent of the Gross National Product in the 1860s to 50 per cent in the 1890s and remained fairly constant until 1914, the share of wages alone stayed at around 40–41 per cent until the end of the 1890s and then fell sharply to 37 per cent between 1900 and 1913. For much of the time, then, wage earners were gaining less than other groups, but much of the advantage probably went to the class that was being recruited from the working class, the growing body of people on small salaries or profits, clerks, workers in retailing or wholesale distribution, young people at the bottom end of professions like teaching. The proportion of national income received by this 'intermediate class' between wage earners and income-tax payers rose from 14 per cent of the whole in 1880 to 17 per cent in 1913. However, despite a squeeze on profits and on farming rents between the mid-1870s and the mid-1890s, for those with capital to invest the demands from all over the world brought good returns.

The professional life offered less remuneration than did investment in industry or commerce, but a great deal more security. The medical man, not yet having fully convinced the world of his importance, or indeed of his respectability, was dependent on the nature of his practice. No doubt a well-connected London practitioner could earn well over £1000, and reputedly a few earned above £5000, but a mixed rural practice, with a few gentry to augment the slight remuneration from the Poor Law Board, would still provide a good income at £600 per annum. For those in largely working-class areas, having to compete in tendering for a contract with the friendly societies or sick clubs £150–£200 was not unusual in 1912. In the Law, for the successful man at the Bar, a few, even in 1850, were earning above £5000. Probably £1000 was nearer the mark for the reasonably successful, though it could take time to start earning any income at all, and many a London barrister supplemented his income with journalism. An up-and-coming young Birkenhead barrister, F. E. Smith, made £529 in 1900 at the age of twenty-eight, a sum large enough for him to consider getting married.[21] The upper limit of a solicitor's professional earnings was likely to be £2000, but he could usually earn additional 'honoraria' for performing a variety of functions in the community.

The incomes to be made in the professions were generally higher than those in the expanding civil service or in industrial management. They were more likely to be in the range from £500 to £1000. To earn over £1000 per annum even in 1914, therefore, was to enter the ranks of the comfortably off middle class. The lower end of the middle class probably lay somewhere between £200 and £300. It would have been a rash gentleman, and an even rasher young lady, in the eyes of her peers, who agreed to set up house in mid-century on an income of less than £200 per annum, and that prolific issuer of advice to the young middle class in the decade before 1914, Mrs C. S. Peel, confined it to those earning more than £250 a year.[22] The presumption was that earnings would rise fairly steadily. For the young middle-class family, expectations were more important than immediate earnings and it was for this that the prospective father-in-law looked.

At the bottom end of the middle class, among the ever-growing army of clerks and other white-collar workers, much probably depended upon the individual firm. With profits squeezed between the 1870s and 1896 there were unlikely to be many increases in salary. This was not too important in a period of falling prices, but with prices rising after 1896 it may be that those on salaries were feeling the squeeze. However as T. R. Gourvish has shown, among London railway clerks and others in banking and insurance regular increments in salary kept well ahead of price rises. His sample of clerks on the South-Eastern and Clapham Railway showed a rise in real earnings of 161 per cent between 1890 and 1914, a position that was in marked contrast to other grades of railway worker.[23]

The evidence from more detailed studies, then, does not overthrow the picture that emerges from the national statistics, of an improvement for most people in their standard of living from the 1860s to the end of the century, mainly as a result of the dramatic price fall. In Edwardian Britain the position was less bright for many and the pinch of rising prices was being felt, but for a substantial number of others standards of living continued to rise. How individuals and families fared depended upon a variety of factors. Ingenuity and initiative in finding alternative sources of income were important, but so was the luck of being in a firm that gave reasonably secure employment, or of having the contacts to assist in finding alternative employment, or the good fortune to live in an area that retained prosperity.

3. Patterns of Consumption: Food

A man's wage would not buy bread for a family, let alone any meat.... Now in the seventies the men brought a bit of cheese as well as an onion. When they ate at home they might have suet pudding with scraps of bacon rolled in it and mushrooms, too, once or twice a year and then it was the richest of dishes.

M. K. Ashby, *Joseph Ashby of Tysoe* (Cambridge, 1961) pp. 36–7.

As the standard of living of the British population rose in the late nineteenth century, families had more to spend on a variety of goods and services. Their first priority was increased consumption of food. As Engels's law asserts, there is a limit to what any family can spend on food, and as income rises the proportion of expenditure that goes on food tends to decline. However, the increased *per capita* consumption of even staple foods in the last half of the nineteenth century is an indication of how many families were just reaching the position where Engels's law applied. It also took time for methods of distribution to develop to meet a growing demand, but by the 1880s and 1890s a much greater variety of foods was available.

Like the rest of western Europe, the British diet from the Middle Ages till the later decades of the nineteenth century depended for the bulk of its protein and calories upon wheat and other cereals. Only with the improvements of the late nineteenth century was the switch made to a diet in which animal products were the staple. Throughout the period flour remained a basic item and its consumption, for all purposes, rose from 200 lb. per head per annum in the 1880s to 220 lb. in the early twentieth century.[1] One would expect a rising standard of living to be accompanied by a decline in bread consumption. One must assume, therefore, that an increasing proportion of the flour was going into cakes and biscuits rather than into bread. The loaf of bread, however, was probably still the principal single component of the working-class diet up to 1914, with the amount consumed being in inverse proportion to the standard of living.

A still cheaper alternative to bread was potatoes. They too loomed less large in the average working-class diet in 1914 than they had in 1850, but were still important. Estimates of consumption per head still indicate a rise, from 176 lb. per year in 1889–93 to 189 lb. in 1904–8.[2] Perhaps at least some of the increased production is attributable to the attraction of chips, as from the 1870s the rest of the nation began to appreciate the delights of a delicacy previously confined to Lancashire to accompany their fried fish.

Meat consumption – more than half of which was beef – rose from 96 lb. *per capita* per annum in the mid–1880s to 111 lb. in the last four years before the war.[3] Home production could not meet the rising demand, and by the 1890s 0·5 million live animals were being imported to be slaughtered in Britain. New techniques of canning brought cheap Australian, South and North American preserved meats to the British tables, though not always to the poorest ones. Resistance to the delights of 'corned beef' persisted for many years, although it retailed at less than half the price of fresh beef. A similar resistance met chilled and frozen meats from the 1880s onwards. There was hostility from both the butchers and the customers. But sound marketing and competitive prices brought a breakthrough by the beginning of the present century. Bacon retained popularity throughout the period. It had for long been the traditional meat in rural areas. The pig had so many advantages: it was relatively easily fed, it required little room and its meat could be preserved by smoking or salting. William Cobbett had seen a pig in every cottage as 'the infallible mark of a happy people', and half a century later the killing of the fattened pig was still the centre of the rural family's year. It was a time when the larder was filled, gifts were given and the 'pig feast' held, 'when fathers and mothers, sisters and brothers, married children and grandchildren who lived within walking distance arrived to dinner'.[4] The tastes of the country were carried to the towns, and urban demand for bacon and ham grew steadily. Bacon had the particular attraction for poorer families that not only was there bacon, which thinly sliced could be made to go a long way, but there was also the left-over dripping to add flavour to the next day's bread and potatoes. It was probably again an indication of greater affluence that there was a marked change in taste away from fatty English bacon to leaner Irish and American, and – particularly important from the late 1880s onwards – Danish.

Further protein was provided, in what was still a diet of excessive carbohydrates, by an increased consumption of fish. The consumption of fish seems always to have been high, even though fresh fish was not available away from the coastal towns until the second half of the century. Inland cities, like Birmingham, had to eat their fish cured, dried, pickled or salted until the development of railways and the use of ice combined to open up the whole country to the delights of Scotch salmon or Aberdeen herring. Ancient ports were revitalised to meet the ever-growing demand. By the 1890s 25 lb. of fish per annum were being devoured per head of population. Twenty years later this had increased to 30 lb.[5] There were substantial regional variations in fish consumption. In some areas there was a persistent prejudice against fish as being of little nutritional value, while in other areas its efficacy for the brain was much commended. The rapid spread of fish and chip shops no doubt helped to overcome old prejudices.

Nutritionally one of the most significant growths in consumption was in milk, where there was a rise from the late 1880s from 15 gallons per annum to 22 gallons per head per annum in 1907–13: still well short of the daily 'pinta' but vital for improved health. The quality of milk still left a great deal to be desired and, at the end of the century, Seebohm Rowntree reported that sediment could still be found in York's milk. It is little wonder that working-class suspicion of milk as a beverage persisted. A committee of the Royal Statistical Society in 1902 found that weekly consumption of liquid milk was 0·8 pint among labourers' families, rising to 1·8 pints among artisans, compared with between 3·8 pints and 6 pints in upper- and middle-class families.[6] The price remained at a fairly constant 2d per pint from 1892 to 1914, certainly a good buy from a nutritional point of view, but dearer than the 8d tin of condensed milk that could produce 5 pints or more when water was added. Condensed milk was widely used from the 1870s onwards, and, despite warnings, was frequently fed to infants and children as a substitute for fresh milk, though some of the cheaper tins contained little more than a solution of cane sugar. Condensed milk contributed to both rickets and epidemic diarrhoea. Despite some educational work in post-natal clinics, there was little significant improvement in infant feeding methods before 1914.[7]

A declining proportion of milk was used in the production of butter and cheese. By 1908, 87 per cent of butter and 76 per cent of cheese were imported. *Per capita* consumption of butter rose from 11 lb. per year in the late 1880s to 13 lb. at the turn of the century, as Danish and colonial butter came in.[8] Cheeses were mainly factory-made cheddar from Canada, from which 71 per cent of cheese imports came, from New Zealand and the United States.

Butter was able to hold its own against the growing competition of margarine. From the mid-1870s until the Margarine Act of 1887, margarine was sold as 'butterine' and indeed, by the less scrupulous, as butter. Retailing at between 6d and 10d per lb. it was considerably cheaper than butter at 1s or 1s 4d per lb., but again there was resistance to novelty. The advance of the new product was not helped by rumours that, like cheap candles, it was made from fatty refuse salvaged from the surface of the river Thames.[9] By 1887 Lipton's shops were selling only 3–4 tons of butterine per week compared with 25–30 tons of butter, and only 1 per cent of the C.W.S.'s butter dealings were in butterine.[10] The clear identification of butterine as 'margarine' as a result of the 1887 Act, does not seem to have harmed the product and consumption more than doubled between then and 1914. None the less, it was still a mere 6·5 lb. *per capita per annum.*

Among the most substantial rises was the consumption of tea from 2 lb. at the time of the Great Exhibition, where there were no tearooms to sustain the awed thousands, to 6 lb. by the turn of the century, by which time J. Lyon was mopping up the Exhibition trade and the A. B. C. was quenching the thirst of daily imbibers. Coffee never challenged tea as the nation's beverage, with consumption always at well under 1 lb. per head, and from the 1890s cocoa began to make a small impact. Whatever the beverage, however, it was drunk sweetly. *Per capita* consumption of sugar had risen from 41 lb. in 1861 to over 87 lb. by 1914.

The most spectacular fall in food consumption in the period was of alcohol. Beer consumption had risen very rapidly from under 20 gallons per head in 1850 to 34 gallons in 1875–6. Forty years of temperance campaigning, the development of alternative entertainments to the public house, the availability of substitute beverages and, perhaps, Mr Gladstone's licensing legislation, all contributed to a turning point in the mid-1870s. The figure fell gradually to under 28 gallons per head in 1886, rose to over 32 gallons in 1900, but from then on it entered a more or less continuous decline to 27 gallons in 1914. Spirit consumption too declined; it fluctuated round a gallon per head from 1850 until around 1902, when there was a substantial fall to under 0·7 gallons in 1914.[11]

The above were largely the staples of any diet. By the end of the century, however, the luxuries of a previous generation were becoming the necessities of the next. If we take fruit as an example, oranges, lemons, melons and pineapples were a delicacy for the very rich before the mid-century and, among all classes, were treated with some caution as being bad for the digestion. In the 1850s and 1860s steamers and clippers provided the means of bringing fruit with sufficient speed to be saleable, and of widening the area of supply. Oranges, formerly from Spain and Portugal, now came from the Azores, Malta and Crete, while 200,000 pineapples were coming from the West Indies every year. In the mid-century oranges were still enough of a novelty to be sold in streets and theatres. By 1900, however, over 5 million cwt. were being imported with consumption at 14·7 lb. per head of population. In the first decade of the twentieth century the exotic banana pushed its way rapidly into the national consciousness, with 6·7 million bunches being imported each year from 1909 to 1913, about 9 bananas per head of population.[12] The quantity consumed in 1914 was about six times more than that in 1900.

Most domestic fruit was used to make jam, which formed a high proportion of the nation's sugar consumption. Jam made bread more palatable for working-class families, though, as mothers complained, it encouraged them to eat more slices of bread. However, it was better than treacle, which tended to cause diarrhoea and it could be a substitute for rather than an accompaniment to butter. From the 1870s the demand for fruit increased. The Kentish orchards, after generations of cider-making, began to switch to dessert fruit. The Vale of Evesham switched from growing potatoes to supplying fruit for the West Midlands and London. Later, household names like Chivers, Tiptree and Beach began to expand their orchard holdings. New vegetables, such as tomatoes, were also being produced, though no doubt the warning about tomatoes that Flora Thompson received at Lark Rise was repeated elsewhere – 'Don't 'ee go trying to eat it, now . . . . It'll only make 'ee sick. I know because I had one of the nasty horrid things at our Minnies'.'[13]

An urban population requires lighter food than a rural one, and this accounted for many of the changes in food consumption habits in the second half of the nineteenth century. Eggs were an ideal way of providing nutrition with lightness. Consumption of eggs rose from 45 per annum in the 1880s to 100 per annum in 1913, but the increase in consumption was confined almost entirely to the better-off sections of the population. A bacon and egg breakfast was by the 1880s becoming fashionable among the middle classes, but in the published diets of the poorer classes eggs hardly feature at all. Perhaps this was because the poor had had unpleasant experiences with eggs. Even in the early twentieth century there was no effective commercial egg-producing industry in Britian, and eggs were sold as surplus from the farm in a very haphazard way. There was an assumption that eggs could not be marketed at a profit unless they were produced as a subsidiary. Vast quantities of eggs were imported – £9 million worth in 1914 – from as far away as Russia, to be sold after a journey of three or four weeks as 'fresh eggs'.[14]

Family Budgets

Figures on *per capita* consumption do not really show how the 'average' family in any income group actually spent its money. Various budgets, real and constructed, are available at different times throughout the period and some examples will illustrate developments.

In 1921 Miss W. A. Mackenzie constructed hypothetical budgets for families at different levels of income in 1860, 1880 and 1914. Her lowest decile family, man, wife and three children, earning 13s per week in 1860, 17s in 1880 and 20s 6d in 1914, would spend over 60 per cent of their income on food: 8s 10¼d in 1860, 11s 3¼d in 1880 and 12s 7¾d in 1914. At a slightly better-off level, a family with a wage of 15s 6d in 1860 would be earning 21s 4d by 1880 and 26s 10d by 1914. Here the proportion spent on food was somewhat less, but still high: 10s 4¼d in 1860, 12s 11¼d in 1880 and 17s 4¼d in 1914. For her median family, 13s 9d out of a wage of 20s 6d was being spent on food in 1860, 16s out of a wage of 22s 6d in 1880 and 22s 7d out of a wage of 35s 6d in 1914. Finally for her upper quartile family, 17s 6d out of a wage of 27s 6d went on food in 1860, 19s 11¼d out of 32s in 1880 and 25s 4½d out of 45s 3d in 1914.[15]

The first scientific attempts to measure food consumption were undertaken in the early 1860s by Dr Edward Smith. He collected weekly budgets of 509 agricultural labourers and 125 poorly paid industrial workers, like silk weavers, needlewomen, glovestickers, shoemakers and stocking weavers, from all over the British Isles. He found some interesting contrasts in patterns of consumption between silk weavers in Spitalfields, Bethnal Green, Coventry and Macclesfield. Bread loomed large in the meals of these poor families, 9½ lb. per adult per week on average. In Coventry and Macclesfield, though not in London, some bread was still baked at home, and in one-third of his sample no flour was purchased at all. An average quantity of 10½ lb. of potatoes was consumed by each family, over 2 lb. per adult per week. Only in Coventry did some of the silk weavers have gardens to grow a few vegetables.

Butter was generally used to accompany bread, and was eaten by all but three of Smith's forty-two families of silk weavers. The average consumption of fats weekly was 4½ oz., just over one third of present-day consumption. Occasionally treacle was taken as an alternative to butter, but was regarded as uneconomical. The London workers generally consumed meat weekly, a finding that fits with that of Mayhew, who claimed that the London costermongers invariably had a Sunday joint. A quarter of those in Macclesfield and one-sixth of those in Coventry, however, never bought meat. Altogether he found that 14·8 oz. of meat per week were consumed by each adult in Bethnal Green, 9·4 oz. in Spitalfields, 5·3 oz. in Coventry and 3·25 oz. in Macclesfield. Bacon was popular, 'because the dripping which ran from it could be given to the children while the bacon itself could be eaten by the adults'. Sheep's head had the same economical character-istics. Smith found that very little fish was consumed, just an oc-casional plaice, whiting, or dried herring.

A surprisingly large quantity of milk was drunk – 4½ pints per family per week. But most of this was in Coventry and Macclesfield, where seven times as much was consumed as in Bethnal Green. In London, however, the milk was new milk, elsewhere it was generally skimmed milk. About half the families bought small quantities of cheese, a treat consumed 'chiefly by the husband', as was the rare egg. Tea drinking was universal, 0·45 oz. per adult per week; cocoa was drunk sometimes in London, but not in Macclesfield or Coventry; most families drank beer, as much as 5 pints per week.

The average total cost of food for the silk weavers was 10s 2½d per family or 2s 2½d per adult, and this varied from 1s 8½d per adult in Macclesfield, 1s 11¾d in Coventry to 3s 5½d in Spitalfields and 2s 9¾d in Bethnal Green. The difference was not due so much to vari-ations in prices between London and elsewhere as to the different selection of foods. Londoners consumed more sugar, fats, meat and tea, while in the provinces the poor ate more bread and skimmed milk.

Smith concluded, 'the average quantity of food supplied is too little for health and strength' and, as Sir John Simon, the Government's Medical Officer commented, it reflected widespread deprivation.

It must be remembered that privation of food is very reluctantly borne, and that, as a rule, great poorness of diet will only come when other privations have preceded it. Long before insufficiency of diet is a matter of hygienic concern, long before the physiologist would think of counting the grains of nitrogen and carbon which intervene between life and starvation, the household will have been utterly destitute of material comfort: – clothing and fuel will have been scantier than food, – against inclemencies of weather there will have been no adequate protection, dwelling space will have been stinted to the degree in which over-crowding produces or increases disease, – of household utensils and furniture there will have been scarcely any, – even cleanliness will have been found costly and difficult, and if there still be self-respectful endeavours to maintain it, every such endeavour will represent additional pangs of hunger.[16]

Food was the major part of any working-class budget: the lower the income the higher the proportion of expenditure on food. As Leone Levi calculated in 1885, 71 per cent of working-class earnings went on food and drink, compared with only 44 per cent of middle-class earnings. This was clearly borne out in the Board of Trade returns on expenditure made in 1889. Admittedly from a small sample, the Board of Trade showed that the average proportion of income expended on bread, flour, butcher's meat, groceries and other provisions for different income groups was as shown below.[17]

Income	Proportion of income on food (%)
£28–40	87·42
£40–50	56·30
£50–60	63·26
£60–70	58·14
£70–80	56·03
£80–90	51·10
£90–100	66·73
£100–110	42·49
£125	44·06
£150	34·81

In the various budgets examined in 1889 it was found that skilled engineers, earning around £1 10s per week, would spend from 2s to 5s of that on meat, while unskilled labourers were likely to spend only between 1s 3d and 3s, though a London gas-stoker in the sample spent just as much as the best-paid engineer. 4d–6d per week was the average spent on jam and treacle in the survey, but the Scots showed their characteristic sweet-toothedness by spending 6d to 8d.

In a study of family budgets in 1901, the *Cornhill Magazine* took as its typical workman someone in receipt of good weekly wages, 30s per

week, who lived in London near work, and had three children of
school age. The wife was careful, shopping in the cheapest markets of
Rye Lane, Peckham or in the Old Kent Road, on Saturday evening or
Sunday morning, when things were cheapest. Her weekly food budget
came to 12s 4½d.

¼ lb. tea would normally do the week at	4½d
¼ lb. coffee	3d
1 lb. loaf sugar	2d
3 lb. moist sugar	3d
3 lb. jam (cheap 'mixed household' made from fruit that had been partly bled to make jelly	7½d
½ lb. butter	6d
8 eggs	6d
1 lb. bacon	8d
½ lb. cheddar cheese (probably American)	3d
6–7 lb. meat for the Sunday joint	2s 6d

This was the meat for the week. Served hot on Sunday, it could be
served cold for two more days and with some additions make a stew
on the fourth day.

¼ lb. suet	2d
fish, for Saturday night supper and breakfast and tea on Monday and Tuesday	10d
potatoes	3d
greens	3d
3 loaves of bread	7½d
½ quartern of flour	3d

Later in the week a further 1s 3d would be spent on bread, 2s on fish
and sausages and 9d for extra vegetables to add to the stew.[18]

Twelve years later, an Oxfordshire agricultural labourer with three
sons and a daughter, all aged under nine was still trying to feed himself
and his family on 8s a week.

1 lb. Quaker Oats	3d
3 lb. sugar	6d
28 lb. bread	3s 2½d
¼ lb. tea	4½d

2 lb. margarine	1s 0d
5 lb. brisket (frozen) and ½ lb. suet	2s 0d
⅛ stone flour	3d
¼ lb. currants	1d
condensed milk	3½d
salt and baking powder	1d

He, at least, could supplement this from his garden and allotment. In that November week in 1912 when the budget was recorded the family consumed 38 lb. of their own potatoes, 7 lb. of their own greens, 1 lb. carrots and 1 lb. turnips.[19]

At some times of the year there would be more produce from the garden and in autumn there were likely to be windfalls from fruit trees and wild fruit to make jam. But, as more than one mother pointed out to the investigators, 'If they eat jam, it includes more bread.'[20] Yet there clearly had been quite an improvement, as M. Davies found in her study of the Wiltshire village of Corsley. Thirty years before, 1 oz. of tea or coffee and 1 lb. of sugar would be bought to last a whole week. By the 1890s the same families were taking ¼ lb. of tea and 3 lb. of sugar.[21]

In the same year as Rowntree and Kendall were examining the plight of the rural labourer, Mrs Pember Reeves found a not dissimilar situation among the urban poor in London. A family of a man, wife and six children, living on 24s per week, might have as little as 8s 7d to expend on food. Some families were spending less than 3d a day on food, although nutritionally 6d was a bare minimum for an individual. The following menu of a London carter, earning from 19s to 23s 6d a week was not untypical.[22] (See Table 3.1 opposite)

Such budgets and menus can readily be duplicated, showing a multitude of variations in the spending of 10s or £1 by frugal housewives. In his analysis of the hundreds of budgets published between 1886 and 1914, Dr D. J. Oddy showed that a typical family income was between 20s and 34s per week, and that expenditure on food ranged from 10s to 20s per week, a percentage of as low as 36·6 per cent and as high as 96 per cent. A 1904 survey of urban families made the norm 60·7 per cent, but the Scottish pattern involved a higher expenditure: 72·6 per cent in Edinburgh at the turn of the century and 73·9 per cent in Glasgow in 1912. Between one-fifth and one-third of all food expenditure was on bread and between one-quarter and one-third on various meats.[23]

There were many difficulties for the working-class wife when it came to purchasing food. Firstly it had to be bought in small quan-

TABLE 3.1

	Breakfast	Dinner	Tea
Sunday	1 loaf, 1 oz. butter, ½ oz. tea, ¼d worth tinned milk, ½d worth sugar. Kippers for the man.	Hashed beef, batter pudding, greens, potatoes.	Same as breakfast, but shrimps for the man.
Monday	The same	Beef, cold with pickles.	1 loaf, marmalade, tea, 2 eggs for the man.
Tuesday	Same, with 2d worth of cocoa and bloaters for the man.	Bread, dripping, cheese and tomatoes.	Same, with fish and fried potatoes for the man.
Wednesday	Same, with corned beef.	Boiled bacon, beans and potatoes.	Same as breakfast with cold bacon.
Thursday	Loaf, jam, tea	Mutton chops, greens, potatoes.	Loaf, 1 oz. butter, tea.
Friday	Same.	Sausages and potatoes.	Loaf, jam, tea.
Saturday	Loaf, 1 oz. butter, cocoa.	Pudding of pieces, greens, potatoes.	Loaf, butter, tea.

tities. Not only was cash not available to allow bulk purchases, but, even if it had been, adequate storage space was lacking in the typical working-class cottage or flat. Any food left lying around for too long was bound to attract mice and cockroaches. Therefore food had to be bought as it was needed. It was not just the 'slovenly and improvident', as the *Cornhill* believed, who bought tea, sugar, butter and bread in halfpenny worths, although those who did so had to pay for the convenience. Cheapness had to be worked for, with long walks from the village to the nearest market town, or from one part of London to another to get the bargains. Meat could be got from the meat bazaars in places like Clare Market, and was at its cheapest in the evening. Late on Saturday night was the best time, and butchers in poor areas often stayed open as late as 1 a.m. on Sunday morning to catch the poor customer and to sell off perishable stock.[24]

Limitations were also placed on working-class eating habits by the difficulties of cooking. Not all working-class houses, by any means, had an oven. If they had it was likely to be expensive to heat. Most food was cooked in the pot, which greatly restricted choice. To middle-class observers many working-class wives seemed less than frugal in their cooking, but there was usually a logic in their methods. For example, porridge was rarely made in poor English homes, and yet nutritionally and economically, it seemed to have much to recommend it. However, the working-class wife knew that opposed to that was the inconvenience of long cooking, constant stirring and the cost of milk to accompany it. It was the difficulty of cooking, with probably in some cases ignorance of methods and general inconvenience of cooking, that made ready-cooked meats so popular among the urban poor. Ready-cooked meat stalls, generally of doubtful hygiene, remained popular throughout the period. Fish and chips caught on for the same reason, and the many canned and preserved foodstuffs that came in the later nineteenth and in the twentieth centuries, although relatively expensive, none the less attracted the working class. Middle-class observers shook their heads at the way poor women bought 'tins of salmon and potted meat, and various other preserved delicacies, rather than take the trouble to cook a wholesome meal of fresh food',[25] with probably a disastrous effect on their health, but, as always, there was a certain logic in it.

Food loomed less large in the budgets of the better off, though they were still conscious of price. The third quarter of the century saw many complaints of rising costs. It was claimed in 1875 that it cost between £30 and £50 more each year to keep a table as well-furnished as it would have been thirty years before. Butcher's meat, it was asserted, had more than doubled in price in forty years, and game, fowl and rabbits were all more expensive. These complaints were being made in the aftermath of the cattle plague of the 1860s, which had decimated British livestock. Dairy produce was affected by the same situation. Butter in 1875 was 2s per lb., double what it had been thirty years before. However, there had been some major price falls, in the main due to the fiscal policies of Peel and Gladstone. The duty on sugar was progressively reduced from as much as 63s per cwt. in 1842 until it was removed completely in 1874; tea duty went down from 2s per lb. to under 1s by 1875 and coffee from 1s 3d per lb. to 9d. The sources of supply were also extended, which affected price. Thus tea was one-half or one-third of its price a generation before. The increasingly fashionable light wines had also gained from tariff arrangements with France and the expansion of vineyards. All in all it was calculated that a middle-class family could expect to expend one-quarter of its income on food.[26]

A quarter of a century later there were more detailed analyses. The ever-helpful Mrs Peel calculated that a family of four or more could feed themselves plainly, but sufficiently, on 8s 6d per head per week. For 'nice living' 10s per head was necessary, for 'good living' 12s 6d and for 'very good living' 17s 6d per head per week.[27]

To Mrs Peel, 'small means' were £300 per annum. To those mechanics, clerks, civil servants, sanitary inspectors and others striving after respectability on an income of £150–£200 a year, in a flat in Finsbury, Lambeth or Southwark, or in an inexpensive house in one of the cheaper suburbs of Clapham, Forest Gate, Kilburn or Walthamstow, things were a good deal tighter. There were train fares to be added to the rent, 6d, a day or £7 per annum, if a season ticket could be afforded. This had the advantage that it allowed more frequent travel up to town, but many lines offered no seasons for third-class passengers. The *Cornhill* gave an example of the budget of a forty-year-old solicitor's clerk with two children:

Meat and fish	7s
Greengrocery	1s 3d
Milk	2s 6d
Bread	1s 6d
Grocery	6s 0d

This meant a total food expenditure of 18s 3d per week, £47 9s per annum. In Mrs Peel's samples, a husband and wife with no family, on an income of £250 and living in the suburbs of a northern town, would spend £78 on food, including food for the maid. A husband, wife, two boys and two servants, with an income of £380, living in west London, would have to trim their expenditure on food to about 7s per head per week, an annual expenditure of £110.

Like her working-class neighbour, the lower-middle-class housewife had to exercise great caution in her shopping. Buying from the travelling salesman could add to the price of food in the suburbs. The wise wife asked her husband to buy food from the cheaper central stores or from the street markets near the City. There would probably be a cooked breakfast of bacon and eggs for the husband, though not necessarily for the wife. The 'traditional' British breakfast had just become traditional during the 1860s, and the decline in the price of imported bacon in the following decades helped to establish it. In the cities the husband was likely to have his lunch out at a dining-room, or by the end of the 1880s at one of the increasing numbers of tea-rooms of the Aerated Bread Company. The evening meal would be high tea – bread and jam, cake and a dish of macaroni and cheese or anchovy toast. The husband might get an extra dish, but no one, least of all the wife and children, was liable to be over-fed.

Although far above starvation level, many middle-class families probably lived very meanly, especially if they entertained from time to time. The third quarter of the century had seen a change in the pattern of middle-class life. Higher standards of cuisine were expected; more lavish entertaining was fashionable; afternoon teas for the ladies and more frequent dinner parties became the norm. In order to meet the cost of public display sacrifices must have been made in private. Only a small proportion were really comfortably off. In 1860 just over 0·25 million people were in the tax-paying bracket with incomes above £160. Half a century later there were just over a million. Less that half of these admitted to an income of more than £400 per annum. In other words, as Peter Laslett has commented, much of the life-style of the middle class, so familiar in novels and reminiscences was 'largely a matter of aspiration, imitation and snobbery'. In order to maintain the 'paraphernalia of gentility' caution and frugality had to be the order of most days. An image of prosperity must have frequently been projected that went no further than the hall, dining-room and drawing-room. 'A third of the population', as Laslett again has remarked, 'was trying to live in a way that only a seventeenth of the population could live.'[28]

As in the working class, children probably suffered most. George Bernard Shaw decried the sacrifices made for 'respectability':

> We are revolted at the heartlessness of the man who starves his wife to provide cutlets for his pet dog; but we applaud the widow who starves her children, physically and morally, in order to bring them up respectable and be respectable herself. In the poor middle class this is a crying evil; boys who have the making of strong artisans in them degenerate into underfed clerks.[29]

Their meals would be extremely frugal, with plenty of porridge, bread and milk, fried bread, toast and dripping. Jam was very much for the special occasion and it was more often treacle than syrup. The lower middle classes took to frozen meat more rapidly than others and there was plenty of advice on how to cook and disguise it. As with all sections of the population, the middle classes gained from the falling prices of foodstuffs in the last quarter of the century, and they were the main consumers of the factory-prepared foods – soups, sauces, potted and tinned meats, jams, preserves – that came into greater use at the same time. It was they who made use of convenience foods like packet jellies and powdered gelatine, or ready-cut lump sugar and castor sugar, prepared and chopped suet, or stoned raisins. It was among the middle class that new eating habits, like the introduction of afternoon tea, appeared, and this meant biscuits and slab cake. Biscuits until then had been largely the accompaniment of a late-evening glass of wine. By the 1870s Ginger Nuts, Osbornes, Alberts, Balmorals and an ever-increasing variety of other biscuits were consumed in ever greater quantities.

Moving into the even more affluent income brackets, one could more or less eat what one chose, or at any rate what the cook chose. At income levels of around £700 or £800 a year or more one would employ a cook on £20 per year, and she would normally do the shopping. This was likely to push up the cost of food, since the cook would expect a commission from the shopkeepers for giving them her custom. Five per cent was not an uncommon level of commission, which was what some butchers selling frozen meat paid to cooks to win them over to the delights of foreign meat.[30] There was also likely to be a great deal of wastage due to over-buying in an establishment of any size, and cooks had a considerable side-line in selling left-overs. The costing of food and control over servants were management problems which the middle-class housewife had to solve if she was to remain comfortably within her income.

There is still a great deal that we do not know about the diet of Britain's population in the years before the First World War. A rising standard of living brought with it increased expenditure on food, but the patterns of that expenditure are not necessarily straightforward. People are generally conservative in their food habits and cling to tastes shaped in childhood. Women learned their cooking from their mothers and not until the twentieth century was well advanced were there many opportunities for them to develop and enlarge upon skills learnt in adolescence. Lack of money obviously limited the amount of experimentation with cooking that could be undertaken, but even in better-off homes which relied upon servants to cook the meals there would be no great variety or elaboration. No doubt the increasing attraction of dining out can be at least partly explained by the dull monotony of home cooking.

Changes in diet were also restricted by what was available, and it seems likely that when real wages began to rise after mid-century there was a limit to what foods were available on which to spend increased earnings. Two areas were attractive: sugar and meat. Both of these could bring relief to a monotonous grain or potato-based diet. They were also generally associated with the better off and, therefore, were regarded as being worthy of emulation. But although reductions in sugar duty, from the 1840s onwards, increased the supply and lowered the price, it was not until 1874 that the duty was removed completely, opening the way to cheap jam and confectionery. There were also limits to how quickly meat production could expand and there were serious shortages in the 1860s. It was not until the 1870s that access to foreign supplies, plus increased home production, brought the price down. Among the few foodstuffs for which it was possible to adjust production speedily and which had a well developed distribution network to meet increased demand were beer and spirits. Therefore, much of the early rise in real wages probably went on increased alcohol consumption. Only during the late 1870s was a wider range of alternatives made available and then drink consumption began to fall. And only after this were urban workers generally able to obtain access to increased quantities of meat, milk, dairy produce and vegetables.[31]

While a rising standard of living brought with it increased expenditure on food, it did not necessarily bring with it diets that were more healthy than before. The extra money for food was spent on more sugar-based products, all of which no doubt made many meals more palatable, but which in themselves probably did harm rather than good to the nation's health. When there was more money to spend it was likely to go on better cuts of meat or on expensive convenience food. Ignorance, false propaganda and fashion all too often led people to sacrifice the nutritionally sound for the expensive and the easy. Such was the pattern that emerged, even at the bottom of the social scale, in Rowntree's study of the working class of York, and the Charity Organisation Society and its supporters never tired of pointing out misdirected working-class expenditure on foodstuffs as well as on other items. A recent study of Lancaster and Barrow, on the other hand, based upon oral evidence, presents a rather different picture in which cost-conscious housewives bought cheap, but nutritious, tradional foods. While in York vegetables hardly feature at all in working-class meals, the Lancastrians made a wide range of vegetables a central part of their diet.[32] As so often happens, there are evident dangers in trying to generalise either nationally or in terms of class.

Behind the clear improvement in the amount of basic foods that were consumed a great deal of undernourishment still persisted. There clearly were many people, a majority of them probably women and children, who spent a great deal of their day feeling hungry. Death rates among children aged between 1 and 4 years were 18·4 per thousand. This was a considerable fall from the 31·2 per thousand of the 1870s, but as D. J. Oddy has pointed out it was well above the 10

per thousand which the World Health Organisation takes as a
threshold for indications of malnutrition in developing countries.[33]

4. Patterns of Consumption: Shelter

To young people... I would strongly recommend a house some little way out of London. Rents are less; smut and blacks are conspicuous by their absence; a small garden, or even a tiny conservatory, are not an impossibility; and if 'Edwin' has to pay for his season-ticket, that is nothing in comparison with his being able to sleep in fresh air, to have a game of tennis in summer, or a friendly evening of music, chess or games in the winter, without expense... Mrs J. E. Panton, *From Kitchen to Garret* (1888).

There was nothing in this miserable room save a tiny saucepan on an empty stove. There was no fire, no warmth or light, no furniture. A Covent Garden flower-seller's home *c.* 1900, in O. C. Malvery, *The Soul Market*, 6th edn (n.d.).

After bodily sustenance the next priority for all classes was accommodation, and here again the poor suffered for their poverty. Just before the First World War a middle-class, well-to-do man, earning £2000 a year, might pay £250 in rent, rates and taxes, one-eighth of his income. The comfortably off gentleman on £500 a year might pay £85, one-sixth of his income. The working man on 24s a week might pay 8s on rent and rates, one–third of his income.

Rents, of course, varied greatly within towns and between different parts of the country, as did the quality of accommodation available. Rents were, however, out of line with the general price trend and continued to rise, in some cases quite steeply, during the last quarter of the century, when other prices were falling. Much of the gain of falling food prices was eaten up by rent increases. On the other hand, as Mrs Gauldie has pointed out, for the very poorest tenants rents remained fairly static. An Irish family in Holborn in 1840 could get a room for 1s or 1s 6d a week; seventy years later it was still possible to find a mean hovel at about that rental.[1]

Generally what one paid for was space. There was remarkably little variation in the price per room: 1s per room plus an additional 6d was common. For 1s or 1s 6d there would be a bare room without a sink and in some cases without a fireplace. Twice that rent would pay for two rooms, an attic, access to a water supply and the use of a communal privy. 4s 6d to 6s would, assuming the tenant had the necessary 'respectability', bring entry to a 'model' dwelling, courtesy of Peabody, Waterlow or the Improved Industrial Dwellings Company in London, designed in what C. F. G. Masterman called the 'later desolate' style. In Leeds 4s 6d to 6s would pay for four rooms in a back to back, the 'superior' ones consisting of 'a living room on one side of the door, and a scullery on the other, a bedroom over each, and usually a third attic bedroom with dormer windows'.[2] In Oxford, in 1912, for the same money one could get two up and two down, or even three up and two down, water laid on, a share of a wash-house and a small garden.[3] For more than 6s it was possible to move to a suburban working-man's cottage, with maybe five bedrooms, but to this had to be added the cost of travel to work.

It was only in the last thirty years of the century, with the development of suburban working-men's trains, that movement out of central areas was possible. Before then the working-man's ideal was a house in which he could lie in bed until he heard the first work bell at ten to six in the morning, and where he could eat all his meals.[4] Many of those houses, however, were destroyed by the mid-century civic improvements and by railway expansion into the heart of the main towns. Their inhabitants were forced into ever-more crowded rookeries. Thomas Wright has left a description of one such:

> There was, as I have already observed, twenty houses in the Court – ten on each side – and each house consisted of four small apartments, two upstairs, and two downstairs, of an average size of eleven feet by ten; and yet in eighteen of these houses there were two, and in some instances three, families living, each house having an average of *at least* ten inhabitants, and every apartment being used at night as a sleeping room.[5]

By 1912, however, 40 per cent of suburban commuters within a six to eight mile radius of central London were working-class men, and 25 per cent of all suburban railway passengers were buying workmen's tickets. They were likely to be living in ill-designed, jerry-built working-class estates, built by a small builder working on tight estimates:

> His bricks will be porous, his timber 'shaky', his mortar deficient in lime, his plaster destitute of hair, his woodwork and joinery of the most unsatisfactory kind, and his sanitary appliances of the cheapest quality.[6]

In the 1880s on average a working-class family was spending 16 per cent of its income on rent, thirty years later the proportion was even higher, if Mrs Pember Reeves's figures are accepted. For a family of six in Lambeth rent would be 8s to 9s a week for three or four rooms, 6s to 7s for two rooms, 3s 6d for one room.[7] This does, however, seem high. A Board of Trade enquiry into the cost of living of the working class found that in England and Wales the predominant weekly rent and rates in 1905 were: for two rooms, 3s to 3s 6d; for three rooms, 3s 9d to 4s 6d; for four rooms, 4s 6d to 5s 6d; for six rooms, 6s 6d to 7s 9d. London rents were considerably higher than those elsewhere: 19 per cent more than in Croydon, 38 per cent more than in Manchester, and 45 per cent more than in Macclesfield. Scottish rents, particularly in Edinburgh, were higher than in comparable English towns. For a single room in Edinburgh 2s to 2s 6d a week was common; for two rooms the range was 3s 10d to 4s 3d, and for three, 5s 2d to 6s 5d. In smaller towns like Greenock, Dundee, Falkirk and Paisley, it cost 10 per cent less, in Kilmarnock and Aberdeen 15 per cent less, and in Perth and Galashields 20 to 30 per cent less.[8]

To take one final example, Lady Florence Bell, in her study of the Tees-side iron town of Middlesbrough in the first decade of the present century, found that out of 700 houses, 30 cost under 3s 6d a week, 180 cost from 3s 6d to 4s, 254 from 4s to 5s, 76 between 5s and 6s, 62 between 6s and 7s 6d and 21 over 7s 6d. Only three men had bought and were living in their own houses.[9] Few could aspire to home ownership, with the cheapest of houses costing over £100. In some areas there were effective building societies which encouraged artisan investors, but a record of fraud against working-class investors over the years deterred such investors and made the working class suspicious of building societies.

Rent in the towns was generally collected weekly or fortnightly, and landlords kept a careful check on arrears. Philanthropists, like Octavia Hill, put regular payment of rent at the heart of the social control of her tenantry, but even in the Peabody 'models', catering for the regularly employed and respectable, two or three weeks rent arrears had to be allowed before eviction took place. In the country rents were very much lower, 1s 6d to 2s a week being fairly common, with perhaps an additional 5s per annum rental for an allotment. None the less, there too, arrears were a problem. The rent would usually be paid yearly or half yearly, and Rowntree and Kendall found in their study of rural conditions at the beginning of the century that hardly any of the labourers they examined laid aside anything towards rent. Rather they depended on extra earnings, like the harvest bonus or the sale of garden produce to meet the payments.[10] In towns another way of helping to pay the rent was to take in lodgers. About a third of the houses in Middlesbrough in Lady Bell's study took in lodgers. They would pay 12s to 15s a week for board, lodging and washing, giving the landlady a profit of perhaps 2s or 3s, a very useful addition to income.[11] It seems to have been slightly cheaper to be a lodger in London. When Olive Malvery was doing her investigations into the London poor she was able to get board and lodging for 6s.[12]

The working-class house would be heated by a coal and wood fire, and for the less than destitute by a black range with side oven. Coal fell in price throughout the period from around 30s a ton in 1850, to 27s in 1872, to 20s by 1902, and to 16s by 1913. None the less it remained an expensive item for the working-class family. Lack of storage space meant that coal had to be purchased by the hundred-weight or less, making it even more expensive. Rowntree and Kendall's agricultural labourers were paying about 1s 4d a week for a hundredweight of coal in 1912, while others buying by the ton and saving through a 'coal club' could get a ton for 16s 6d. At the turn of the century about 2s per week on coal and wood for fuel seems to have been the normal outlay. During winter, when the fire was on most of the time, all the cooking would be done on it, but by the end of the century the paraffin stove offered a cheaper means of cooking and was becoming increasingly popular. In many cities the gas industry had expanded, particularly from the late 1860s onwards, when private works were taken over by the municipalities. This brought a fall in the price of gas, and in some cities like Glasgow and Manchester it was possible to hire gas stoves from the municipal gas department. None the less, paraffin at 9d to 1s per gallon was attractively cheap.

James 'Paraffin' Young's discovery, in 1847, of the refining process which produced paraffin contributed to a domestic revolution in the second half of the nineteenth century. It was particularly important for lighting. Until the 1870s and 1880s candles were the usual means of lighting, having replaced the tallow dip in the 1830s. At first the candle made from tallow was expensive at 1s per lb, but new techniques for removing colour and smell from fats, fish oil and palm oil brought cheapness, if not great light. After 1871 paraffin wax was mainly used, but already oil lamps were offering an alternative. Paraffin oil used with a flat wick produced an unparalleled amount of light, and between 1859 and 1870 some eighty patents were taken out on aspects of the oil lamp, producing improved burners, wicks and draught design. Lamps were expensive to buy, however, and it could cost 6d a week to light a house adequately, which was a large part of many working-class budgets. Expense did, of course, vary with the time of year, but since Lady Bell believed that the 2d per week that her Middlesbrough families expended on oil was quite adequate, it is probable that candles still remained popular. In addition the cheaper lamps were smoky and a problem to clean.

The actual furnishings and fittings in any house depended on a variety of factors: present and past income, versatility of the wife, attitudes of the husband, aspirations of the family, the benevolence of local philanthropy and luck. Luck was always important: the luck of having tables, chairs, dressers, beds, sofas passed on by friends, relatives or parents; the luck of not having to pawn them in hard times; the luck of better times which allowed them to be taken out of pawn. In Flora Thompson's Lark Rise, there were marked differences in life style among those with the same 10s a week income.

> In nearly all the cottages there was but one room downstairs, and many of these were poor and bare, with only a table and a few chairs and stools for furniture and a superannuated potato sack thrown down by way of a hearthrug. Other rooms were bright and cosy, with dressers and crockery, cushioned chairs, pictures on the walls and brightly coloured hand-made rugs on the floor. In these there would be pots of geraniums, fuschias, and old-fashioned, sweet-smelling musk on the window-sills. In the older cottages there were grandfather clocks, gate-legged tables, and rows of pewter, relics of a time when life was easier for country folk.[13]

The *Morning Chronicle* reporter had noted a similar phenomenon in Manchester in 1859.

> Nothing struck me more, while visiting and comparing notes in the different operative districts of Manchester, than the regularity with which the better style of house and the better style of furniture went together; it being always kept in mind that, so far as wages are concerned, the inhabitants of one locality are almost, if not quite, on a

par with those of another. But a superior room seemed by a sort of natural sequence, to attract the superior class of furniture. A very fair proportion of what was deal in Ancoats was mahogany in Hulme. Yet the people of Hulme get no higher wages than the people of Ancoats. The secret is that they live in better built houses, and consequently take more pride in their dwellings.[14]

It is really impossible to describe a 'typical' working-class home. The bare room, with nothing but a heap of rags in it to act as a bed, is well attested to at any period. In the 1860s Wright wrote of the 'simply horrible' conditions of many of the working class, living in dwellings that were 'inferior to most stables' – 'any master of fox-hounds would be indignant if he were asked to kennel his hounds in such foul dens for a night'.[15] The avid 'slummers' of the 1880s and 1890s found similar conditions in the poor areas of any great city twenty years after Wright, and another twenty years on Olive Malvery, visiting the home of a Covent Garden flower-seller, found 'nothing in this miserable room ... no fire, no warmth or light, no furniture'.[16]

It is very difficult to penetrate behind the curtains in a seemingly more prosperous working-class home. Away from the slums and courts real poverty lay behind a comfortable exterior. Wright wrote of those who 'though they may be without a chair to sit upon, and their bedding may consist of a pile of rags, they will have a curtain for their window, they will keep their ragged children out of sight as much as possible, and they will endure direct hardship rather than seek aid from the hand of charity'.[17] And many other investigators found that the home behind the clean and tidy window curtains and the 'outward air of cleanliness', did not bear closer inspection.[18] There is more than one story of philanthropists calling at two houses next door to each other in each of which there was temporary distress. In one 'the poverty was accentuated by dirt, rags, and disorder, and in the other it was hidden from superficial observers by cleanliness, well-dusted furniture, a few strips of carefully preserved carpet, and a general determination to put the best side foremost'. It was the former that received the hand-out, while the latter got a mere commendation: 'A pleasure to see a house look so nice after the sad scenes of poverty we have witnessed among your neighbours.'[19] The same concern about appearance was to be found among the journalist Stephen Reynolds's friends in early twentieth-century Devon. In that part of the world there was the unwritten rule that it was bad manners to go into other people's kitchens during a meal: 'If they have to go hungry give them at least a chance of not letting it be known.'[20] At the same time in

Salford the need to seem 'respectable' was all important, with a draped lace curtain 'a necessity for any family with pretensions to class', and oil cloth on the floor, if only in the kitchen.[21]

It must be asked if the popular image of the clean, comfortable, well but simply-furnished cottage of the artisan was more a product of the novelists' imagination than of reality. Lack of space meant disorder, dirt and clutter. Tony Widgery's kitchen, scullery, eating-room, sitting-room, reception-room, store-room, wash-house in Devon was probably not unusual.

The kitchen is not a very light room; its low small-paned window is in the N. wall. Then going round the room, the courting chair stands in the N E corner, below some shelves laden with fancy china and souvenirs – and tackle. The kitchener, which opens out into quite a comfortable fireplace, is let into the E. wall, and close beside it is the provision cupboard, so situated that the cockroaches, having ample food and warmth, shall wax fat and multiply. Next, behind a low dirty door in the S. wall, is the coalhole, then the high dresser, and then the door to the narrow front passage, beneath the ceiling of which are lodged masts, spars and sails. The W. wall of the kitchen is decorated with Tony's Oddfellow 'cistificate', with old almanacs and with a number of small pictures, all more or less askew.

There is an abundance of chairs, most of them with a cushion on the seat, all of them more or less broken by the children's racket. Over the pictures on the warm W. wall – against which, on the other side, the neighbour's kitchener stands – is a line of clean underclothing, hung there to air. The dresser is littered with fishing lines as well as with dry provisions and its proper complement of odd pieces of china. Beneath the table and each of the larger chairs are boots and slippers in various stages of polish or decay. Every jug not in daily use, every pot and vase, and half the many drawers, contain lines, copper nails, sail thimbles and needles, spare blocks and pulleys, rope-ends and twine. But most characteristic of the kitchen (the household teapot excepted) are the navy-blue garments and jerseys, drying along the line and flung over chairs, together with innumerable photographs of Tony and all his kin, the greater number of them in seafaring rig.[22]

Much of the clutter was brought about by necessity, the lack of cupboard space, the lack of wardrobes. These last were largely unknown in working-class homes before the twentieth century, hence the attraction of the pawn shop as a place to hang one's best clothes, though some Manchester operatives' houses had a nondescript piece of furniture which doubled as a bed by night and a wardrobe by day.[23] But some of the clutter was self-imposed. Late Victorian fashion dictated that as much as possible of one's worldly possessions should be on display. The young Flora Thompson noticed how domestic servants picked up the styles and fashions of their employers and when they returned to marry in the village they sought 'to obtain things as near as possible like those in the houses in which they had been employed'.

Instead of the hard windsor chairs of her childhood's home, she would have small 'parlour' chairs with round backs and seats covered with horsehair or American cloth. The deal centre table would be covered with a brightly coloured woollen cloth between meals and cookery operations. On the chest of drawers which served as a sideboard, her wedding presents from her employers and fellow servants would be displayed – a best tea service, a shaded lamp, a case of silver teaspoons with the lid propped open, or a pair of owl pepper-boxes with green-glass eyes and holes at the top of the head for the pepper to come through. Somewhere in the room would be seen a few books and a vase or two of flowers. The two wicker arm-chairs by the hearth would have cushions and anti-macassars of the bride's own working.[24]

The fact that possessions were so often on display must have had the effect of encouraging demand. The chipped or cracked vase or cup had to be replaced; the too-often repaired table covering had to go. It encouraged duplication, with the 'good set' kept for display and visitors and the less good for everyday use. The ambition of many was to have a parlour, where the finest possessions could be displayed to the discriminating visitor, but which was rarely used by the family.

Bedrooms were likely to be fully utilised, with beds filling the room so that it was necessary to climb over them to reach one's own corner. Beds could be sprung, or just mattresses, or a pile of rags. The *Morning Chronicle* reporter who visited miners in Northumberland and Durham in 1859 noticed in particular the beds and the chests-of-drawers, noting that 'in a great proportion of cases neither of these would be out of place in a house of some pretensions'. 'The bedstead is very frequently of carved and turned mahogany, and the bed, clean, soft, and comfortable with white furniture and a quilted coverlet.'[25] Many Scottish houses had the advantage that the bed was built into the wall, saving the cost of having to purchase one and in addition providing extra seating. Very few blankets were likely to be available, and sacks, old coats and curtains were added to provide warmth. If there were any pretensions to respectability then sheets would probably be kept in reasonably good condition and certainly well repaired, since the wash-day display could matter to one's social standing.

For most working-class families the furnishing of a house was probably done gradually, using the second-hand market. Saving before marriage was necessary to fit out the house which probably delayed the age at which couples married. A young couple from a Northumberland mining community at the end of the 1850s would generally go to a furniture broker in Newcastle or Sunderland, with perhaps £10 cash.[26] A considerable part of their 'plenishing', as it was called, would be obtained on credit and paid off by instalments. The pattern in Oxfordshire in the 1880s was for the bride to buy the house furnishings from her savings in service. Some idea of the kind of savings required can be obtained from the complete 'house of furniture' suitable for a one-up, one-down house, offered for twelve guineas early in the twentieth century.[27]

	£	s	d
One leather couch or sofa	1	6	0
One hardwood armchair		9	6
One hardwood rocking chair		9	6
Four best kitchen chairs		15	6
One square table		10	6
3½ × 4 yards oil cloth		14	0
One cloth hearth rug		4	9
One kitchen fender		6	6
One set kitchen fire-irons		4	6
One ashpan		2	11
One full-size brass-mounted bedstead	1	12	6
One double woven wire mattress		14	6
One flock bed bolster and pillows		16	6
3 ft 6 in. enclosed dressing-table with fixed glass	1	15	0
Ditto washstand with tile back	1	9	0
Two cane seat chairs		7	0
2½ × 4 yards oil cloth		10	0
Two bedside rugs		3	10
	12	12	0

The quality of such furniture was not likely to be particularly good. Most commentators seem agreed that new furniture was of poor finish, and fairly quickly the chairs would start to creak, the veneer would blister and the drawers cease to open as the green wood warped.

At slightly above basic level one could aspire to various refinements. Clocks were, of course, essential in an industrial society. It was remarked that, 'No Manchester operative would be without one a moment longer than he can help.' Northumberland miners similarly laid great store by their clocks.[28] A cottage piano at around £24 at the turn of the century or, particularly in Scotland, a small harmonium, were popular, though the new gramophone was already having a deleterious effect on musical self-help. Alternatively, one might spend a windfall on the chiffonier, the owning of which was the acme of respectability and which would be 'placed where it could be seen through the open street door'.

Pots, pans, utensils and crockery would be built up by a family over the years. Few would be new and pans would be frequently repaired. The wise housewife would pay her 4d a week to the 'crockery club' to build up a stock. Many of the basic items were very cheap. Michael Marks's stall in Leeds market in the mid-1880s had cups, saucers, teapots, tumblers, plates, pudding bowls amid the abundance of penny items.

One feature of the working-class house in an industrial city would probably have been the dirt and grime, which seeped in through ill-fitting windows and doors or was carried in from work. No campaign was more persistently pursued than the attempts to make 'the great unwashed' more conscious of their noses. Cleanliness was, after all, next to godliness in the middle-class scheme of things. But, then, godliness was not really a pursuit to which the working class devoted much attention. Cleanliness was hardly possible and not often a great concern in the working-class home. Consumption of soap certainly increased throughout the century from the days when the Duke of Wellington had popularised a daily bath among the upper classes, but when W. H. Lever set out to capture the working-class market in the 1880s and 1890s he had first to educate his customers with a pamphlet, *Sunlight Soap and How to Use It*.[29] By the time Lady Bell was preparing her study of Middlesbrough, the 5d or 6d a week which was being expended by working-class families on soap, soda, polish, grate cleaning and blacking seems to have been not untypical, though in 1913 rural labourers were spending on average a mere 2½d. One of Lever's early slogans was 'Why does a woman look old sooner than a man?', showing an awareness of the Sisyphean task that any working-class wife or domestic servant faced, in the battle against dirt.

Middle-Class Housing

For the middle- and upper-class family there was a wide choice of available accommodation. In the nineteenth century, in London at any rate, it was more common to rent than to buy and rents rose considerably from the 1850s onwards, though probably just keeping pace with rising incomes. About 12 per cent of a middle-class income was spent on rents, and Mrs Peel's advice to those setting up house was not to spend more than 10 per cent on rent with a third more on rates and taxes.[30] For somewhere between £80 and £110 per annum a young couple could have a large flat with three or four bedrooms, three public rooms and a bathroom. Most of the newer houses and even cheap flats had bathrooms from the 1890s onwards. Earlier they had been most unusual. As a child in the 1870s in Islington Molly Hughes had not seen a bathroom, and in her experience a tin bath was kept in each bedroom.[31]

In the twentieth century there were more opportunities for the middle class to buy their houses in the ever-developing suburbs. Along the recently opened Hampstead underground line in 1910 there was a choice which ranged from a small semi-detached at £385 to an elegant architect-designed mansion at £3000 in the healthy Hampstead Garden Suburb. Golders Green prices were from £350 to £650 for a semi-detached house, and six-bedroomed terraced houses in Belsize Park could be acquired for £800. Four bedrooms and a boxroom in Highgate cost £525 and, further out, in Hendon a house could be bought for £300: £25 cash down and £2 8s per month for fourteen years.[32] Prices and rents were both a great deal higher in London than in provincial cities, but in London the choice and variety of available housing was much wider.

One paid in middle-class housing for the area, for the finish in the house and for space, both inside and around the house. Space outside was important since it gave privacy and privacy mattered to the middle class. Was it because they did not want neighbours to pry beneath their, often superficial, affluence? Space mattered inside because there were bound to be servants. The cost of domestic labour had remained remarkably cheap over the decades. In 1860 a housekeeper or butler would cost £45–£50 per annum, a cook £20, a housemaid £18–£20, a scullery maid £10. Fifty years later, an experienced butler could still be got for just over £50. The family on 'small means' of £300 a year in the suburbs of a large provicinal town could still get an all-purpose maid for £16 per annum.[33] In a family with £800 a year in Bayswater, the cook was still only paid £20 per annum in 1901 and the house parlourmaid £18.[34]

The 'servant problem' loomed large in the middle-class mind: the 'problem' being the difficulty of obtaining servants. It was becoming necessary to rely on outside aid, like the boys of the London brigade who would come in to do scrubbing, cleaning of knives and boots and to wash up. Domestic servants were beginning to be selective and to demand improved conditions. Everywhere at the turn of the century the complaint was that working-class girls showed no enthusiasm for domestic service and turned instead to shops and factories. Perhaps Mrs Peel is right when she says that the attraction of the alternatives was 'not because the work is lighter or the pay better, but because in those professions she has the full use of her hours of liberty, and more important reason than all, she enjoys a higher social position'.[35] However, one suspects that a middle class caught in the pincers of a slowly rising income and rapidly rising expectations failed to remunerate their servants adequately and so lost them.

How a house was furnished depended on income and taste. It helped, of course, if the bride's father bought the basic necessities.[36] In his *Manual of Domestic Economy* in 1857, J. H. Walsh showed how to furnish a hall, staircase, kitchen, dining-room, drawing-room, library, three bedrooms, two servants' rooms and a nursery for £585, but there were cheap furnishing warehouses from which a ten-roomed house could be furnished for under £300.[37] Fashion after the mid-nineteenth century dictated the familiar Victorian furniture, heavy oak and mahogany chairs and tables and sideboards, elaborately ornamented settees and couches with, as a critic of 1864 declared, a 'generally puffy and blown out appearance' and probably shrouded in chintz covering. Carpets were beginning to be fitted as prices were lowered. In 1875 a good Brussels carpet cost 4s 6d a yard compared with 5s 3d in 1850 and, as a result, the same critic was complaining that 'every nook and cranny' was now being covered. Walls were being hung with heavy wall-papers, dark in the dining-room, light in the drawing-room, with window curtains a yard too long so that they could be looped at either side, the whole effect combining to produce a dark and gloomy appearance.

By the end of the century a great deal had changed. William Morris and a few others had opened the eyes of the Victorians to the 'peculiar ugliness' of their domestic lives. Wall-papers were brightening. Colour-wash was making them unnecessary in bedrooms. Parquet surrounds were gaining ground from fitted carpets, and linoleum and American oil cloth were becoming popular for bedrooms.

Of course, what more than anything else brought brightness into the Victorian household was the revolution in lighting. A duplex paraffin lamp or a central draught lamp could provide fifty candle power, but there were table lamps, hand lamps, wall lamps and reading lamps of every description, with globes and pillars that reflect the elaborateness of Victorian taste. By the beginning of the present century, Von Webbach's experiments had resulted in the incandescent mantle, which brought major improvements in luminosity and the Famos and Aladdin lamps. The application of pressure brought the Primus from Sweden and the Coleman from the United States to compete with the British Tilley and Veritas. It helped greatly to have servants to look after the oil lamps, with their glass and brass to be polished, wicks to be trimmed, chimneys to be cleaned and founts to be kept filled. With anything from a dozen to thirty lamps in a house, it must have been, second only to blacking the fireplace, the most unpleasant of a housemaid's tasks.

The introduction of gas was an even bigger step forward, but in the 1890s it was still regarded as expensive and rather messy, though municipal ownership of gas works in many cities had brought the cost down. By 1910, however, the Gas Light and Coke Company, London's private gas supplier, was reminding would-be house furnishers that gas lighting was 'Artistic, Hygienic, Best for the Eyes, and the Cheapest Method of Artificial Illumination'. By this time electricity was beginning to make some impact. As demand increased, the cost fell. Almost all the Hampstead Garden Suburb houses had electric fittings, and increasing numbers of plumbers and decorators were setting up as jobbing electricians, often at great hazard to life and property. The average cost of installation was 23s to 25s per light, and running charges in London were 4d to 6d per unit (one unit equalled eight candle power for thirty-five hours).[38] The relatively high cost of electricity was still a deterrent to many in the early twentieth century, but its convenience and cleanliness made it very attractive as a source of light. The introduction of the oven thermometer after 1903 made it more attractive as a means of cooking, but its widespread acceptance for that purpose did not really come until some time after the First World War. One problem with electric light was that it could so very easily be wasted and advice was given on how to save money (but surely to lose servants): 'It may also be useful to have the switch of the servants' quarters in the mistress's bedroom, so that if she suspects the domestics of reading in bed their lights can be put out.'[39] Most cooking would be done on a kitchener or range. These varied in size and complexity, but a medium-size one would cost anything between £8 and £18 at the turn of the century. Gas or oil stoves might also be used. Heating would be by open grate, with which every room including the hall, would be fitted. Many hours were spent blacking the ranges and grates, with patent blackeners, like Zebra polish, which sold at 1d per box. The price of grates and ranges had fallen by almost 50 per cent in the last half of the nineteenth century, and a much wider choice of style and design was available, but the fundamental problem of cleaning them was never solved.

There was little alternative to scouring grates, but the 'servant problem' gave the search for labour-saving devices a certain urgency. By 1914 some important new ones were available. There were carpet sweepers from Bissell's of the United States, ranging in price from 9s 9d to 17s 3d and, after 1905, a portable vacuum cleaner at £12 to £15. This last needed two people to operate it, but after 1906 an electrically operated one-man (or rather maid) model was available for £35.[40] Yet these were exceptional luxuries, and the problem of keeping house was a massive one as the inevitable grime found its way among the packed ornaments and furniture. It was not just arbiters of fashion who encouraged less clutter and increasing simplicity in the late nineteenth and early twentieth centuries, but middle-class housewives faced with the problem of doing more and more of their own work.

5. Patterns of Consumption: Clothing

> It will not perhaps realise all the dreams of fancy, but it will put an end to that slavery to the needle under which so many English girls have grown crooked and sallow and miserable.
>
> Harriet Martineau, commenting on the sewing machine in 1857.

Clothing came after food and shelter in the order of priorities for expenditure. It is difficult to give any kind of 'norm' for expenditure on clothing over time. Professor Asa Briggs has estimated that in 1845 a working man spent 6 per cent of his income on clothes, by 1890 8 or 9 per cent, and by 1904 12 per cent.[1] This, however, seems something of an over-estimate when compared with the calculations made by Miss W. A. Mackenzie for representative families. Her lowest decile family of man, wife and three children, earning 13s in 1860, 17s in 1880 and 20s 6d in 1914, spent 9d, 1s and 1s per week respectively on clothing. Her median family, earning 20s 6d in 1860, 22s 6d in 1880 and 35s 6d in 1914, spent 1s 6d, 2s and 2s 6d respectively: and her upper quartile family, earning 27s 6d, in 1860, 32s in 1880 and 45s 3d in 1914, spent 2s, 2s 6d and 3s respectively on clothing. In no case was this more than 8 per cent.

Returns on working-class expenditure in 1889 showed Northumberland miners spending from £3 to £12 per year on boots and clothing from incomes that ranged from £1 0s 7d per week to £1 4s 10d. Joiners in the sample earning between £1 9s 3d and £1 9s 9d per week were spending between £5 and £10, and engineers from £8 to £15 on slightly higher incomes. These proportions are nearer Professor Briggs's figures, and the 1889 sample showed that on the whole the higher the income the greater the proportion spent on clothing.[2] (See Table 5.1.)

In the *Cornhill*'s workman's budget of 1901 the expenditure on clothing out of a 30s per week income was 2s, that is 7 per cent. The lower-middle-class family on £160 per annum spent £25 on clothing,

Table 5.1

Average income	Percentage expenditure on clothing
£28–40	2·15
£40–50	13·46
£50–60	10·25
£60–70	9·13
£70–80	14·62
£80–90	9·17
£90–100	9·65
£100–110	10·46
£125	16·00
£150	8·66

16 per cent. Rowntree's study of York showed families investigated there expending just over 6 per cent of their income on clothes, though he believed that 6d per adult and 5d per child per week was the minimum necessary for a clothing allowance, that is from £5 17s per annum for a family with three children to over £9 for a family with six children. Mrs Pember Reeves's families on 'round about a pound a week' were spending less than that. One typical family of father, mother and six children spend a mere £3 5s 5½d in a fifteen-month period on clothes. Most of the women cotton weavers in a survey published in 1911 spent around 3s 6d a week on clothes.[3]

The time to buy clothes in poor households was in the summer when less money was needed for fuel. It is, however, doubtful if any but a small proportion of the working class bought new clothes before the 1870s. They were dependent on the second-hand clothes' dealers, hand-me-downs and charity. As a writer in 1860 noted,

Worn clothes were of course always procurable in the purlieus of Whitechapel and St Giles's. A nobleman's or wealthy commoner's cast off garments went to his domestics, and from the domestics to the old clothesman, and from the old clothesman to the mechanics. and from the mechanics to the sweepers at the street crossings.[4]

Agricultural labourers' wives in Oxfordshire in the 1880s were still largely dependent on clothes sent home by their daughters in service. This did not mean that fashion was ignored. Clothes had to be only 'a year or two behind outside standards' and the bustle was necessary even when carrying swill to the pigs.[5] Rowntree and Kendall's rural budgets of 1913 showed that respectable labourers in regular work were largely dependent on charity for their dress.[6] Only perhaps on leaving school, using the pennies saved in the school savings scheme, would a 'Sunday' suit be purchased for a boy and a dress for a girl to go into domestic service with.[7]

There was a market for some working-class ready-made clothing even in the 1850s and 1860s. These were produced by the slop tailors of the East End and were in a shapeless style and of indifferent quality. In many ways refurbished old clothes were probably better. The great advantage of having a set of reasonably respectable 'Sunday clothes' was that they could be a most useful source of capital, if pawned on a Monday morning and redeemed late on Saturday night. Corduroy and moleskin were the most popular materials for working-men's clothes, though miners wore coarse flannel. A broad-ribbed corduroy waistcoat with fustian back and sleeves and dark 'cable cord' trousers was standard wear for a London costermonger in the 1850s. The small cloth cap was a must, with a hat only for Sunday, and, to set off the whole rig-out, a gay neckerchief. Women wore printed cotton gowns with petticoats to the ankles and a velveteen or straw bonnet.[8] A covering for the head was *de rigueur* for both sexes. From the slop tailor, trousers would cost anything from 9s 6d to £1, a waistcoat 10s and a great coat £2 10s. The cost of a pit suit 'of good material and fair workmanship' in Newcastle in 1859 was about £1.

Boots and shoes were a major problem. Most working-men needed fairly solid ones and 1s a week might be paid into a 'boot club' to ensure a regular supply. Many got their boots from the 'boiled' boot shops where old boots were patched, polished and sold cheaply. The hard-wearing and relatively cheap clogs of Lancashire mill towns were a great boon, but by the end of the century distinctly unfashionable. Men needed decent boots for work and compulsory education meant that children had to obtain a pair of shoes or boots at least for school hours. For women, however, decent footwear came well down the list of family priorities. One reason why working-women's skirts remained so long and were rarely lifted out of the mud was that they were embarrassed to show off the battered, ill-fitting boots that were likely to be their footwear. The mark of a 'real lady' was a short skirt (within reason, of course) and neat boots.

The clothing industry was revolutionised by the introduction of the sewing machine, first seen at the Great Exhibition of 1851, but really coming in when I. M. Singer opened his works at Glasgow in 1856. Others followed, like the Jones Company, building on the patents of Elias Howe, but always second to Singer's. The introduction of the sewing machine brought the industrial revolution to the ready-made clothes and footwear industries. Yet, paradoxically, at the same time it strengthened domestic clothes-making. The sewing machine allowed clothes to be made at home more easily and more professionally.

The careful wife made the family clothes, buying flannel at 2s 6d per yard for shirts; otherwise a good flannel shirt would cost anything from 6s 6d to 9s 6d, and probably two would be needed in a year. Flannelette was popular too because it was warm, soft, unshrinkable and cheap. A child's dress in it could be provided for 6d. It did not wear well, but it was more popular than cotton, both for the warmth it gave and because of theories that gas and fumes 'ate' cotton material. Most girls would have learned the rudiments of sewing at school, using suitably functional material provided by the philanthropic, as Flora Thompson recalled:

> roomy chemises and wide-legged drawers made of unbleached calico, beautifully sewn, but without an inch of trimming; harsh, but strong flannel petticoats and worsted stockings that would almost stand up with no legs in them.[9]

But the even more important development that grew from the sewing machine and from other inventions like the band-saw was the industry of ready-made clothing. By the 1880s and 1890s, old-clothes dealers had moved across to becoming new clothes makers and a wide choice of cheap new clothing became available to the masses. Less was now made at home. For 10s 6d one could buy a pair of working trousers, 'heavy rebarbative garments that would stand erect even without a tenant', and a pair of light boots could be bought for the same price.[10] 2s 11d would buy a flannelette shirt, but it was not likely to last. Greatly preferable was an ex-army one from the pawnshop at anything from 2s 6d to 3s 9d, or a new good quality flannel one at from 6s 6d to 9s 6d.[11] For around £5 the young mill girl in 1910 could fit herself out.[12] (See Table 5.2.)

By the first decade of the twentieth century a proportion of the working class not only had the opportunity of being well clad, but could clothe themselves from an increasing variety and range of items. There was now enough choice for the working-class girl to be able to concern herself with fashion and style and not solely with price.

As one moves up the social and income scale, clothes have always been touched by the dictates of fashion. The clerk in the city, passing comfortable on £200 per annum, had to spend considerable sums on his clothes. A smart suit and well-shod feet were essential if he wished

Table 5.2

Mill skirt	3s 3d	Combinations	3s 5d
Tweed skirt	9s 9d	Nightdress	3s 6d
Mill blouse	2s 11d	Underbodice	1s 11d
Wollen blouse	7s	Knickers	3s 9d
Net blouse	6s 11d	Mill apron	2s 2d
Hat	4s 11d	Footing stockings	3s
Hat	10s 6d	Stockings	1s 9d
Trimming	1s	Clogs	4s
Shawl	8s 11d	Corset	2s 10d
Cloth for coat	12s 7d	Handkerchief	5½d
Boots	10s 9d		

to keep his job. He would probably have two or three pairs of boots in use and, in a 1901 budget, just such a clerk spent 4 per cent of his income on boots alone.[13] Throughout the period from 1850 to 1914 he would continue to wear a frock coat to work, with a stiff-collared white shirt. And after the 1860s he would have had a bowler hat. By the end of the nineteenth century, however, he would have had a lounge suit for informal wear. In order for the husband to be maintained in the necessary sartorial sobriety, the wife would have to be her own dressmaker and the dressmaker for her children. A boy's suit made at home would cost 10s, made by a tailor it would cost a guinea. Material for a flannel blouse would be 4s, to have it made up by a professional would add another 3s 6d. With her sewing machine and the paper patterns available in many women's magazines or, after 1873, from Butterick and others, even within a lower-middle-class budget a woman could make some nod towards the dictates of fashion. Mrs Peel calculated that £45 would be the necessary expenditure on clothes for a family on around £300 per annum.[14] On incomes around £700–£800 she believed £80 was typical. However, at the lower end of the middle-class income scale, the obtaining of clothes adequate to maintain the appearances that went with social aspirations must have been a major problem.

When cost ceased to matter, fashion dominated. A spin-off from the inventiveness of the Great Exhibition was the mechanical substitute for starched petticoats to support that 'indelicate, expensive, dangerous and hideous article called Crinoline' (the words are Queen Victoria's). The expansion of the Sheffield steel industry came just in time to supply the rolled steel to make the cage.[15] The voluminous dresses necessitated shawls, rather than overcoats, and the mid-century brought a flourishing in the demand for Paisley shawls and other traditional patterns from India, China and France. Draughts and delicacy necessitated developments in underclothing in the shape of pantaloons and trousers. Mrs Amelia Bloomer was merely building on a well-established trend. Despite its inconvenience to others, and, presumably because of its comfort to the wearer, the crinoline had a remarkable longevity. However, by the late 1860s it had given way to the rather simpler bustle, which persisted for a decade. New materials for dresses were experimented with, like wool, alpaca and velveteen, and, with the invention of aniline dyes, new bright colours, like royal blue, purple, green and red became fashionable. Morris, Burne-Jones, Millais and others, via Liberty & Company, tried to wean Victorian ladies away from excesses and some way towards the flowing simplicity depicted in their paintings. Yet they could not eliminate the fascination with trimmings – lace ruffles, fringes, frogging – nor with hats, which from the mid-1850s were replacing bonnets and caps. The demand for dead birds to supply the ornamental feathers for these hats was insatiable; some twenty to thirty million a year were imported. By 1884 the battle for simplicity had been lost and the bustle was back for a time. But, by the last decade of the century, with more and more middle-class ladies working for a living before marriage, more practical apparel was in demand. A skirt and high-necked blouse became the uniform of the 'typewriter' and of the elementary school teacher, and they were likely to be ready-made. By 1900 the Americans had taken over the market in shirt-waists, as fitted blouses were called. The ready-made clothing industry in the United States quickly caught on to the need for accurate sizings in both clothes and shoes and forced it upon the more conservative British clothing industry.

Until the middle years of the century ladies had their clothes made by one of the numerous dressmakers and milliners who proliferated in any town. From the 1860s onwards, however, the opportunities to buy ready-made clothes increased. First only the overcoats or special clothes for a trip to India or hike in the Highlands were bought in this way, but quickly the sheer convenience and relative cheapness of other ready-made items won the market. By the 1870s underclothes, traditionally sewn at home, were being machine-produced, though as late as 1907 the Army & Navy Stores were still distinguishing between hand-made and machine-made underclothes. There was little to choose between them with regard to price: a hand-made article was perhaps a shilling dearer.

Underclothes were made of cotton, with flannel popular for petticoats. From the 1880s, however, dedicated followers of fashion were caught up in Dr Jaeger's 'sanitary woollen movement', and woollen vests, drawers and combinations provided a welcome insulation against the inadequacies of Victorian domestic heating. Not everyone approved. The *Lancet* in 1879 still regarded drawers as 'unnecessary' and 'in many ways detrimental to health and morals'. Mrs Ada Ballin, a leading dress reformer warned of other hazards:

> Many people . . . think it is advisable to change underclothing at night. If this is done, great care is needed to prevent chill. If the woollen vest is changed, its place must be supplied by one of equal thickness and warmth.[16]

Woollen stockings were also in demand by the 1880s and cotton ones, on which the Midland hosiery industry had been built, were confined to the cheapest markets. Wool had the disadvantage of shrinking, and new mixtures were sought which would eliminate this. The wool and cotton mix of Viyella was one of the most successful of these, coming in at the end of the 1890s, and in the twentieth century was in wide use for underwear, shirts, blouses and the increasingly popular pyjamas.

No commentary on Victorian and Edwardian clothing is complete without some reference to mourning weeds. There was nothing new in ostentatious obsequies for the dead. Daniel Defoe had commented that during the seemingly endless periods of mourning for the children of Queen Anne, ladies draped themselves in black to give the impression that they were at court and shop-girls draped themselves in black to give the impression that they were ladies. Queen Victoria's obsession with the dead Albert strengthened well-established tendencies, and the etiquette of mourning became an obsession. There was an insatiable demand for black. By the early 1850s there were four 'Mourning Warehouses' in Regent Street alone. The bereaved went from crape, to plain black to half black for varied lengths of time: two years for a husband, sixteen months for a father, three weeks for the parents of a husband's first wife. The dresses, bonnets, and petticoats of a widow had to be trimmed and covered with crape, with parasols and muffs to match. There was a custom that guests at a funeral were presented with a pair of black kid gloves.[17] By the 1880s and 1890s there was something of a rebellion against the nation's equivalent to suttee, but the ladies' journals continued to fill their pages with guidance on correct procedures.

Such elaboration was not practical for the working class, but a funeral was a major social event in any working-class family. To put on a 'proper' funeral was important, to ensure that the deceased was 'buried with ham' and 'put away splendidly'.[18] There clearly was a great deal of social pressure to persuade people to spend on funerals. They were a public display at which the deceased's worth was presented for public judgement. The middle-class model was followed as much as possible, often at great cost.

> In the matter of mourning the strictest forms are observed. Black clothing is not merely a sign of respect, but a distinct element of *sacrifice* can still be traced in it. Hearing that a poor woman was about to buy 'new black' for her mother, I said to her daughter, who was grieving over the expense: 'It need not cost very much. It is so short a time since your little brother died that she must have plenty of mourning.' The girl stared at me in blank astonishment at my ignorance, and I learnt for the first time that *new* clothes are indispensable for each death in a family. If you already possess mourning there is no credit in wearing it; even a pair of black kid gloves already bought and 'lying by' must not be used.[19]

This was the experience of a district nurse in early twentieth-century London, and she noted the harsh irony of families spending as much on mourning weeds for a grandfather who died in the workhouse as would have kept him out of the workhouse in the first place. However, the cash for the funeral and the mourning clothes came from the life-insurance policies to which the working class avidly subscribed in a grim determination to avoid, even in death, the clutches of the Poor Law. The Poor Law authorities of one north-east union publicised what may not have been a typical case of a recently widowed mother who had applied for relief after having spent the £10 she had received from her friendly society: £2 10s 0d for the coffin, £1 for cab expenses, £5 for funeral clothing, and £2 on sundries.[20]

6. Patterns of Consumption: Luxuries

> I think the mass of our people are beginning to find other ways of expending some portion of the time and money which used previously to be spent in the public house. No change has been more remarkable in the habits of the people than the growing attendance in the last fifteen years at outdoor games and sports, and large places of public entertainment like theatres, music-halls and so forth, do not lend themselves to consumption of drink, or offer it as their chief attraction.
>
> Austen Chamberlain, in House of Commons, 10 April 1905

Despite increased expenditure on rents, food and clothing, the actual money surplus left in a family's budget increased steadily from 1850 to 1914. Again taking W. A. Mackenzie's model budgets as a starting point, after paying for food, rent, fuel and clothing her lowest decile family had 10¾d per week left for 'sundries' in 1860, 1s 8¾d in 1880 and 1s 10¾d in 1914; her median family's residue was 1s 3d in 1860, 3s 5¼d in 1880 and 3s 11d in 1914; and her upper quartile family's was 3s in 1860, 3s 6¾d in 1880 and 8s 10½d in 1914. With more to spend there was a wider range of items to spend on, though traditional pleasures did not die.

Drinking and Smoking

Drink and tobacco were the main working-class luxuries in the nineteenth century, as they were in the twentieth. 56 per cent of the population consumed alcohol in one form or another, with women drinking, on average, half as much as men. At the end of the nineteenth century, each male drinker was consuming 73 gallons of beer, 2·4 gallons of spirits and just under one gallon of wine, per annum.[1]

The pub offered warmth, company and an escape from overcrowded and desolate homes. Indeed it could be argued, as did the habitués of the pub in Lark Rise, that evenings in the taproom were indeed a saving, 'for with no man in the house, the fire at home could be let die down and the rest of the family could go to bed when the room got cold'.[2] With beer at 2½d a pint, and spirits at around 3s 4d a pint, pleasure and refreshment could be obtained fairly cheaply. In addition beer was still delivered to the home in rural areas. M. F. Davies, in her study of the Wiltshire village of Corsley in 1905–6, found that at least eight brewers supplied casks of beer and ale to labourers' houses. Home brewing also continued to an unknown extent, for the home-made barrel of ale and the illicit bottle of whisky or poteen from some Scottish or Irish glen have no place in the available official statistics.

Drink had always loomed large in the working-class budget. Beer and ale consumption in England and Wales and whisky consumption in Scotland were woven into the traditions and customs of the workplace. In some cases beer was supplied by the employer or a visiting contractor. New apprentices, new journeymen, birth and marriage were all celebrated in the workshop with drink. It is probable that some of these customs were declining under pressure from the advance of industrialism. Certainly working-class leaders in the trade unions were active in trying to dissociate organised working-class activity from the public house. Not until the 1870s was there much sign that they were achieving any success. Even then traditional activities like the celebration of 'Saint Monday' remained a part of the life style of some of the working class.

having had a 'spree' on the Saturday night, and taken numerous hairs of the dog that bit them on the Sunday without experiencing that benefit which is popularly supposed to result from such a proceeding, [they] avail themselves of the circumstances of Monday being a holiday to have an appropriate and characteristic wind-up of their weekly spree by a day's idling and drinking.[3]

By eleven on a Monday morning they would be ensconced in the bar drinking, smoking and playing dominoes.

Just what proportion of an average working-class family's income was spent on drink is difficult to assess. Working-men were not likely to expose themselves to the moral reproaches of middle-class investigators by admitting to excessive consumption of alcohol. Flora Thompson's neighbours were spending 7d per week at the 'Wagon and Horses' and making a half-pint last the evening. In London the *Cornhill* reckoned on 2*s* 4*d* per week on drink, with a pint for man and wife each day.[4] Professor John Burnett has calculated that the average working-class household was spending £15 to £20 a year on alcohol, which in many cases meant a quarter to a half of their income.[5] This tallies with the findings of Charles Booth, who believed that a quarter of working-class earnings was going on drink, and with Rowntree, who believed that it was one-sixth overall, but that drink was 'the predominant factor' in pushing 28 per cent of York wage-earners in 1899 into secondary poverty.

Contemporary literature is full of stereotypes of the drunken workman spending his wages on drink. Yet few could have had the necessary resources to buy enough to get really drunk. Only occasionally with some sudden windfall was there a chance to have 'a famous fuddle', and a major cause of drunkenness may well have been bad liquor rather than too much liquor. Things no doubt improved greatly after the 1850s, when it was still quite common for vitriol, cocculus indicus, gentian and other drugs to be found added to beer to give it strength. The legislation of the Adulteration of Food, Drink and Drugs Act of the 1870s helped greatly in limiting this, and Professor Burnett believes that beer adulteration ceased to exist by 1880, except for some judicious watering.[6] On the other hand, in 1900 there was a major poisoning outbreak as a result of arsenical contamination of brewing sugar, and there was a persistent belief among the working class that adulterated drink was still being sold by unscrupulous publicans. 'There's many a poor man falls into the hands of the police, not because he's drunk too much, but because the scoundrels have sold him rank liquor,' Devon fishermen believed in 1912, 'and the poorer he is the more likely he is to be served with what's no better than poison.'[7] Their advice was to stick to gin in a strange pub, because, being cheap, it was least likely to be adulterated. Rum, a strong-smelling imported drink, was very likely to have been tampered with.

By the twentieth century beer was not what it had been. Porter and 'hard old beer' had given way to a paler, less alcoholic beverage. As always it is difficult to distinguish between a change in taste forcing a change in the brewers, or the brewers' desire to cut costs while maintaining constant price levels forcing a change in consumers' tastes. The change, whatever the reason, does seem to have helped to reduce the amount of drunkenness among the working class. How much of the improvement was due to the impact of the temperance movement is hard to say. Certainly there was still no shortage of pubs: 1 to every 393 persons in London, 1 to 279 in Liverpool, 1 to 215 in Birmingham,

1 to 176 in Sheffield, 1 to 168 in Manchester.[8]

If the temperance movement had a definite success, it was in driving the middle classes from the pubs. The movement did not stop them drinking, but by the 1860s the respectable were drinking at home. They would obtain their drink through the off-licences which tended to concentrate in the well-to-do suburbs.[9] Mrs Peel found that her lower-middle-class families spent £5 to £7 on wine, beer and spirits in a year and a family with an income of £700 a year would spend around £10. With whisky at 36s a dozen bottles, claret 15s a dozen, port 42s a dozen and brandy 5s a bottle, this was hardly abstemious.

Tobacco was less the subject of philanthropic strictures to the working class, though it was regarded as an unnecessary extravagance. Expenditure on tobacco rose from £13·5 million in 1870 to £42 million in 1915. In 1851 *per capita* consumption of tobacco was 16 oz.: by 1914 it was 3 lb., an increase of 300 per cent. In 1900 3·5 per cent of consumers' retail expenditure went on tobacco.[10] In the 1860s Thomas Wright believed that 1oz. tobacco a day was fairly common among his skilled associates. Most of them were smokers and found ways round the workshop ban on smoking, to 'have a smoke' unseen in 'curious holes and corners'.[11] At 5d for 1½ oz. of shag, 1 oz. a day was a great deal for a working-man and 3 oz. a week, which was the average among the Middlesbrough ironworkers in 1907, was probably nearer the norm.

In the 1850s most tobacco was smoked in pipes: nearly 60 per cent. 30 per cent was rolled for cigars and 10 per cent was taken as snuff. But the last two were not for the working class. The working-man smoked his Best Bird's Eye or his Bishop's Blaze in a short-stemmed clay 'cuttie' at work or in the 'churchwarden' in the evening, the best being made from Broseley clay. Only on high days and holidays would he treat himself to some 'matchless Havanas' at 7 for a shilling. Cigars had quickly become popular in the 1850s, when the complaint was that 'men smoke nowadays whilst they are occupied in working or hunting, riding in carriages, or otherwise employed'.[12] The briar pipe came from Corsica via France in about 1859, but it was not until the vulcanite mouthpiece was developed to replace horn ones at the end of the 1870s that briars came to be widely adopted. At 7s each in 1879 they were beyond the means of most working-men, and it was not until the 1890s and into this century that they began to seriously challenge the clay pipe.

However, the real revolution in the late nineteenth century was the replacement of the pipe by the cigarette as the working-man's 'smoke'. Small quantities of cigarettes were made in Britain from about the 1840s onwards, though it seems to have been regarded as very much a foreign habit. Robert Gloag's factory in Walworth in 1856 is usually credited with having produced the first commercial cigarettes. The Crimean War helped to stimulate a liking for Turkish tobacco, and cigarettes, wrapped in tissue and with a cane mouth-piece, were produced. The demand remained very small and it was not until the end of the American Civil War, when the new flue-cured bright tobacco came in, that popular cigarettes began to be produced. The earlier air-cured and fire-cured tobacco was really too strong for cigarettes, but the discovery of the process of producing the mild bright yellow leaf and its exploitation by Washington Duke in Virginia changed all that. The Virginian cigarette appealed to British taste.

W. D. & H. O. Wills moved to cigarette production in 1870, when their London factory produced Bristol cigarettes, and by 1879 they were offering over twenty different brands. Hand-rolled, these cigarettes were still relatively expensive, but in 1883 Wills bought the rights of the cigarette-making machine that James A. Bonsack of Salem, Virginia had patented two years earlier. By 1890 an improved Bonsack machine could produce 300 cigarettes a minute.[13] The first British machine-produced cigarettes were Three Castles, Gold Flake and Louisville, all of which were on the market early in 1884. Then, in July 1888, Wild Woodbine and Cinderella were launched: five for a penny. The cigarette for the mass market had arrived, and by the autumn of the same year the *Oxford Times* was rebuking girls of sixteen or eighteen for 'smoking cigars or cigarettes' in the open.[14] By the end of the following year, the sale of 1*d* cigarettes (27,830,000) had surpassed that of all other Wills's cigarettes (23,608,950).[15] By 1900, 12 per cent of all British tobacco sales were of cigarettes, compared with a mere 0·5 per cent a decade earlier. Woodbine led the way with a phenomenal rate of growth in the early 1890s: 53 million in 1891, 98 million in 1892 and 159 million in 1893. Not until 1900 was Woodbine challenged, but not threatened, in the 1*d* for 5 market, by Ogden's Tabs.

Slightly up the market, Ogden's had a big success in the 1890s with their Guinea Gold at 3*d* for 10, though here they were challenged by Wills's Capstan, introduced in 1893 at 2½*d* for 10. The Nottingham firm of John Player & Son competed in this same market with their Gold Leaf Navy Cut from 1886 and the Player's Medium Navy Cut from 1900. So much handier to carry, so much more convenient to light, so much more rapidly extinguished when the foreman came, and now so cheap, cigarettes inevitably came to replace the pipe in the workman's mouth.

By the beginning of the present century smoking in public was becoming much more acceptable. By then it was not just the 'fast' young ladies who smoked, though it could still shock. Margot Asquith's smoking was still regarded as 'a terrible thing' by her stepsons in 1903. In 1912 her husband's colleague, Reginald McKenna, perturbed the young Compton Mackenzie by appearing on his way to the House with top-hat, frock coat and large curved pipe between his teeth.[16] Such remaining rules of tobacco etiquette as there were did not survive the war. Even by 1914 the ubiquitous corner tobacconist was patronised by male and female alike, of all classes. There were tobaccos for every taste and pocket.

Reading

A quiet smoke over a pint of ale in the corner public house of an evening was the main leisure pursuit of the working man, but from the mid-nineteenth century he was presented with an increasing range of alternatives in the form of mind-improving classes, body-improving sports and temperament-improving entertainments.

From the 1820s there had been mechanics' institutes and improving lectures for the working class, to provide them with 'useful knowledge' and an understanding of their place in the economy. Such activities increased in the mid-nineteenth-century decades as trade unions encouraged their members towards mutual improvement. Numerous reading rooms and meeting rooms intended to lure the working class out of the pubs were provided. In many cases the unions built these themselves, but middle-class temperance philanthropists were the main force behind them. Not all such enterprises were entirely successful. Not all workers cared for 'the books, the quiet games, the instructive lectures, the improving talk, the large national views, the tea, coffee, buns, and bread and butter' which such places offered, and preferred 'the stronger drinks and, as they think, the more vigorous style of talk and lines of action they find elsewhere'.[17] None the less, for many future leaders of the working class the books and lectures of the improving societies opened up new horizons, freeing them from the confines of their mean homes. The guided use of their literacy gave many workers new perspectives on their position in society and on the condition of their fellow workers.

By 1851, 62 per cent of the nation's population were literate, in that they could sign their names in the marriage register. Twenty years later, before the new school boards had had time to have an effect, the rate was 77 per cent. Not until twenty years after that can the impact of extended elementary schooling first be seen. Between 1881 and 1891 the level of literacy rose by nearly 9 per cent, by which time 93 per cent of the population were literate. Throughout the whole of our period, always keeping in mind the poor quality of much of the education provided in the elementary schools, there was a substantial demand for reading matter.

The quality of the reading matter for the masses had for long been the subject of middle-class concern. For decades there had been broadsheets and ballads, hot from the presses of Seven Dials, with their details of gory murders, the latest execution, the most recent Royal marriage. The doyen of the broadsheet printers, James Catnach, had reputedly sold 1,166,000 copies of the *Last Dying Confession of William Cader, the murderer of Maria Marten* in 1828.[18] When the facts did not offer sufficient titillation there was a wealth of pornographic street literature to turn to. Equally subject to middle-class criticism by the 1880s was the thriving trade in fictional romantic adventures. Those catering for the tastes of the working-class readership had quickly appreciated that crime and romance were the most successful ingredients. The Sunday newspapers thrived because they combined both. By the mid-nineteenth century, with *Lloyd's Weekly Newspaper* and the *News of the World* in the vanguard, the Sunday newspaper was established as the core of working-class reading. In a study of a London working-class parish in 1843, out of 1439 families 616 had newspapers: 283 took *Bell's Weekly Despatch*: 79 took the *Sunday Times*; 23 *Bell's Life in London*; 15 the *Penny Sunday Times* and 13 the *Weekly Chronicle*.[19] Sixty years later some of the names were different: The *Referee* (established 1877), The *People* (established 1881), the *Sunday Chronicle* (established 1885). But *Lloyd's* and the *News of the World* were still there. The mixture was the same as it had always been: a little radical politics, a lot of crime reporting and a romantic serial. Even in poor households, however, the Sunday papers were important, and among the Middlesbrough workmen anything from 1*d* to as much as 6*d* was spent on them. Circulations rose steadily. With the reduction of the price to 1*d* when newspaper duty was removed in 1861, *Lloyd's Weekly Newspaper* sales rose to 170,000, two years later it was 350,000 and twenty years later it was around 0·75 million, rising by the 1890s to over 1 million.[20]

To the despair of generations of philanthropists, educators and moral improvers the ever-more literate public sought not 'improving' tracts but reading matter 'to keep their eyes busy while their brains took a rest'. Religious organisations, the temperance movement and optimistic individuals had all sought to combat what they regarded as the pernicious nature of working-class reading matter with penny tracts and penny magazines preaching wholesomeness and improvement. The working class were nothing if not catholic in their reading tastes. The *Morning Chronicle* of 1859 reported the contents of the Manchester wholesaler Abel Haywood's shop in Oldham Street:

Masses of penny novels and comic songs and recreation books are jumbled with sectarian pamphlets and democratic essays. Educational books abound in every variety. Loads of cheap reprints of American authors seldom or never heard of among the upper, reading classes here, are mingled with editions of early Puritan divines. Double columned translations from Sue, Dumas, Sand, Paul Feval and Frederick Soube jostle with dream-books, scriptural commentaries, Pinnoch's Guides and quantities of cheap music, sacred Methodists and Little Warblers. Altogether the literary chaos is very significant of the restless and all devouring literary appetite which it supplies.[21]

The decisive breakthrough which George Newnes made in the 1880s was to see that there was a market for wholesome literature for the working class that did not include moralising. His *Tit-Bits*, launched in October 1881, with its rag bag of items culled from books, journals and newspapers, was an immediate success with clerks and artisans. It satisfied a craving for factual information, and with competitions and publicity stunts gave an air of excitement to the whole process of reading. Its success bred imitators, like Alfred Harmsworth's *Answers* in 1888 and Cyril Pearson's *Pearson's Weekly* in 1890. Harmsworth had been a freelance contributor to *Tit-Bits*, and Cyril Pearson had won a *Tit-Bits* general knowledge contest, for which the prize was training in the paper's office. By 1900 these three bitter rivals, *Tit-Bits* with its green cover, *Answers* with its orange cover and *Pearson's Weekly* with its pink one were together selling over two million copies. What Harmsworth told his readers was true of all three,

We are a sort of Universal Information provider. Anyone who reads our paper for a year will be able to converse on many subjects on which he was entirely ignorant. He will have a good stock of anecdotes and jokes and will indeed be a pleasant companion.[22]

The simplified, attractive presentation, with regular sensationalism to catch the public's eye, which was pioneered by the weeklies, began to affect the dailies, as the full potential of the working-class market was gradually realised. In 1888 T. P. O'Connor launched the *Star* as a halfpenny evening paper, modelled on the American press with bold headlines, short paragraphs and only one daily article of any length. By 1894 there were four 'halfpenny evenings' in London: the *Echo*, the *Star*, the *Sun* (another T. P. O'Connor creation) and the *Evening News and Post*. In the following year Alfred Harmsworth experimented with a halfpenny daily in Glasgow, and in May 1896 launched the *Daily Mail*, whose success was immediate and spectacular. Within three years its circulation was over 0·5 million, within four, over 700,000. For four years the *Mail* had the monopoly of the daily halfpenny market, but in 1900 Pearson launched the *Daily Express*, which followed the American pattern of having news on the front page. These two, the *Mail* and the *Express*, peddling a mixture of sensation, patriotism and sentimentality, were in the vanguard of a regiment of dailies which sought the magic formula that would scoop the mass market in readership. None, however, succeeded in altering working-class enthusiasm for Sunday papers.

One can, of course, cite plenty of examples of working-men who devoted their leisure hours to self improvement. For them new worlds were opened in the pages of such publications as *Cassell's Popular Educator* in the 1850s, Newnes's *Penny Library of Famous Books* in the 1890s, or the glorious *Everyman Library* throughout the twentieth century, but they reached only a few of the working class. As typical was the reading of children's *Comic Cuts*, *Chips* or *Lot O' Fun*, of the useful *Winning Post* and *Sporting Life* and, in the constant search for melodrama and sensationalism, of the *Illustrated Police Budget*. For working-men's wives the preferred reading was 'something about love, with a dash of religion in it'.[23] No education could kill the hold of such penny dreadfuls as *Through Weal and Woe*, *The Rightful Heir*, or *Mary, the Poacher's Wife*, which depicted a society divided between the poor, but honest, and the rich and beautiful, and not much in between, and where moral lessons were drawn and hammered home to the reader. The pioneers of the new journalism were well aware of the potential of the women's market. Harmsworth launched a penny weekly for woman, *Forget-Me-Not*, in 1891 and the circulation quickly rose to over 80,000, and both the *Mail* and the *Express* had sections for women readers. The attempt by Alfred Harmsworth to publish the *Daily Mirror* in 1903 as a paper edited by women for women readers proved to be a mistake, or, at any rate, premature.

Within months the women were ousted and the *Mirror* had become the first tabloid 'for Men and Women'.[24]

One does not want to draw too sharp a distinction between the reading habits of the middle classes and those of the working classes. Newspapers like the *Mail* and the *Express* had a substantial lower-middle-class readership before they attracted large numbers of the working class. However, many newspapers survived on a relatively small and almost exclusively middle-class readership. The expansion of the 1*d* daily from the mid-1850s, both in London and in most provincial towns, brought daily newspapers into middle-class homes. In the 1870s the *Daily Telegraph*, with a circulation of around 200,000, and the *Daily News* at around 150,000 were the two most popular. Most middle-class men, however, probably stuck to the local newspapers, which in many towns were numerous enough to reflect most nuances of political opinion.

The middle-class reader also had the choice of a wide range of weekly, fortnightly, monthly and quarterly periodicals. Of 630 magazines published in 1873, 253 were published under religious auspices.[25] They tended to pander to the Victorian cult of the family: *Family Herald, Good Words, Household Words*. The 1860s saw a whole range of shilling monthlies following in the wake of the *Cornhill Magazine*, aimed at a literate, middle-class readership which lacked the income to purchase one of the heavier 2*s* or 2*s* 6*d* monthlies. Most of these monthlies offered their readers fiction serials, often of a very high quality, but they also catered for the information seeker that Newnes was to notice was such an important part of the mass reading audience.

In published middle-class budgets books and papers tended to be lumped in with other miscellaneous items of expenditure under the heading small expenditure. Mrs Peel advised her newly-weds on small means to allow £7 or £8 for books, papers, stamps and stationery. The *Cornhill*'s lower-middle-class budget allowed £4 10*s* for newspapers and books. What this meant was probably a daily newspaper, an occasional halfpenny evening, a monthly magazine, and perhaps an occasional child's magazine, preferably of the 'improving kind' like the *Boy's Own Paper*, first published in 1879, but more likely the more adventurous *Marvel, Wonder* or *Union Jack*. This would leave little for books. When books were bought it was probably for a train journey. From the mid-1850s 'yellow backs' appeared to cater for the ever increasing travelling public with cheap reprints of books at 2*s* or 1*s*. By 1898 Routledge's shilling Railway Library had a list of 1300 titles. By the 1880s and 1890s intense competition had brought cheap editions down to 3*d* in paperback, and by the turn of the century Newnes and others were offering abridged versions of the classics at a penny.

The middle-class family interested in new novels of quality would use the library. In the mid-nineteenth century few could consider purchasing the verbose and price-inflated three-decker novels at 10*s* 6*d* a volume. Rather they would pay their £2 to Mudie's Library or to W. H. Smith's Library. From 1900 Boot's Book-lovers' Library was catering for an even larger readership. The power of the libraries was broken in the 1890s, when the three-decker finally disappeared and new books cost 5*s* or 6*s*. The new prices stimulated a wider readership with first editions being printed in 40, 50, 60 and even 70 thousands instead of the few hundreds of the three decker.

High Days and Holidays

An important stimulus to consumer demand was the development of entertainments and holidays for the populace. These not only created a demand for services, but by making the population more mobile brought an awareness of the goods and services which were available. The country visitor coming to the town was made aware of a treasure house; the town visitor coming to the city was made aware of the limits of small-town retailing. Not only that, but time out put people in the frame of mind to spend, whether on a trip out to the pub or a week in Blackpool. Retailers were aware that people saved for high days and holidays, and these were the times to catch customers in an expansive mood. By the 1860s more and more working men were getting a Saturday half-holiday, and gradually the modern week-end, as a period of odd jobs and leisure, was taking shape. The supply of entertainments expanded to satisfy the new demand.

The public house remained the favourite place in which to pass a Saturday evening, the grime of the week having been washed off and the shopping done. In spite of growing competition from alternative meeting places, the pub was likely to be the main social centre in which the activities of a working-class community took place. This remained the case even when pubs became more commercialised, as they increasingly did throughout the period. Saturday was the time when the working-class family had the cash to think of splashing out on extras. Perhaps three or four times a year a trip to the 'gods' of the theatre was the fancy, carefully armed with a supply of drink and food. It was considered wise to take one's own food, for theatre food was likely to be 'of a sickly and poisonous, rather than an ambrosial character', according to Thomas Wright in the 1860s: 'ale and porter, originally bad, shaken in being carried about until it has become muddy to the sight, and abominable to the taste; rotten fruit, and biscuits stale to the degree of semi-putrefaction'.[26] The public preference, at any rate in the gallery, was for tragedy and melodrama: 'something deep' was much preferred to comedy or farce. The fun came in the general noise and uproar which accompanied the play and the barracking of the poor actors.

To a large extent the working class were spectators at an entertainment aimed at the middle classes in the theatre. Not so in the music hall. Here was the authentic working-class entertainment that had indeed grown out of pub entertainments. In the 1860s and 1870s the halls were really large public houses and, as they developed and became more professional, they still supplied alcoholic refreshment. Best remembered are halls like the Alhambra and the Empire of Edwardian London, where stars like Marie Lloyd, Vesta Tilley and Little Tich made their name, but it was in the provinces that the music hall had its real strength. Early twentieth-century Middlesbrough had ten halls in full swing, with seating capacity ranging from 350 to 2000.[27] For prices ranging from $2d$ to $6d$ and even, in one or two, to $2s$, warmth, companionship and an incredible variety of singing, conjuring, juggling and comedy was on offer. By 1910 a sinister threat to such places was becoming apparent as they were converted to show moving pictures, at any rate on Sundays, when live entertainment was restricted.

Working-men's clubs also offered a variety of music-hall entertainment. Most of these had been founded in the mid-nineteenth century as temperance, mutual improvement organisations, where aristocratic and middle-class patrons sought to lead the working class along the path of middle-class respectability. By the 1880s and 1890s, however, they had shed their patrons, acquired a beer licence and reduced improving talks to an interlude between songs, recitations, melodramas, comedies, billiards matches and dancing classes. Run by the members, restricted in membership, these clubs offered all the advantages of the public house, with the added assurance of unadulterated beer and comparative cheapness.

For some, the week-end did not end on Sunday, but extended into Monday. 'Saint Monday' as a holiday had a long tradition as industrialised workers asserted their desire for leisure. All the disciplines of the early factory system had failed to eliminate it, and throughout the nineteenth century employers complained of Monday absenteeism.

At the first C. W. S. boot and shoe factory in Leicester in 1874, 40 per cent of the riveters were absent every Monday from March to June, 17 per cent every Tuesday and 12 per cent every Wednesday.[28] In 1867 Thomas Wright talked of it as 'a recognised institution' and of the wide range of entertainments offered for the 'Saint Mondayites'.[29] Day trips to the seaside were run on a Monday throughout the summer, as were trips to the Crystal Palace and other public recreation grounds. Athletics meetings, boxing matches and dog-racing were popular in the 1860s, often spontaneously organised. The great attraction of any of these was the thrill of betting on the winner. All the evidence shows that gambling was on the increase, in spite of the moral censure it attracted and of the legal obstacles put in its way. From 1853 onwards betting shops and, less successfully, betting lists in pubs were suppressed. On-course betting was allowed.

Alternative entertainment came in the 1870s with the growth of football clubs and the enclosing of race courses, when a serious effort was made to attract paying spectators. Both these, however, held their fixtures mainly on a Saturday and did nothing to encourage the Saint Mondayites. Attendances grew rapidly. In 1891 the average attendance at a main London football ground was around 7000, twenty years later it was nearer 30,000 and about three-quarter of a million amateurs were playing football for recreation;[30] similarly with horse racing: the enclosure of Sandown in 1877 was rapidly followed by other enclosed courses around the main cities to attract the holiday crowd.[31]

Most areas had their traditional holiday periods when the local races would be held and the fair would come to town. Many traditional fairs expanded in the nineteenth century, catering for the better off and more leisured working class. Sally Alexander, in her fascinating study of Oxford's St Giles's Fair, lists some of the cornucopia of goods available – dolls, toys, sweets, gingerbread, cakes, glass and china ornaments, cheap tools and jewellery, photographs, ices, canaries, potato peelers, name stamps, baskets, brooms, mats, lace, gloves, curtain material – the whole range of the cheap jack, offering anything 'calculated to please the eye, gratify the appetite, and extract money from the pocket'.[32] It was at the fair one learned of novelties, like the appearance on the gingerbread stall, alongside the gingerbread babies, brown and white peppermint humbugs and sticks of pink-and-white rock, of a box of 'thin, dark brown slabs packed in pink paper', which a wordly cousin might identify as chocolate.[33] Mainly, however, the fair offered cheapness at its various penny stalls. As an 'Oxford Lady' recounted in 1908: 'I bought two screw-drivers, a thing to put in a pie dish, a saucepan with a lid, a looking glass, and some little cake tins, all for a penny each, except the cake tins which were four for a penny.'[34]

Besides the traditional local fair days and race days, there were the wakes weeks of Lancashire, the Bowlingtide holidays of the Yorkshire woollen industry and the fair holidays of Glasgow. In addition most workers had at least a day and sometimes three or four at Christmas, Easter and Whitsun, and there was often an annual works outing. In most cases these holidays meant loss of pay, but for salaried employees holidays with pay were coming in during the 1860s; railwaymen on the Great Northern line were granted such holidays in 1872; a large chemical firm gave paid holidays to their workforce in 1884 and the large West End retail houses gave them from the 1890s onwards.[35]

Both the pleasure steamer and the railway transformed such holidays into a time for going away from home. The Nottingham Mechanics' Institute pioneered the first rail excursion in 1840 with a workmen's trip to Leicester, but it was the Great Exhibition of 1851 which revealed the demand for excursion trips. Six million people visited the site in Hyde Park in the summer of 1851. The London and North Western Railway alone carried 774,910 excursion passengers to and from London between June and October in 1851, at 5s return from Leeds. By the mid-1860s day excursions were being run from London at holiday times to almost all the south-coast ports: 3s 6d by 'covered carriage', 4s 6d second class to Margate, Ramsgate, Folkestone, Dover or Hastings.[36] Holiday towns for industrial areas began to develop, with their serried ranks of guest houses where the discipline of the workshop was replaced by the discipline of the landlady: Weston-super-Mare for Bristol (1s 6d from Bristol), Tynemouth for Tyneside, Tenby and Barry for south Wales, Saltburn for Middlesbrough, Blackpool for Lancashire. The complaint of the publicans and retailers at the holiday resorts was that the excursionists had little to spend, since all their money had been spent on the rail fare and admission to the pier.[37] On a day trip a picnic was popular, and a further attraction of Saint Monday outings was that Sunday's cold leftovers could fill the sandwiches. At Weston an excursion hall outside the station was provided where tea could be bought at $1\frac{1}{2}d$ per cup or one could eat one's own provisions. In spite of the complaints, however, the resorts grew, and with them their tea-rooms and ice-cream parlours. By the turn of the century excursion tickets were available for football fans on many lines, and a big match always brought good business to the shopkeepers.

There seems no way of knowing what proportion of the working class actually took holidays away from home. Few of the published budgets contained any allowance for holidays, and an occasional trip to relatives was the most that the poor with families could hope for. It was the arrival of a family that probably put an end to regular holidays for a young couple. Some unmarried working girls in the 1911 survey spent as much as £5 on 'holidays and picnics'. A Lancashire cotton weaver on 28s 10d a week spent five days at the seaside in September at a cost of 30s, and a week at a town near the coast in June at a cost of £3.

Even if it was only a minority who did take holidays, trips and excursions opened up new worlds and a whole new range of experiences. They brought an awareness of the ever-increasing variety of things that could be purchased. They created pressures on the family to spend more money, not just on Brummagen penny items, clearly marked that they were a present from somewhere, but on suitable clothes to go on holiday, on pyjamas to wear in the guest house, on suitcases to carry the clothes. The greater the mobility, the wider the range of consumption. Holidays and outings, therefore, not only created a specialist demand of their own, but stimulated a general demand.

New Entertainments

For the middle class, from the mid-nineteenth century onwards holidays became part of the accepted pattern of genteel life and had to be budgeted for. The seaside held as much fascination for the middle classes as for the workers, but, as if some barely repressed puritanism still insisted that leisure was basically wrong, the favourite resort usually had to provide some recuperative powers in its water. The middle-class watering places – Brighton, Bournemouth, Torquay, Torbay and Scarborough on the coast, Cheltenham, Malvern, Harrogate and Leamington inland – all set out to be exclusive. Not for them the day trippers who could afford to spend nothing more than their penny on the pier; not if they could be avoided. Here were the fashionable clothiers, the expensive shops. Yet the principle was the same as with the working class: a change of air encouraged spending. Of course, as the domestic watering places became crowded, the discriminating turned to the mainland of Europe and sought to recreate the Brighton and Eastbourne of an earlier period at Nice, Biarritz or even Ostend. A holiday in Europe was probably cheaper than one at a really fashionable domestic resort in the years before 1914.

For the more dynamic members of the middle class, particularly those at the lower end of that stratum, there were increased possibilities for leisure at the cricket and bowling clubs. By the end of the century the tennis clubs, growing from their phenomenally successful invention in the 1870s, already had it within their power to endow the clerk's or shopkeeper's son with middle-class gentility. Yet more successful was the bicycle. The high-wheeled 'penny farthing', coming in the 1870s, had an immediate success. Henry Sturmey's *Indispensable Bicyclist's Handbook* of 1879 listed some 300 different machines made by about sixty firms, mostly in Coventry, Birmingham and London, but also in Cheltenham, King's Lynn, and elsewhere. By 1880 there were 230 cycling clubs in Britain, and knickerbocker-clad gentlemen hurtled through the country lanes with an anxious expression, known as 'bicyclist's face', as they balanced somewhat precariously on the high wheel. Newspaper prophecies that the pastime would produce 'a hunchbacked and torture-faced future generation' did nothing to deter enthusiasm. Even at prices around £20, 40,000 'ordinaries' were being produced. From the mid-1880s for a mere nine guineas one could purchase the less worrying 'safety' bicycle, and it was from then that the real boom began. Now ladies too could partake of the sport and, from the end of the next decade, the journey was even smoother on the pneumatic tyre which J. B. Dunlop re-invented and patented in 1888. By the turn of the century the Nottingham firm of Raleigh alone was producing 12,000 bicycles a year.[38]

It was in the first decade of this century that bicycling changed from being a largely middle-class pursuit to being a working-class enthusiasm and necessity. It was a measure of its ever-widening popularity that the early socialists saw cycling clubs as a means of attracting working-class youth. 'Clarion' cycling clubs were among the most successful of Robert Blatchford's many contributions to socialism, and Clarion members could buy their bicycles through the club for eight or ten guineas, or by monthly instalments.[39] With constant refinements in the bicycle a second-hand market quickly grew up, which brought cycles within the reach of those who could never hope to aspire to a fully-equipped Rudge at ten guineas.

Bicycles required better road surfaces and signposts, improvements that were under way by the time the motor car came along. The motor-car industry was well established in France before British entrepreneurs interested themselves in it in 1896, but its growth in Britain was rapid. At prices ranging from £150 for a one-cylinder 'Voiturette' to £700 for a luxury machine, the car was limited to a fairly narrow social group. None the less by 1909 there were 40,000 cars registered in London alone, more than in the whole of France. Twelve driving lessons could be obtained for three guineas, and a Daimler with driver could be hired also for three guineas.[40] The intense interest aroused was clear from the success of the weekly paper *The Motor* which had a circulation of 40,000 in 1909.[41] Clearly, Jack Tanner in George Bernard Shaw's *Man and Superman* was not alone in being a slave to the automobile. It had so many advantages. It was fast: Shaw's 'new man', 'Enry Straker, could drive from Hyde Park Corner to Richmond in twenty-one minutes in 1903 (though the American steam car took a mere seventeen minutes). It was cheap: a small car could run for as little as 4*d* per mile, while it was difficult to maintain a pony and trap for less than 6*d* a mile.[42] By 1914 many famous car names were already around. An Austin 10 could be bought for £325, a Morris Oxford for £175, a Singer 10 for £185.[43] Motorised transport had become commercially essential and socially highly desirable.

Both bicycles and cars spawned a huge market in accessories. In 1907 discerning cyclists could buy from the Army & Navy Stores bags, bells, brushes, carriers, lamps, polish, pumps, repair outfits, spanners, stands and waterproofs all made for cyclists. They could keep their machines shining with Cyclebright Paste and note their speed with a cyclometer. To wear he (or she) could choose from cycling capes, corsets, drawers, gloves, jackets, knickers, stockings, suits, and could round off the day with a snack from a cycling tea valise. The motorist needed to clad himself in cap, coat, gloves, goggles, overcoat and scarf with apron and dustcoat and carry tools, fire 'extincteur', oil and grease. Pratt's A-Grade Motor Car spirit could be obtained from most chemists at 1*s* 3*d* a gallon, or between the *petit pois* and the pickles at the Army & Navy grocery department.

For different sections of society the bicycle and then the motor car had a liberating effect. They gave to people a freedom of movement and the opportunity to explore town or city. Indeed more than one critic warned of the way in which cycling could produce the dangerous 'intoxication that comes from unfettered liberty'.[44] This was especially so among those young women who, ignoring the abuse of children and males, took to the road in the 'rational dress' of knickerbockers. However, for both 'new men' and 'new women' the bicycle opened up a world of experience undreamed of by their parents.

Part II

The Stimulation of Demand

7. The Credit System

As soon as houses in the street were occupied there swept down upon us a flock of human vultures eager to obtain as much money as they could possibly screw out of the people. These tallymen, who were generally either Jews or Scotsmen, were insurance agents, sewing-machine agents, furniture-on-the-hire-system agents, and so forth. All had something to sell on the easiest possible terms; in fact, one might suppose, taking them on their own valuation, that they were merely stray philanthropists, wandering about the world endeavouring to make life easier for those less fortunate than themselves.

O. C. Malvery, *The Soul Market*, 6th edn (n.d). p. 730

'Revolution' is not too strong a word to describe the transformation that took place in many areas of retailing in the half-century before 1914. The relatively small specialist shop and the even smaller local general shop remained typical, but the emergence of multiple shops, specialist retailers and of the all-embracing department stores, totally transformed the attitudes and practices of shopkeepers at all levels and opened up a completely new shopping experience for customers. The retailing trade was adjusting to a new and increased demand, but shopkeepers were also coming to realise that they had a function in not only satisfying demand, but also in stimulating it and, if necessary, altering taste and fashion. They realised that even in the smallest budgets there was an order of priorities which, under sales pressure, could be altered.

The traditional, and in some ways the most effective, bait that the shopkeeper could offer was credit, and the giving of credit was at the heart of retailing, at all levels of the market, in the second half of the nineteenth century. Shops in working-class areas gave credit, as in many cases they had to if they were to survive. By the end of a normal week, and especially at times of unemployment or sickness, even careful working-class families were likely to find themselves without the resources to buy even the basic necessities. The shopkeeper, as part of the working-class community, had to respond to the needs of that community and tread a delicate path between generosity and firmness. Not to give credit was to lose business, to give too much credit was the quickest way to Carey Street. As the son of a slum corner-shopkeeper recalled, his mother 'had to assess with careful judgement the honesty, class standing and financial resources of all tick customers':

> how many mouths had the woman to feed? Was the husband ailing? Tuberculosis in the house, perhaps. If TB took one it always claimed others; the breadwinner next time, maybe. Did the male partner drink heavily? Was he a bad time keeper at work? Did they patronise the pawnshop? If so, how far were they committed? Were their relations known good payers? And last, had they already 'blued' some other shop in the district, and for how much?[1]

If credit was granted then there would probably be an upper limit of say no more than five shillings a week – again the shopkeeper's judgement on what was realistic was essential. The outstanding bill, or, at the worst, part of it, would be settled on Saturday pay night, and any arrears would be paid off from the occasional windfall. In Salford the dividend from the co-operative, which did not give credit, would be used to pay off any arrears at the small shop. For many families it was a constant battle of balancing the importunings of one creditor against those of another, and it tested a housewife's ingenuity to find ways of getting credit. To do this often meant journeys of considerable length. For example, an Oxfordshire labourer's wife, with an income of 13s a week in 1913, covered a wide radius to build up debts of £10. There was no hope of such debts being completely paid off. As she said, 'when they worry, we have to pay a bit off and go short'.[2] More commonly they just built up debts with the landlord by failing to pay the rent.

Most shopkeepers in working-class areas tried to anticipate some of the difficulties by using the club system. Housewives could pay small weekly sums into the shop for some major item. For example, there were boot clubs, crockery clubs, coal clubs and Christmas clubs to encourage saving. This was aimed at the frugal, of course, but, as Dr John Foster had pointed out, the whole credit system was a pressure on the working-class family towards 'respectability', because only the respectable could expect credit.[3] Indeed, in some areas, to be 'taken on at a tick shop' was a sign of social advancement among one's peers.

While the poor, through little fault of their own, might sink into debt, the slightly more comfortable working classes were encouraged to embrace debt. A witness to the Select Committee on Manufacturers and Trade in 1833 reported on the credit system for buying cloth as it operated in Lancashire.[4] There were, at that time, about twenty Manchester-based firms employing travellers, mainly 'Scotchmen', who went round selling cloth on credit:

> If I were to give an order to a Scotchman when he called, he would, upon the following Saturday, send it to me, and the next day he calls. Afterwards I begin to pay from 2s to 10s at a time according to the amount of the order.

Goods bought in this way were considerably dearer than those bought from shops. The witness claimed that the lowest charge was 50 per cent above the shop rate, and that some went as high as 100 per cent. Three-quarters of a century later the interest on the hire-purchase of sewing machines was at a similar level and even higher. With payments of 5s a month over three years, the selling price was often three times the cost price.[5]

The evidence seems to suggest that the tally system, or a more formalised system of hire purchase, was in fact growing from the 1860s and 1870s onwards, often accompanied by the prototype of high-pressure salesmanship. Presumably it was expanding because it was succeeding. The literary evidence that exists, paradoxically, is largely of failure. Flora Thompson recalled the enterprising furniture salesman in the Oxfordshire of the 1880s who persuaded first one and then almost all the other wives in a village, where the wage was 10s a week, that their lives could not be complete without a wooden wash-stand and a zinc bath. To be without these was to be humiliated in front of a visiting relative from the town or the doctor, looking for somewhere to wash his hands.

> Then the fortnightly payments began. One-and-six was the specified instalment, and, for the first few fortnights, this was forthcoming. But it was so difficult to get that eighteenpence together. A few pence had always to be used out of the first week's ninepence, then in the second week some urgent need for cash would occur. The instalments fell to a shilling. Then to sixpence. A few gave up the struggle and defaulted.[6]

At least the furniture salesman could reasonably have expected to make something from the transaction. The young and foolish brewers' traveller who persuaded the same villagers that what they needed for a perfect Christmas was a nine-gallon cask of ale, payable three months later, deserved to fail and to have to end in the County Court trying to get 2*d* a week from the debtors. He ought to have learned from the funeral contractors, who gave no credit, that dead men, human or oak, are bad risks.

The tallyman, or 'Johnny Fortnightly' was never popular – a situation exacerbated, no doubt, by the high proportion among them of Scots and Jews.[7] A working-man of the 1860s has left a graphic description of how one working-class court dealt with the 'enemy'.

After the street vendors of tea and breakfast relishes, the potmen of neighbouring public houses, and the parish doctor, the most frequent visitors to our Court are tallymen. This by no means respected class of tradesmen are said to realise an enormous profit upon their sales; but however this may be in a general way, they certainly get much more traffic than profit in our Court. No one individual ever keeps the Court long in his rounds; but the force of competition, or a spirit of recklessness, always induces some new man to try his fortune in it; and for a time each fresh adventurer is heartily welcomed, and favoured with liberal orders, until he begins to ask for money, when he is at once put down as a most unwelcome visitor, and one to be at all times received with a 'not at home', which is carried out by the following 'strategic movement': as the children of the Court are not sent to school, there are always a number of them playing about; and being brought up in the way that they are likely to go, they are early instructed to combine business with pleasure by keeping a sharp look-out for the tallyman while they are at play, and giving timely notice of his approach. By this means an alarm is given whenever a tallyman, who is immediately recognised by his parcel, comes in sight. Doors are then instantly shut, silence is proclaimed, and scouts are stationed at bedroom-windows on both sides of the Court. By the time these dispositions for the reception of the invader have been made, he will have arrived at the door of one of his debtors, and sounded a summons upon it. To this call to a parley there is of course no reply from the garrison, and a louder, more prolonged summons, with something of a threat in it, is then given. Should it happen that those next door to the attached house are not indebted to that particular tallyman, they will come out and gravely tell the plundered individual that 'There is no one at home there, sir'; a piece of intelligence which he receives with an evident air of disbelief, but with which he is nevertheless obliged to be content, as there is no appearance of life about the house to contradict the statement. But, as a rule, it is not convenient for any of the inhabitants of our Court to hold any discourse whatever with a tallyman who is in search of money; and in this case he is just allowed to knock at the door until he is tired, and raises the siege, when his retreat is signalled to the garrison by the scout at the opposite bedroom window; but it is not until one of the children, who has been 'told off', to follow up the retreat, and see that it is not a feigned one, has returned from his mission, that the lately besieged parties venture out.[8]

When all such subtle strategy failed, the much-maligned tallyman was quite likely to be subject to violence from his impecunious customers.

The difficulty with the tally system was that the customer had to accept the tallyman's price, and she had no way of knowing how extortionate it was. Secondly she was buying without having seen the actual article, only a sample. The quality of the goods delivered could be different from the sample. Finally there was always the pressure to buy more. The system no doubt allowed many to obtain what otherwise was outside their reach, but it only needed illness, loss of job, failure to maintain payments and all was lost. The more unscrupulous firms seem to have assumed that they were going to seize back a high proportion of their goods once part of the instalments had been paid and there was a large second-hand furniture trade in seized goods.[9]

An altogether more satisfactory system was operated by some shops, which by the end of the century were supplying the working class with ready-made clothes and footwear. This was the ticket system. Men bought credit notes worth £1 for perhaps 18s from some of these shops and sold them for 21s, payable in instalments of 1s per week. The great advantage of this system was that the housewife, armed with her ticket, could see the actual goods she was going to buy displayed, with price tickets.[10]

There were other less recommended ways of obtaining credit, by means of the money-lender and the pawnbroker. Both charged exceptionally high rates of interest. For example, costermongers in London might hire a barrow from a barrow yard at 1s per week. They might also borrow money from the barrow-owner to buy their vegetables. The rate charged for this was 2d a week.[11] This seems to have been the usual rate in the first decade of the century, and rates could rise to 3d in the shilling per week for long-term borrowing. There were various other refinements to ensnare the needy. For example, in Liverpool many money-lenders kept small shops or hawked fish and, occasionally, meat. They would insist that part of the loan had to be taken in kind. Thus, in order to obtain 2s in cash, the borrower might have to take 1s worth of fish as well. The debt then became 3s 4d.[12]

The pawnbroker offered much more moderate terms. In Liverpool in 1870 the charge was ½d per month on every complete half-crown lent. On larger pledges, over two guineas and under £10 in value, the charge was 3d per month per pound.[13] Thirty or forty years later in Liverpool the charge was usually ½d on 2s or less and another ½d on redeeming, which seems to have been fairly normal.

The law laid down that interest charged by pawnbrokers could not exceed 12·5 per cent, but there were all kinds of ways of getting round this with additional charges, for example 1d for the pawn ticket, 1d for accommodating items in a drawer or for hanging up an article. In this way the interest could rise to 200 per cent. There might also be the additional expense of paying a commission to a middle man (or more usually, a woman), the 'leaver', who took other people's clothes to pawn and reputedly got the best price.[14]

The majority of pledgings were small. In returns from thirty of the Liverpool pawnshops in 1869, 702,657 pledges were under 2s 6d, 638,477 between 2s 6d and 10s and only 74,530 between 10s and £10.[15] Monday was the favourite pawning day, when Sunday clothes went in to pawn to be redeemed on Saturday evening. In many cases this was done not just for the money, but because the typical working-class house lacked adequate storage space for good clothes. The wardrobe was hardly known, and cupboard space was limited and dirty. In Glasgow, with its 109 licensed pawnshops, and its countless, unlicensed 'wee pawns' compared with London's 425, a yet more vicious deprivation trap could be observed. Blankets were sometimes pledged in the morning to raise money to buy fish or fruit, which were sold during the day, and the blankets were then redeemed in the evening.[16]

Credit, from whatever source, allowed people to buy things they would not otherwise obtain. It probably also encouraged them to buy things they might well have done without. With the poorer section of the population, however, credit was largely for necessities. The result for many families was an overwhelming burden of debt. Eleanor Rathbone has left us with a sample of one Liverpool labourer's liabilities.[17] His wage was 24s per week and the family were 'decent people, well thought of by the clergy man'. In October 1908 his liabilities were:

Balance still due of loan of £4 from well-to-do friend in 1907 to meet debt contracted during illness	£1	2s	0d
Paying at rate 1s or 6d a week; no interest.			
Balance still due of loan from Loan Company, borrowed when out of work in 1908 at 8s interest on whole.	£2	5s	0d
Paying at rate of 2s 6d a week, plus 6d a week towards arrears.			
Debt to Money Lender contracted by wife when X was in half-time. Paying 3s 4d a week interest.	£1	0s	0d
Owing to Doctor.	£1	8s	0d
Paying 4s a month by order of Court			
Back Rent.	£1	10s	0d
Paying 1s a week.			
Interest on lodger's shawl, usually pawned on Monday for 7s 4d redeemed on Friday for 7s 8d.	£0	0s	4d
Interest on friend's bundle, usually pawned on Monday for 6s 4d redeemed on Friday for 6s 8d.	£0	0s	4d
Six weeks arrears on Weekly Burial Club, subscription 1s 10d.	£0	13s	0d
Coal Bill.	£0	3s	6d
No payment being made at date.			
Boots.	£0	4s	0d
No payment being made at date.			

There was really no complete way out of such a burden of debt. The struggle had always to be merely to minimise it. Little wonder that it often resulted in a devil-may-care drunkenness or in violence of husband against the unfortunate wife who had to battle to make ends meet.

Credit and the search for credit were by no means confined to the working class, of course. The relationship between shopkeeper and wholesaler was based on credit of a fortnight, a month or a quarter, and the small shopkeeper in a poor area had exactly the same kind of problem as his customers in balancing one creditor against another and keeping the commercial travellers on the 'hop'.[18]

Credit was just as necessary for the middle-class family on a tight budget, though failure to live within one's means was seen as a much greater moral lapse for such a family than among the working class. Also, it was probably more difficult for the lower-middle-class family to obtain credit than for any other group. They lacked the community contact of the little corner shop and they lacked the credit worthiness that would give them an account at the high-class shop. The irony of the whole credit system was that the better off the customer the more extensive the credit he could get. A year was the normal time for high-class tradesmen or shopkeepers to be kept waiting for settlement of accounts. Few indeed, if they wished to keep custom, would dare to send out their bills in under a year. In some cases the situation was worse. A dressmaker planning to set up in business on her own to cater for ladies of fashion needed capital to keep herself for three years, 'because society ladies seldom pay their dressmakers' bills before two or three years'.[19]

Any shopkeeper seeking to cater for the 'carriage trade' had similar problems. It could prove impossible for the tailor or the hatter to get his money out of an impecunious aristocrat, yet that same aristocrat could destroy a shopkeeper's reputation by an ostentatious boycott. The high-class shopkeeper depended on his reputation and the number of carriages parked outside his shop. The shopkeeper's response to such problems was to inflate his prices and increase his profit margin.

Many of the new retailers who appeared in the 1870s and 1880s made it their first priority to break out of the vicious circle of credit. They demanded cash payments for all goods, and under no circumstances gave credit. In this way they ensured a regular flow of cash and were in a position to cut their costs, since a major part of their book-work was eliminated. None the less, it is surprising how many, by the early twentieth century when they were successfully established, did begin to give credit and allow weekly or monthly accounts. Perhaps it was a measure of customer pressure for credit, but probably it was a reflection of a swing back to the middle-class market by many of the new shops. Only with a very few items did a system of hire-purchase develop before 1914. Sewing machines had been sold on this basis from their first introduction, and when large items like pianos and harmoniums became popular they too were usually sold by hire-purchase. It was not, however, until between the wars that this system was widely adopted as one of the most effective means of stimulating demand.

The better-off middle class could also look to the banks for credit. Developments in banking, particularly the spread of joint-stock banking with limited liability after 1862, probably made it easier for many to obtain overdrafts. Banking amalgamations, which were especially common in the 1890s, brought competition for customers as the banks strove to achieve influence and territorial domination. Such sources of credit were, however, available to only a very few, and among those who were trying to reach the middle class or to cling on to a middle-class status just achieved there was probably a wariness of taking on debts of any kind.

8. Pack, Stall and Shop

'Don't ask the price, it's a penny.' Slogan used by Michael Marks at his Leeds market stall *c*. 1886.

Among the most effective ways in which demand for goods was stimulated were developments in retailing. The 'retailing revolution' as it has been called was far from complete by 1914, but a major transformation was well under way. There were three main aspects to this revolution: the displacement of hawkers, fairs and street markets by the fixed shop; the growth in the size of shops and in the variety of their stock; and the increasing number of multiple-branch retailing firms.

In the streets of Henry Mayhew's London of the 1850s, the cries of the street-seller were everywhere:

'So-old again,' roars one. 'Chestnuts all 'ot, a penny a score,' bawls another. 'An 'aypenny a skin, blacking,' squeaks a boy. 'Buy, buy, buy, buy, buy – bu-u-uy!' cries the butcher. 'Half-quire of paper for a penny,' bellows the street stationer. 'An 'aypenny a lot ing-uns.' 'Twopence a pound grapes.' 'Three a penny Yarmouth bloaters.' 'Who'll buy a bonnet for fourpence?' 'Pick 'em out cheap here! Three pair for a halfpenny, bootlaces.' 'Now's your time! beautiful whelks, a penny a lot.' 'Here's ha'porths,' shouts the perambulating confectioner. 'Come and look at 'em! here's toasters!' bellows one with a Yarmouth bloater stuck on a toasting-fork. 'Penny a lot, fine russets,' calls the apple woman.[1]

This babel was at its worst in the street markets such as at the New Cut in Lambeth or down Lambeth Walk, at the Brill in Somers' Town or along Hampstead Road or Tottenham Court Road, or in the notorious Clare Market, all thronged to capacity on Saturday pay-night. The stalls were lit by candles, perhaps stuck into a turnip, or even by an old-fashioned grease lamp, though 'the new self-generating gas lamp' was beginning to make its appearance. Amid the stalls were those who carried their wares in a pack or on a tray.

Street trading was not confined to markets, and the street-sellers daily wandered a regular fifteen miles through residential streets, selling their myriad of wares. Mayhew calculated that there were more than 43,000 street-sellers in the London of 1851, a number swollen by the recent influx of near-destitute Irish. Although there was a hard-core of traditional street-sellers, those who had been born to costermongering, the street was the last refuge of the unemployed and the unemployable, the artisan who had hit hard times, the drunkard, the blind, the limbless. One did not need much capital to try one's hand at private enterprise. A barrow could be hired for 3d or 4d a day, a basket for 1d, scales for 2d and a set of weights for 1d. Stock could be obtained on credit or with a loan from the money-lender.[2] The range of possible specialisms was wide. First there were 30,000 costermongers – men, women and children of all ages, engaged in selling fish, fruit, vegetables, game, poultry and flowers. The original costermongers had sold the Suffolk 'coster' apples, and home-grown fruit and vegetables remained their main stock, bought in the markets of Covent Garden, Spitalfields or the Borough. By the 1850s increasing quantities of imported fruit were coming in, pineapples, melons, grapes, oranges, nuts, which could be purchased from the brokers. But the born coster preferred home-grown fruit, and oranges and nuts were left to the Irish.

After fruit and vegetables, fish was the main item for sale. The coming of the railways had brought more fresh fish from wider areas. Billingsgate had expanded and the price of fish had fallen sharply, overcoming working-class prejudice against it. Herrings were cheapest and most popular, and the smell constantly pervaded the homes of the poor. Mayhew calculated that the street-sellers alone sold 210 million pounds of herring in London, followed by plaice, mackerel and, for a short season, sprats. There was considerable demand for oysters, at four a penny, a demand that grew to a peak in the early 1860s until price and depleted oyster beds pushed them into the luxury class. The fish dealer who had got rid of his stock of 'wet fish' would probably turn to 'dry fish' that had been cured and salted – salt cod, smoked haddock, salt herrings. Many of these came from Scotland, but in other cases smoking and drying was a way of giving a second lease of life to 'wet' fish that had failed to go in the previous week. Many a 'Scotch haddie' had never been within sight of Scotland.

Because of the seasonal nature of their trade most of the costermongers did not specialise, but moved to whatever was the most plentiful or the most lucrative. Probably it would be fish in January and February, when 8s a week were the average earnings. March and April tended to be the bleakest of months, when they might scratch a living of 4s–6s a week selling garden plants. Things were likely to pick up in May with new supplies of fresh fish, and earnings would be up to 12s a week. The summer brought the boom months, with new potatoes, peas and beans in June, cherries, strawberries, raspberries, currants in July and plums and apples in August and September. Then earnings would rise to 6s, 7s and even 8s a day. 30s a week was a low average throughout July. By October the apples were getting scarcer and the days shorter. However, with an 'r' in the month a reasonable trade could be done in oysters, earning perhaps 1s or 1s 6d a day. In November and December the concentration was again on fish, but the pre-Christmas rush brought a switch to holly and ivy, oranges and lemons, and the coster's earnings might rise to 3s or 4s a day in Christmas week.[3]

A second large group of street-traders in Mayhew's London (4000 of them) sold eatables and drinkables. Lacking adequate means of cooking food, the poorest section of the working class had always depended upon buying their food ready-cooked. The streets offered a wide range of delicacies. For the main course one could have 'hot-eels, pickled whelks, oysters, sheep's trotters, pea soup, fried fish, ham sandwiches, hot green peas, kidney puddings, boiled meat pud-dings, beef, mutton, kidney and eel pies, and baked potatoes'.[4] The last had become popular since the late 1830s, and potato cans for keeping them hot could be purchased from about 50s, though for ten guineas one could have a brass one, mounted with German silver. It is probable that baked potatoes were used as an accompaniment to fried fish, which had a long history as a street food. The great advantage of frying fish in batter was that it temporarily halted decay and it hid the original appearance of the fish. The fish for frying would be the fresh fishmonger's end-of-day (or end-of-week) stocks, which because of appearance and smell could not last another day at his stall.

The quality of food provided by the street-hawkers was of the poorest kind. The meat dishes were made from scraps and offal for which the butcher had no use or, just as likely, from decayed and tainted meat, that had lain around too long. A good sprinkling of hot pepper could disguise the strongest taste. However, as meat prices fell in the 1850s, the pieman was less likely to be met with cries of 'Mee-yow' or 'Bow-wow-wow', as customers impugned the nature of the contents.[5]

To follow the main course the street offered a feast of sweet dishes –

fruit tarts and mince pies, plum duff and currant cake, gingerbread-nuts and Chelsea buns, candies, rocks and oranges, and, just coming in, street ices. A few of the pastries and buns would be made and sold by bakers, but in most cases the street-seller bought his trayful from wholesalers. About a dozen Jewish pastry cooks in Whitechapel supplied the street-traders at 4d a dozen.[6] The range of candied items on sale was likely to have been produced by the seller. It was a relatively easy starter for the would-be coster. As the future 'Lord' George Sanger discovered, ten pounds of coarse moist sugar at 7d a lb., with some oil of peppermint, boiled hard makes passable mint rock to sell at ½d a lump.[7] Add a few herbs and one had cough drops.

The street drinks were tea, coffee, cocoa, ginger-beer, lemonade, sherbet, elder cordial, peppermint water, curds and whey, rice milk and fresh milk. These street traders were catering for what, in terms of the London poor, was the 'luxury' trade, for the working-class equivalent to the 'diners-out'. Mayhew gives a breakdown of the economics of a coffee-stall of the 1850s:

I usually buy 10 ounces of coffee a night. That costs, when good, 1s. 0½d. With this I should make five gallons of coffee, such as I sell in the street, which would require 3 quarts of milk, at 3d. per quart, and 1½ lb. of sugar, at 3½d per lb., there is some at 3d. This would come to 2s. 2¾d.; and allowing 1¼d. for a quarter peck of charcoal to keep the coffee hot, it would give 2s. 4d. for the cost of five gallons of coffee. This I should sell at about 1½d. per pint; so that the five gallons would produce me 5s., or 2s. 8d. clear. I generally get rid of one quartern loaf and 6oz. of butter with this quantity of coffee, and for this I pay 5d. the loaf and 3d. the butter, making 8d.; and these I make into twenty-eight slices at ½d. per slice; so that the whole brings me in 1s. 2d., or about 6d. clear. Added to this, I sell a 4 lb cake which costs me 3½d. per lb., 1s. 2d. the entire cake; and this in twenty-eight slices, at 1d. per slice, would yield 2s. 4d., or 1s. 2d. clear; so that altogether my clear gains would be 4s. 4d. upon an expenditure of 2s. 2d. – say 200 per cent.[8]

Other beverages to be found were home-made concoctions of doubtful content or lemonades bought from manufacturers in Ratcliffe Highway or in the Commercial Road – though the contents were equally doubtful. In St James's Park of a summer's day one could obtain milk straight from one of the grazing cows, or there were street milk-sellers with a pair of cans and a yoke, who had purchased the milk at Smithfield, or at one of the other markets or from one of the town dairies. In Hampstead and Highgate water was carried and sold in this way, 1½d for two pails full, seven gallons.[9]

Yet another large group of street-sellers were those selling manufactured articles in metal, glass, china and cloth. Mayhew calculated that there were 4000 of these. The list of their wares is endless – razors, knives, tea-trays, candlesticks, tools, lucifer matches, rat poison, grease-removing potions, sheets, laces, cotton threads, cigars, pipes, snuff-boxes, dolls, toys, firewood, pincushions and so on, anything that was portable. This group differed from the food retailers in that many of them preferred barter to cash. The 'crock-seller' with his tray loaded with 5s to 15s worth of tea-sets, vases, cruets, plates and jugs would look for old clothes in exchange.

A good tea-service we generally give ... for a left-off suit of clothes, hat and boots – they must all be in a decent condition to be worth that. We give a sugar-basin for an old coat, and a runner for a pair of old Wellington boots. For a glass milk-jug I should expect a waistcoat and trousers, and they must be tidy ones too. But there's nothing so saleable as a pair of old boots to us. There is always a market for old boots, when there is not for old clothes. You can any day get a dinner out of old Wellingtons.[10]

The 'crock-seller' would then take his bundle of clothes to the second-hand clothes exchange in Houndsditch. From there the woollen ones would find their way to the shoddy mills of Dewsbury or back into streets in the second-hand clothes stalls. Manufactured goods to sell or exchange were bought from wholesale warehouses. There were, for example, about 150 glass and crockery 'swag shops' around Spitalfields, where Staffordshire pottery and Lancashire glass was kept in large quantities. Around Bishopsgate one would find the haberdashery 'swag shops' and 'print brokers'.

In poor areas, naturally enough, there was always a market for second-hand goods of all kinds, but particularly for clothes. Indeed part of the tailoring and shoemaking trades existed on refurbishing old clothes. A silk hat could be touched up with velvet and dye to look like new, until it was in a shower of rain. 'Slop' tailors re-seated trousers and drawers, darned stockings and re-lined dresses. Boots and shoes were in the hands of 'translators', 'slop' cordwainers, who took an old pair of boots and with some fixing, patching and polishing produced something that looked only partly worn.[11] The 'slop' workers in some cases sold their own, while others worked for a wholesaler who supplied the street-sellers with their stock.

Another considerable group of street-sellers were the purveyors of street literature: ballads, songs, broadsheets, tales of murders, rapes and 'shocking events' – confessions and dying words of some notorious villain. There was a publishing industry catering for the masses that had no contact at all with the respectable establishments of Albermarle Street or Paternoster Row.

Finally there were thousands of others selling everything saleable. 2000 people were involved in selling watercress, chickweed, groundsel, plantain and turf, catering for the Victorian fascination with caged birds. There were 300 sellers of live animals, dogs, birds, goldfish, squirrels, tortoises, leverets and snails. The dog-selling profession could be quite a lucrative one, and Mayhew calculated that some were able to make as much as £8 a week. At the other end of the scale were the sellers of trees, shrubs, flowers, salt, sand and shells, of combs and colanders, of matches and shoelaces. There is no end to the list that can be compiled.

There was not much difference between the itinerant street-seller and the seller with a fixed stall in the market. A stall of one's own was obviously the ambition of most street-sellers, but in many cases the hawker wandering through the streets crying his wares was the husband of the lady running the stall in the street market. Likewise the butcher hawking his meat from a tray, or the fisherman selling his dried fish, was the stall-holder trying to get rid of the remains of his stock. It was in the streets, then, that the working class bought their food, their clothes, their cutlery and their crockery. In the 1850s there were a few retailers catering for the working class who had fixed shops, but working-class housewives were on the whole suspicious of shops. They could not be persuaded that they could buy as cheaply in shops, and they were 'apt to think shopkeepers are rich and street-sellers poor, and that they may as well encourage the poor'.[12] In working-class areas shops and street-sellers existed in relative harmony, with the housewife buying her fish and vegetables in the street, but her bacon and cheese at the cheesemonger's, her tea and sugar at the grocer's, her firewood at the oilman's, and her beef at the butcher's, all of whom would have shops behind the stalls and barrows. When the police were called in and the street-traders moved on, it was a sure sign that an area was moving up in the world and that the shopkeepers had their eye on a better class of market.[13]

The pattern of street trading, as described in London by Mayhew, was to be found on a lesser scale in any major city. In smaller towns, where there were not wholesale markets, the major variation would be that a large number of the traders would be producers: the farmer brought his fruit, vegetables and milk into town, the grazier would also be the butcher. The pack, the barrow and the stall continued to play an important part in the system, but it was a declining part. City costermongers had in the past travelled to rural areas around the city. For the London trader a country round broke the monotony of the year. The extension of the railway network, however, more or less put a stop to such outings. Local dealers could now supply their own market. By the 1880s the wandering 'packman' with his barrow of trinkets, baubles, cheap china and tinware, the naphtha lamps on the side of his barrow flaring, and his ready line of 'patter', brought excitement and novelty to an isolated hamlet, but he was seen less and less.[14] It was still possible in the mid-1880s for a refugee from the pogroms of Tsarist Russia, Michael Marks, to begin his retailing career as a packman in the isolated villages of the West Riding, but he quickly moved to a stall at the Tuesday and Saturday market in Kirkgate in Leeds, then to the Castleford and Wakefield markets on the other days of the week.[15] People now travelled to the town, and it was less necessary for the retailer to go to them.

In many provincial towns the markets were becoming formalised and regularised. Frequently they were municipally owned, with what amounted to permanent sites held by the stall-holders. For the wandering 'cheap-jack' and hawker only the round of annual fairs was left, but these were by no means unimportant. At fair time people had extra money to spend and were in a frame of mind to purchase luxuries and follies. It was not just itinerant hawkers and cheap-jacks who joined the gypsies and amusement-booth owners at the fair, but local retailers with fixed shops used market stalls to push their cheap lines. At Oxford's St Giles's Fair in 1892, the local Singer representative did not disdain the stall to sell his sewing machines.[16]

By the end of the nineteenth century the number of itinerant hawkers had been greatly reduced everywhere. Only in the very poorest areas were hawkers of meat and stale bread to be found. Those that still wandered were the poorest, near beggars purveying matches and shoelaces, who expected charity rather than sales, and in some cases were accompanied by a child hired from a baby-minder, to tug the heart of the passers by. The street stall too was less important than it had been fifty years before, but it still played a large part in London retailing. An L. C. C. report of 1893 listed 106 informal and unauthorised street markets. At these there were 5290 barrows and movable stalls. 790 were attached to permanent shops, but the remaining 4500 belonged to costermongers and street-traders. 3469 of the stalls dealt in perishables: vegetables, fruit, flowers, fish, meat, provisions, eggs, confectionery, cakes, coffee, ices; but there were 427 clothing stalls, 531 selling furniture, 290 selling books, pictures, toys and games, 220 selling old clothes and second-hand goods and 353 selling medicines and sundries.[17] The pattern of street retailing had not changed very much in fifty years. Fewer street-sellers combined sale and manufacture and most depended on factory products. There was less ready-cooked food for sale, as standards of cooking had improved and more canned meat was available. The 'slop' workers were producing ready-made new clothes rather than revitalising old. But it was still a shilling a week to hire a barrow, and the barrow-owner still acted as a money-lender and took a handsome dividend. Increasingly, however, the barrow-owners were buying the stock and using the costers as salesmen on a commission basis.[18]

Everywhere there were signs that retailing was passing out of the hands of the small vendor into those of larger firms, but the individual shop was still at the heart of the system in 1914, and indeed much later. In villages and the working-class areas of towns the key shop was the general store – the small corner shop, providing almost all the regular needs of the populace in the necessary small quantities and with reasonable credit. An 1853 shopkeepers' guide lists the stock of such a shop. The grocery section contained tea, coffee, cocoa, chocolate, chicory, spices, barley, patent flour, semolina, sauces, pepper, mustard, bird seed and scent. The chandlery section had black lead, paste-blacking, starch, grits, night-lights, oxalic acid, sweet oil, soda, sandpaper, bath-brick, Fullers' earth, congreve matches, soap, blue, gum, and so on; in the hardware section there were nails, tools, cutlery, tinware, toys, turnery (that is brushes, clothes-pegs and so on), Seidlitz powders, adhesive plaster, ginger-beer, soda-water powders, sherbet powders, ginger-beer powders, baldness pomades, tooth-powders, hair dyes, phosphorous paste for rats, ink and bug-poison. These would be kept in a glorious disarray with little regard to the possibilities of contamination. Fifty or sixty years later things had not changed all that much in the little shop. Robert Roberts's father in Salford banned kippers from his corner shop 'swearing that their "pong", as he called it, amalgamated with the odour from tarry fire-lighters under the counter to give a certain "*je ne sais quoi* to the milk".' while his mother complained that the milk tasted like disinfectant as a result of contact with 'Lively Polly', a powerful washing powder.[19]

The corner shop was manned from six in the morning to eleven at night seven days a week to catch the smallest bit of trade. Little capital was needed for such a shop. Robert Roberts's father bought his for £40 and, as Charles Booth found, it could be stocked for under £2.

Stocks were mainly purchased on a daily basis from larger shops near by which combined wholesaling and retailing. The knack was to balance the books, not to over-extend and to watch the credit system. Booth found that in such a shop the takings would be £3 in a good week and £2 15s on average. The quantities purchased in such a shop were tiny pennyworths and ha'pennyworths, but the profits on such transactions were considerable. The shop Booth examined in the 1890s was in a cellar with 'a wooden screen betwixt door and fire, two tables, a counter, small and large scales and weights, a good corner cupboard, and some odds and ends'. This 14ft by 11ft by 7ft shop, half below street level had cost 40s for the good will and fittings and a rent of 3s 6d a week. Table 8.1 (pp. 104–5) gives its stock on a typical Friday evening.[20]

Such a shop offered a meagre living and the ideal situation was for it to be run by the wife of a working man. The profit margins on many items were high, but on the most common ones, bread and sugar, they were only 14 per cent, with 25 to 30 per cent the average on other standard items. Given risk, credit and the long hours worked the returns were not unreasonable.

A high proportion of the shops in any working-class area would be food shops, since it was on food that the bulk of working-class expenditure went. The typical bakery would be the small shop at the front of the small bakehouse, run by a working baker with the assistance of his wife and perhaps an apprentice or two. In many areas in the mid-nineteenth century the trade was grossly overcrowded. Drury Lane, for example, had eleven bakers' shops at the end of the 1860s, and London as a whole more than three thousand. This competition produced notorious adulteration, with alum the favourite additive. The falling price of flour from the 1870s onwards helped to eliminate the worst aspects, as did public health legislation and the vigilance of public analysts. Bakers still had a bad reputation, however, and the poet Laurie Lee has recalled how in his Cotswold village just before 1914:

> Eight to ten loaves came to the house every day, and they never grew dry. We tore them to pieces with their crusts still warm and their monotony was brightened by the objects we found in them – string, nails, paper, and once a mouse; for these were the days of happy-go-lucky baking.[21]

On the other hand, perhaps we ought to take due note of Professor Mathias's warning that 'Nothing becomes romanticised so much as memories, both individual and collective, about food and drink'.[22] However, there is some confirmation from other sources of persistent low standards in bakehouses. Miss Malvery describes the use of eggs by bakers with a complete disregard to their freshness. Many of the eggs took weeks to travel from as far away as Russia and yet were broken into the mixture with little examination.[23]

The gradual establishment of baking on a scientific basis began in about the 1880s. The 'Healtheries' Exhibition in London in 1884 provided the principal impetus to this development, and training for bakers was introduced. The National Association of Master Bakers set up a school of baking and confectionery at the Borough Polytechnic in London, and there was a similar one attached to the Glasgow and West of Scotland Technical College. These institutions helped to propagate the latest ideas.

The appearance of the standard loaf altered out of all recognition in the last quarter of the century. At the beginning of the period the 4 lb. quartern loaf or the even larger 8 lb. one were still available, though the sizes were no longer fixed by statute. Such bread was generally dirty brown in colour, 'stodgy, soggy, suggesting the idea that some pudding had missed its vocation in life'.[24] In 1872 the first roller flour mill was opened in Glasgow, which began the trend towards finer, whiter bread. From the 1880s till the early twentieth century a whole spate of inventions mechanised baking, doing away wth long hours of fermenting and with the drudgery of hand kneading. Baking on a large scale came in, but the small local baker with a minimum of mechanisation persisted, and the really significant improvements in the quality of bread before 1914 were confined to the middle-class market, supplied in London by firms like Nevill, J. & B. Stevenson and the Civil Service Bread Company.

The combined producer and retailer, typical of the baking trade throughout the period, was also common in the meat trade. Butchering in the mid-nineteenth century was a highly skilled task. The butcher bought the cattle live, slaughtered them, cut them up and sold them. Only in the largest towns like London, Manchester and Glasgow were there wholesale meat markets where the butcher could buy carcass meat. In most areas butchers were closely associated with farmers, a fact that encouraged most of them to be Tory in their politics, and in some cases they fattened animals on their own grazing land. With no refrigeration the butcher had to get rid of his stock as rapidly as possible. Many butchers had shops to cater for the better-off end of the market and set up stalls in working-class areas at the end of the week to cater for the poorer end. Alternatively, the left-over

Table 8.1

Articles	Quantities	Total Value [s d]		Cost price	Sale price	% of profit on cost
Ginger beer	6 dozen	4	0	8d per dozen	1d each	50
Vinegar	1 gallon	0	9	9d per gallon	by ha'porths (say)	100
Salt	–	0	2	2d per loaf	by ha'porths and farthings	100
Mustard	1 dozen	0	8	8d per dozen	1d each	50
Tea	Loose	0	8	1s 4d per lb.	6d per ¼lb.	25
Tea	in oz. and ½ oz. pkts	1	6	1s per lb.	1d per oz.	33
Rice and pearl barley	–	0	4	1½d per lb.	5 oz. for 1d	100
Sugar	12 lb. in packets	1	9	1s 9d per dozen lb.	2d per lb.	14
Currants	–	0	2	1½d per lb.	5 oz. for 1d.	100
Coffee	–	0	6	1s per lb.	4d per ¼ lb.	33
Soap	–	1	1½	4½d per bar	cut into 12 pieces at ½d	33
Blue	2 dozen packets	0	4	2d per dozen	¼d each	50
Blacking	1 dozen packets	0	2½	2½d per dozen	½d each	140
Matches	3 dozen boxes	0	6	2d per dozen	¼d each	50
Candles	1½ packets	1	6	11d per packet of 60	4 for 1d	36
Washing powder	1 dozen packets	0	4½	4½d per dozen	½d each	33
Blacklead	1 dozen packets	0	2	2d per dozen	¼d each	50
Epsom salts	1 dozen packets	0	2	2d per dozen	¼d each	50
Senna	1 dozen packets	0	2	2d per dozen	¼d each	50
Firewood	3 dozen bundles	0	6	2d per dozen	4 for 1d	50
Baking powder	1 dozen packets	0	2	2d per dozen	¼d each	50
Flour	6 packets	0	7½	1s 3d per dozen pkts. (fell later to 1s)	1½d and 2d per packet. (1½d)	50

				£	s	d	
Bread	6 loaves	1s 9d per dozen	2d each	0	7½		14
Margarine	3 lb. (best)	7½d per lb.	10d per lb.	1	10		33
Margarine	2½ lb.	5½d per lb.	8d per lb.	1	3		42
Cheese	3 lb.	5d per lb.	8d per lb.	1	3		60
Eggs	–	6s 6d per 120 in summer	1d each and 2 for 2½d	1	0		25 (about)
Dripping	–	4d per lb.	6d per lb.	1	8		50
Bacon	6¼ lb.	4½d per lb.	8d per lb.	2	8		77
Onions	–	10d or 1s per 20 lb.	1d per lb.	1	0		80
Pickled onions	1½ jars	Home-made	by ha'porths (say)	1	8		100
Jam	–	4d for 2 lb.	6d per lb.	0	9		200
Milk	1 gallon	9d or 10d per gallon	2d per pint	0	9		60
Cotton, tapes, etc.	–	Various	–	1	0		–
Hair oil	–	7d per bottle	by ha'porths	0	7		–
Cigarettes	–	6 doz. for 1s	½d each	–			50
Sweets	–	3d & 4d per lb.	½d for 1½ oz.	3	0		50
Cakes	–	Various kinds	–	1	0		30–50
Tarts	–	4½d per dozen	½d each	0	3		33
				1	16	7½	

Source: C. Booth, *Life and Labour of the People in London: Industry*, vol. III 2nd ser. (1903), p. 254.

meat or the 'block ornaments', the small pieces of meat that butchers cut off from the joint, might be sold off to small general shops or even to street-hawkers. At least until the end of the nineteenth century the hawking of meat ends in the streets was not unknown. Generally, however, the same butcher catered for all sections of the community. Glasgow butchers, whose main trade during the week was the servant-employing classes, kept open until midnight at the end of the week to pick up trade once the public houses had closed.[25]

The traditional pattern of the meat trade began to alter in the 1880s as a result of a number of factors. Firstly the depression in agriculture brought a decline in the number of domestic livestock. Secondly re-frigeration opened up whole new areas of the New World as suppliers; and thirdly improved regulation of the slaughtering of animals brought greater centralisation to the business of killing, and with it the development of larger abattoirs. As a result most butchers became simple retailers.

As early as the 1860s home supplies were not adequate to meet the rising demand for meat, and the cattle plague of the 1860s made the situation even worse. Attempts to solve the problem by retailing horse-meat in a *boucherie hippophagique*[26] stirred little enthusiasm, and the search for alternative suppliers began. The difficulty lay in transportation. Pork was no problem, it could be rubbed in salt, loaded on board ship in the United States, and arrive in Liverpool cured. Beef, on the other hand, required careful preparation and coo-pering, and even then it was likely to deteriorate if any delay occurred. Such salted beef and pork were sold in the poorer areas at 4d or 5d per lb. The tremendous shortfall in domestic supplies as a result of rinderpest slaughterings pushed up prices to such an extent that it encouraged experimentation. Canned meats of various kinds appeared on the market, in some cases imported from Australia, and by the 1870s from the great American canning firms in Chicago and Cincinnati that P. D. Armour and others had initiated. Selling at 5d to 7d per lb., at a time when fresh meat was costing over 1s per lb. the preserved meats had the obvious attraction of cheapness in the late 1860s and early 1870s. Such meats, however, were not sold by the but-chers, but in general shops and by some grocers.

The rise in meat prices in the late 1860s also made it economical to import live cattle from the United States and Canada. By 1877 the New York firm of T. C. Eastman was shipping 1000 cattle a week. Some were slaughtered on arrival, others were fattened and then slaughtered. Both lots were generally sold as Scotch meat.[27] It was Eastmans who, in 1874, successfully shipped the first consignment of chilled meat across the North Atlantic. Two years later the French-man, Charles Tellier, shipped the first cargo of frozen meat through the tropics from Buenos Aires, and in 1880 the first shipment of frozen meat arrived in London from Australia. These developments constituted a revolution of major importance, not just for the British housewife, but for half the world. Imports of frozen and chilled meat rose by leaps and bounds. In 1875 a mere 3098 cwt. of fresh beef (frozen or chilled) arrived from the United States. In 1876 it was over 144,000 cwt. and, by the end of the 1870s, over 0·5 million cwt. By the end of the 1880s the million mark had been passed and by 1896 that had doubled. From the mid-1880s supplies were coming in from Australia, New Zealand and South America. The 500 cwt. from the Argentine in 1884 had become 5 million cwt. by 1910. By the end of the nineteenth century, the United Kingdom was getting a third of its beef and mutton and over half its pig meat from foreign sources.[28]

Not that there was great enthusiasm for the new meat. Once the initial novelty had worn off, frozen meat came up against entrenched prejudices and vested interests. Customers were suspicious of chilled meat, since it lost a certain brightness after thawing and was limp and reputedly difficult to cook. They had reason to be suspicious, as butchers were believed to be passing off old cows and ewes, or slightly tainted meat, as best River Plate or Australian. This belief died hard, and into the twentieth century it was still the current conviction that tubercular sheep and cattle were sold off as foreign meat.[29] On the other hand, given the rapid rate of growth of imports, it is clear that either the prejudice was not as great as has sometimes been suggested, or – and this is more likely – much frozen meat was passing for home produce. The agricultural correspondent of the *Glasgow Herald* was quite convinced that this was the case in 1880. 'I must reiterate my deliberately informed opinion', he wrote, 'that fully 85 per cent of the dead meat which reached this city from America finds its way to consumers through the ordinary channels as home-bred and home-fed beef.'[30]

Traditional butchers went to great lengths to distinguish themselves from the 'hard beef smashers' and as a result the shippers of frozen meat had to set up their own outlets. With frozen meat selling at 2½d to 3d per lb. when it first came in, compared with 9d to 1s per lb. for English meat, it tended to be sold mainly on market stalls. It often fell to lower prices as the frozen-meat retailers tried to sell off their supply as quickly as possible before it went bad. The gradual introduction of refrigeration in butchers' shops further differentiated the shopkeeping butcher from the stall-holder, since there was less need to find an outlet for end-of-week leftovers.

Even cheapness was not enough to break down hostility to frozen meat in some parts of the country, and working-class housewives in Yorkshire, the north east, Wales and Scotland showed a reluctance to experiment.[31] It may be that it was in middle-class homes, where the servants did the shopping and received a discount from the butcher if they took foreign meat, that most frozen meat was eaten.[32] It was really the falling standard of living in the first decade of the century that pushed many into trying frozen meat for the first time. Faced with increasing competition from multiple-branch meat retailers, many of the traditional butchers swallowed their pride and started to sell foreign meat. The traditional producer-retailer butcher persisted in smaller towns well after 1914, but the transformation of the butcher into a mere meat retailer had been largely accomplished.

By the last quarter of the nineteenth century the need for ready-cooked meats was less than it had been in Mayhew's day, and the street-seller of pies and tarts was beginning to disappear. Most people had some means of cooking. However, convenience foods which could be supplied in cans were in demand. Some of the early Australian canned meat was not particularly attractive, 'a large lump of coarse-grained lean meat inclined to separate into coarse fibres, a large lump of unpleasant fat on one side of it – an irregular hollow partly filled with watery fluid'.[33] There was resistance to canned meats, and this resistance spread to the nutritious corned beef which was being imported from South America and the United States. In Nottingham in the mid-1880s there were still many families that lacked a tin-opener. When Jesse Boot offered tins of salmon at 4½d a tin in his Goosegate shop, one of the assistants was kept busy opening the tins for the customers.[34] The working-class partiality for tinned salmon was frequently commented upon, particularly by those who sought to argue that bad management contributed more to the plight of the poor than low incomes.

The favourite ready-cooked meal by the end of the century was fish and chips, and one hesitates to enter into the controversy on the origins of that particular delicacy. When the British fried fish was linked with the French *pommes frites* on a regular basis is impossible to say. One might be tempted to find its roots in some relic of the 'Auld Alliance' if it were not for the strident claims that emanate from both Lancashire and Yorkshire. Significantly the main fish-range manufacturers were, by the 1880s, established in Oldham. Whatever the truth about the pioneers, it is clear that by the end of the 1880s the fish-and-chip shop was a well-established feature of working-class areas, both north and south of the Trent.[35] However in London it was still enough of a novelty for the ever-innovative William Whiteley to offer snacks in his Westbourne Grove store.[36] But the early fish and chip shops, with their smell, their dirt and their grease-coated windows, were for the poor. There was no better bargain than a hot meal for six or eight mouths for sixpence.

Few trades underwent such a major transformation in the last half of the nineteenth century as the grocery trade. Specialism gave way to the all-embracing grocery and provision store and, indeed, in the case of some like Charles Harrod's shop in the Brompton Road, into department stores. In the mid-nineteenth century the grocer proper concentrated on tea, coffee, cocoa, sugar and spices. For soap and candles one went to the chandler, for foreign specialities to the Italian warehouseman, for cheese to the cheesemonger and for paint to the oil and colourman. Within forty years the chandler and the Italian warehousemen had largely disappeared and their custom was absorbed by the grocers. Oil and colourmen had either moved towards groceries by keeping a range of sauces and pickles and soap, tinned foods and jams, or towards hardware, with brushes, china, ironmongery, china and lamps. It was to the oil and colourman that one went for paraffin oil, but he probably kept a cheaper range of food than the grocer. There were still specialist shops, like the cheesemonger and the provision dealer, but they were disappearing. It was in groceries and provisions that the most substantial developments in retailing took place, through the multiple grocery chains, developments which are examined in chapter 9.

9. The Transformation of the Shop

From floor to ceiling the walls are covered with rows of hams, and there is also a large assortment of bacon, butter, and Dunlop, Stilton, Cheddar and American cheese. A substantial horse-shoe counter gives a large space for salesmen, and it is evident that Mr Lipton intends to carry on an extensive business, for we understand that he has a staff of from twelve to fifteen salesmen, besides three cash boys.

Description of Lipton's new branch in Dundee, 1878.

Depot, emporium, bazaar, warehouse – none of these seem to possess the slightest descriptive power. Whiteley's is an immense symposium of the arts and industries of the nation and of the world; a grand review of everything that goes to make life worth living passing in seemingly endless array before critical but bewildered humanity.

Description of Whiteley's, in *Modern London* (1887).

The working class, by shopping in the streets or in the corner store, got neither cheapness nor quality. They paid dearly for their small quantities and for any credit obtained. The quality was abysmal, with frequent adulteration of the most common products to squeeze a few pence more profit from the poor. Nor was there much effort to attract customers, and the only sales technique applied in the better-off shops was servility and deference. From about the 1870s onwards, however, there were signs of change, and of an awareness of new, potentially lucrative markets to be tapped. A few shopkeepers began to perceive that there was a place for cheapness *and* reasonable quality. The change came partly as a response to the demand generated by rising incomes and partly as a response to the supply of goods. A new range, first of foodstuffs and then gradually of manufactured goods, was available in almost limitless quantities as the five continents were opened up by railway and steamboat. For supplies of meat, dairy produce, fruit and vegetables the British consumer could now draw upon the whole world, and within the British Isles goods could be transported rapidly from port to market and from country to town.

In most cases the traditional shopkeepers were slow to make the adjustments that the new conditions of supply and demand necessitated. It was frequently new firms that really made the breakthrough in the late nineteenth and early twentieth centuries, and it tended to be new retailers who were involved in the key development of multiple-shop firms and department stores.

The Multiples

A small number of specialist firms in the grocery and provision trade had developed branches by the middle of the century. In London the Italian warehousemen, Walton, Hassell & Port, had already thirty branches in 1870, while in the north-east the London & Newcastle Tea Company had between ten and twenty branches. However, it was from the 1870s and 1880s, coinciding with high levels of employment in the early years and with the fall in price of foodstuffs from abroad in the later years, that the multiple-branch grocery firm really expanded. By 1885 there were 31 firms in the grocery and provision trade with 10 or more branches, 8 of them with more than 25 branches. By 1895 there were 72 with 10 or more branches, 26 with over 25 branches. Fifteen years later the figures were 114 and 44.[1]

Many of the founders of these firms started in a small way. The most famous of all was Thomas Lipton, born the son of a small provision shopkeeper in Glasgow, but with his horizons widened by four years in the United States. From his first shop in Stobcross Street in 1871, he expanded rapidly, specialising in Irish ham, butter and eggs. By 1880 he had four branches in Glasgow, one in Paisley and one in Greenock, and was opening shops in the three other Scottish cities of Dundee, Aberdeen and Edinburgh. The (as always) spectacular move south of the border came with the opening of the Leeds branch in 1881, and branches in Liverpool, Birmingham, Sunderland, Manchester, Bristol, Cardiff, London, Swansea and Belfast followed in quick succession. By the end of the decade he was undoubtedly 'King of the Dairy Provision Trades', as the *American Dairyman* dubbed him.[2]

Lipton was unusual in many ways, not least in thinking in terms of a national market. Most other firms, although opening branches, confined themselves to particular regions. Massey's, founded in 1872 by Alexander Massey, paralleled Lipton's in a number of ways, specialising in Irish and American dairy produce and later in tea, but before 1914 his branches were confined to the Glasgow area. Templeton's, which was built up in the 1880s by a group of Ayrshire brothers had fifty branches by 1910, over forty of them in Glasgow, the other half-dozen or so being in surrounding towns. Andrew Cochrane, the son of a small farmer from Perthshire, moved into the tea trade in Glasgow in 1881, and by 1914 had almost 100 shops operating. All were in Glasgow and its immediate neighbourhood. William Galbraith's branches moved slowly from Linwood to Paisley in 1884 and then crept into Glasgow along the Paisley road.[3]

A similar pattern emerged along the north-east coast, with family firms like William Duncan's and J. W. Brough's and Willson's expanding slowly and cautiously in Newcastle, Gateshead, South Shields and other Tyneside towns. In Liverpool there was Cooper's, in Manchester John Williams's and in London John Sainsbury' and David Greig'.

Another firm that thought in national terms was that of Julius Drew and J. Musker, which grew from a store in the Edgware Road into a number of grocery and tea stores in London, Birmingham and Leeds, before taking on a new corporate identity in 1888, as Home & Colonial Stores Ltd. In the process of incorporation, and under the dynamic guidance of a solicitor, William Capel Slaughter, they switched from tea as their staple to butter and later margarine. In less than ten years the company had more than 200 branches and in less than a further fifteen years 400 branches.[4] Another firm with national horizons was the Maypole Dairy Company, built on the shops of the Watson brothers and George Jackson. By the time these merged in 1898, there were twenty-five branches in Lancashire and Cheshire, nineteen in Scottish towns as far north as Dundee, and a total of more than 150 scattered throughout England, South Wales, Belfast and Dublin.

There were two kinds of multiples in the grocery and provision trade. The first were high-class grocers, carrying a large range of goods, like John Williams's in Manchester. The second (and these) were the ones which expanded really fast) were geared to the working-class market and concentrated on a limited range of items with mass appeal. Many of the multiple shop firms grew from small beginnings in working-class districts and their dynamic founders were themselves working class, in tune with working-class tastes and attitudes. Experience of the small shop no doubt made many, like Thomas Lipton and William Galbraith, very aware of the problems of the credit system. Many a shop in a working-class area had been overwhelmed by the debts that customers had been allowed to accumulate. Therefore no credit was the golden rule of the new retailers. The alternative offered was cheapness. Gross profit margins were kept at 10 to 15 per cent, one-half or one-third of what a traditional grocer could expect. Costs were kept down by eliminating deliveries and orders, by keeping book-keeping to a minimum, thanks to the refusal of credit, and by making shop fittings fairly simple. Most effective of all, however, was the limitation of the range offered to a few selected items which could be obtained cheaply by bulk purchase. In almost all cases these were imported foodstuffs. Butter, bacon, ham, eggs and later tea and margarine were the staples. Lipton and others were able to sell imported ham at half the price of their rivals, butter at 1*s* instead of 1*s* 8*d* per lb. and, after 1889, tea at 1*s* 2*d* to 1*s* 9*d* per lb. instead of the usual 3*s* to 4*s*.[5]

These items, with bread, were becoming the staples of the working-class diet, and their cheapness at the multiples encouraged increased consumption. In addition the shops were conveniently placed in central working-class areas. They opened at 7 a.m. in time to catch the early morning breakfast trade. In the Clyde shipyards, for example, the pattern was a 6 a.m. start and a break for breakfast at 9 a.m. The working-class housewife did some shopping between 7 and 8 a.m. and was making breakfast for 9 a.m.[6] They also accepted the traditional working-class shopping pattern by staying open until 10 or 11 p.m. or even to midnight on Saturdays.

There was also a recognition that a more prosperous working class was demanding better standards. Lipton was after the working-class housewife, but he offered her the highest standards of service. The shops, in contrast to many, were kept immaculately clean, with assistants in white coats and aprons. For the first time working-class housewives were seen as a market important enough to be courted and catered for. That the demand was there to be won was evident from Lipton's phenomenal success. By the end of the 1870s, in four Glasgow shops, he was selling 1·5 tons of lump butter, 50 cases of roll butter, 1 ton of bacon, 1·5 tons of ham, 0·5 ton of cheese and 16,000 eggs – daily![7]

The range of products sold by the new retailers was gradually extended. Margarine, especially after it had gained a certain respectability after the 1887 enquiry, was an obvious item to appeal to the working class. Certainly by the first decade of this century, most of the prejudice against margarine had gone, though it was still a product for the lower end of the market. Lipton's started selling margarine in the early 1890s, and in 1892 jam was introduced, in 1893 mineral water, in

1895 a limited range of confectionery and in 1898 (and not very successfully) wines and spirits.[8] After 1906 Home & Colonial began expanding their lines – jams, coffee, sauces, jellies, custards, blancmange, baking powder, treacle, self-raising flour, and tinned milk were added to their traditional lines, and this pattern can be seen in other grocery and provision chains. A major exception was the Maypole Dairy, which, as late as 1922, still carried only four lines – butter, margarine, condensed milk and tea.

The small shops had gained from the increasing availability of foodstuffs and the larger range of manufactured foods. They had also gained from the expansion of demand, and there were plenty of opportunities to open new shops in the developing suburbs. However, by the turn of the century, these small shops were facing fierce competition from the multiples. It was no longer unacceptable to be seen buying cheese in Lipton's. Margarine, of course, was bought only for the servants! In 1906 *The Times* was warning of the imminent disappearance of the small grocer, but he showed a remarkable tenacity. In working-class areas it was still essential to get credit, which only the small shop supplied. In middle-class and upper-class areas, the services of ordering, delivering and monthly accounts, which the small shop also supplied, were enough to ensure its survival. The food being sold in some of the small shops was in many cases no different from that of the multiples, as Lipton, Galbraith and others soon developed a wholesale side to supply small shops.

The meat trade saw similar developments to those in groceries, brought about in part by those pressures which had transformed the grocery and provision trade, but also by its own particular circumstances. The butcher who slaughtered his own animals, while certainly not disappearing entirely, increasingly gave way to the retailer who bought carcases in the wholesale market. The coming of frozen meat in the 1880s was important in bringing about multiple-shop retailing in the meat trade.[9] Meat shippers from the United States, Australasia and the Argentine found such hostility among established butchers and in the markets of Smithfield and elsewhere that they were forced to do their own marketing. Also enthusiastic salemanship was required to get the new product across to the public. Eastmans began to buy up stalls and open retailing outlets, and in 1889 they amalgamated with the Glasgow firm of John Bell & Sons. Bell's had existed as a family firm since 1827, and from 1879 had begun to open multiple outlets. When it amalgamated with Eastmans there were 330 shops.[10] Their main rivals were James Nelson & Sons. Nelson's had started as cattle salesmen, and in 1886 had set up a freezing plant in the Argentine. From 1888 the main importers of Antipodean mutton and lamb were Messrs W. & R. Fletcher Ltd. By 1910 this firm had a turnover of £1,483,000 at its 400 branches. The Argenta Meat Company Ltd, founded by G. J. Ward and W. Rushworth, opened its first retailing branch in Oldham in 1895. Fifteen years later it had more than a hundred branches. All the meat multiples depended on a high turnover, with profit margins in some cases as low as 0·5 per cent, but, particularly in the first decade of this century, they were able to break down traditional suspicion of frozen meat by offering cheapness. Six firms – Eastmans Ltd with 1400 shops, James Nelson & Sons Ltd with 1500 shops, the River Plate Meat Company Ltd, the London Central Meat Company Ltd and W. & R. Fletcher each with over 400 shops, and the Argenta Meat Company Ltd with more than 100 shops – between them controlled about 90 per cent of the frozen-meat trade in 1910.[11]

The move towards multiples took place in the retailing of bread also, but to a lesser extent than in meat and groceries, and the real revolution here was in technology rather than in methods of distribution. However, multiple-shop bakery organisations, with branches acting as outlets for the produce of a central bakery, did appear by the end of the century, and in 1915 there were eight firms with more than twenty-five branches each, the largest of which were the City Bakeries Ltd and Kirkland & Sons in Glasgow, J. Miller Ltd in London, and four in Liverpool, James Blackledge & Sons Ltd, George Lunt & Sons Ltd, Richard Taylor & Sons Ltd and Benjamin Sykes & Sons Ltd. The first three Liverpool firms had been founded in the late 1840s, but the other multiples in bread retailing had all appeared during the 1890s and after. By far the most typical bread retailer was still the baker with a small shop at the front of his small bakehouse.

The multiples were the shops of the mass market. They grew from the cheapening of a range of imported goods, and were geared to a limited range of items for mass sale. They were shops that set out to cater specifically for a better-off working class, offering first new staples of the working-class diet, and then steadily broadening their range of goods as those new items which presented the least problems of storage and distribution became available in large enough quantities and cheaply enough. Table 9.1 (p. 116) gives some indication of the pattern of growth of multiples in the food trades. Similar pressures and conditions produced similar developments in other branches of retailing, as Table 9.2 (p. 117) shows.[12]

The multiples were able to undercut many of the prices in traditional shops, and therefore must have had some effect in pushing

Estimates of the Number of Multiple-Shop Firms with more than Ten Branches

Table 9.1

Trade	1880 Number of		1890 Number of		1900 Number of		1910 Number of	
	Firms	Branches	Firms	Branches	Firms	Branches	Firms	Branches
Grocery & Provision	14	108	43	1265	80	3444	114	2870
Meat			8	564	13	2058	23	3828
Bread & Flour								
Confectionery					8	105	21	451
Milk					8	101	20	324
Chocolate & Sugar								
Confectionery							10	308

Table 9.2

Trade	1880 Number of		1890 Number of		1900 Number of		1910 Number of	
	Firms	Branches	Firms	Branches	Firms	Branches	Firms	Branches
Footwear	21	500	45	1231	64	2589	70	3544
Men's and boys' clothing					22	570	38	1085
Women's and girls' clothing							15	572
Chemists' and druggists'					11	410	13	700
Furniture and furnishing							9	128
Household goods					14	359	17	404
Tobacco							8	502
Dyeing and cleaning	3	56	4	90	16	468	24	836

down prices. Perhaps more importantly, however, their style of presentation, their deliberate courting of a mass of consumers, inevitably forced change on all retailers.

In non-food trades multiple-shop firms had developed first among railway bookstalls, when W. H. Smith & Son in England obtained a near monopoly in the years after 1841, just as John Menzies did in Scotland after 1857. The Singer Sewing Machine Company developed a chain of shops to market their sewing machine and its accessories; the first shop was opened in 1856, and they had nearly 400 branches by 1900. Both these developments were the product of special circumstances: Smiths and Menzies because of the needs of the railway companies, and the sewing-machine multiples because of the need for a good after-sales service and because of the difficulties of finding existing retailers willing to carry enough of the relatively expensive stock.

More in line with the pattern in the food trade was the growth of multiples in boot and shoe retailing. From the 1870s onwards the need to find outlets for increased factory production of boots and shoes for the working class brought new retailers, who had none of the traditional cobbler's sensitivity to the monstrosities that the early factories produced, and who were willing to hold stocks to match the output of the factories. Such firms included P. Rabbits & Sons and Pocock Bros in London, R. J. Dick, A. & W. Paterson and John Gray in Scotland, and Scales & Slater in Yorkshire, all dating from the 1870s. In the 1880s others joined them, like Freeman Hardy Willis, Thomas Lilley and Stead & Simpson. Many of these firms were closely associated with particular manufacturing companies, and in 1900, according to J. B. Jefferys, 45 per cent of the branches controlled by the largest retailing firms (that is those with twenty-five or more branches) belonged to firms that undertook both retailing and manufacturing.[13]

The development of the factory system in tailoring and the acceptance of ready-made men's clothing brought the multiple clothes shops. Hepworths of Leeds. Hope Brothers of London and Jamiesons in Scotland appeared in the late 1870s, followed in the 1880s by such firms as G. A. Dunn, the hatters in London, and Ansells in Leeds. A very rapid period of expansion took place between 1890 and 1900, by which time there were twenty-two firms with over ten branches and Hepworths had 126 branches. The rate of growth slowed down in the first decade of the twentieth century, partly as a result of the set-back to real wages in that decade, but also because of too rapid a rate of development which produced over-competition. None the less there was still an increase of more than 100 per cent in the number of branches of firms with more than ten. As in footwear, close links developed between the manufacturing and retailing sides of the clothes trade.

In outerwear the ready-made clothing trade, upon which the multiples depended, was largely confined to men's wear, and only in wool, hosiery and underwear did multiples develop for women's wear. At the forefront of these was the Greenock firm of worsted spinners and hosiery manufacturers, Fleming, Reid & Company whose branches grew from their first in 1881 to over 200 Scotch Wool & Hosiery Shops, as they were called, by 1910. No other firm specialising in women's wear came anywhere near Fleming, Reid in size before 1910. The next largest, the Hosiery Manufacturing Company had only forty branches.[14]

Those multiples selling working-class clothing and footwear pursued the vigorous sales techniques of other multiples. Suits, shirts, caps and overcoats were well displayed, often on the pavement outside the shop. Boots and shoes were hung on poles around the doorways. Prices were clearly displayed, often with the assurance that the prices charged inside would be no different from those on the tickets. Sometimes even a 'hooker-in' was employed to entice anyone who dallied into the shop, and regular use was made of handbills and sandwich-board men to emphasise the cheapness of the goods available.

A close second to food as the major call on the increased purchasing power of the working class was patent medicines, the sales of which rose from £0·5 million in 1850 to £4 million in 1900, and then to £5 million in 1914.[15] The faith placed by the working class in the concoctions of Holloway, Beecham and countless others has still to be studied by historians, but it must be a commentary upon the cost and inadequacies of existing medical services and on the extent to which persistent minor ailments afflicted the working class. Dirt, poor cooking, poor-quality food and ignorance of hygiene must all have brought frequent stomach upsets, which a patent pill was called upon to cure. It was an obvious area for multiple-shop expansion.

The pioneer was Jesse Boot of Nottingham, who in 1874 expanded the sales of his herbalist and grocer's shop to include proprietary medicines. Although the wholesale price of drugs had been falling, often quite dramatically, since the 1830s, local retail chemists working with price agreements rarely passed the gains from this on to the consumers. The Pharmaceutical Society had been able to get the use of the titles 'chemist' and 'druggist' confined to its members, but in 1880 the House of Lords ruled that this restriction did not cover limited companies. Between 1880 and 1894 more than 200 limited liability companies, mainly grocers and provision merchants, were registered for retail trade in drugs. Boot converted to limited liability in July 1883, and began to spread his branches throughout the Midlands and then to all parts of the country. By 1900 there were 181 branches; in 1901 as a result of take-overs there were 251; and in 1914 he had 560 branches. Boot's nearest rivals were Taylor's Drug Co. Ltd of Leeds, which moved into London in 1889, and the Portsmouth firm of Timothy White, which had started as a ship's chandler's store. Day's Southern Drug Company, a Southampton firm, expanded its branches rapidly in the 1890s until it was bought in 1901 by Boot's, which was seeking to break into London. Others such as Lewis & Burrough's, Hodder's in Bristol and Ward's in Leicester expanded more slowly.[16]

Like all multiples, the chemists emphasised the competitiveness of their prices with those of traditional retailers. Boot's in 1884 was selling Epsom salts at 1d per lb. compared with the ½d per oz. charged by some small shops. Soap was offered at 4½d for 2 lb. wrapped, compared with 4d per lb. elsewhere. Jesse Boot showed the same flair for publicity as other pioneering multiple retailers. There were the usual brass bands and sandwich-board men, and the firm was among the first to take full-page advertisements in the press. In December 1904 Boot's bought the whole front page of the *Daily Mail* for ten days.[17]

Boot bought many of his supplies in the 1880s from American drug firms, which were steadily breaking into the British market. Burroughs Wellcome, who had pioneered the compressed pill, and Parke-Davis & Co. were both important suppliers. British companies were often caught between the rivalry that existed between the multiples and the small retailers, and when Boot found he had difficulties with supply he moved into production, opening his first factory in 1888. Other multiples followed in this direction slowly. Once their position as chemists was secure the multiples became rather less concerned with price cutting, and sought to attract custom by extending the range of goods which they held. By 1903, for example, half of Boot's shops had libraries, and many stocked stationery, fancy goods and photographic equipment. As a result there was a great deal less conflict in the trade between the Pharmaceutical Society, representing small traders, and the multiples in the years immediately before 1914 than there had been earlier.

By 1914 there was multiple-shop retailing in all consumer-goods trades and in all parts of the country. The multiples gained cost advantages by bulk purchase of goods, a policy which gave them a powerful bargaining position *vis-à-vis* the manufacturers. In a number of cases the shops were controlled by the producers, while in others firms that started in retailing moved into manufacturing. In both cases the profits of middle-men were eliminated. Retailing on this scale required standardisation, and generally the multiples specialised in a limited number of items, offering in their various branches a standard range of goods. Customers knew the quality they could expect, and the growth of multiples encouraged the development of packaged, branded and standardised products.

The success of multiples stemmed from new selling techniques but also from the rebellion by consumers against the high costs of traditional shopping. There was little of the elaborate salesmanship associated with the traditional shop. Salesmanship was now concentrated in vigorous and frequently spectacular advertising with the emphasis on the cheapness of the goods. The policy was successful in gaining for multiple retailers an ever-greater share of the market. In 1885 this share was negligible: by 1900 only footwear multiples had more than 10 per cent of the whole trade (between 19 and 21 per cent according to Jefferys' estimates). Fifteen years later footwear multiples had 32–4 per cent of the trade: chemists' multiples had 13–15 per cent: bicycles, sewing machines and electrical goods had 12–15 per cent; grocery and provision stores had 12–14 per cent and meat multiples 9–11 per cent.

The Co-operatives

The multiple grocers offered cheapness and quality to the working-class housewife. The other important group that did this, and indeed had been the first to provide some kind of certainty of quality to working-class purchasers, were the co-operative societies. The advantages of bulk buying and of trimming overheads had been appreciated by co-operators long before the Rochdale Pioneers opened their first shop in 1844. In 1760 Woolwich and Chatham shipwrights had their own co-operative corn mill until it was inadvertently burned down (possibly by the local bakers).[18] In the 1790s Hull had an 'anti-mill' run on a co-operative basis; such ventures spread to other parts of Yorkshire, and were generally part of a working-class resistance to the millers' monopoly.[19]

The canny Scots first struck on the idea of co-operative store-keeping, among the weavers of Fenwick in Ayrshire in 1769; and it was the Co-operative Society of the Stirlingshire village of Lennox-town, soon after its formation in 1812, which introduced payments of dividends on purchases. The late 1820s saw co-operatives flourishing, but those modelled on Dr William King's Brighton Co-operative Trading Society, and caught up in the omnivorous Owenite movement, were intended to provide the funds for building a co-operative community. Between 1826 and 1835 250 such societies were formed, mainly in London, Lancashire, Yorkshire and the Midlands, with some scattered from Aberdeen to Exeter.[20] Many, because of their close links with trade unionism, went down in the collapse of unions which happened in 1834 and 1835, and yet others went under amid the distress of such bleak years as 1842. Many of the men who pioneered the most famous of co-operative societies at Rochdale in 1844 were Owenite socialists who had gone through the fire of the early 1830s.

There was little in the organisation of the Rochdale Co-operative Society that was really new. Most of the ideas had been tried by other societies. Rochdale's innovation was to combine these in one society. G. D. H. Cole has listed eight basic Rochdale principles: (1) democratic control, with each member having a vote without any reference to the amount of his investment in the society; (2) membership of the society was open to all who wished to join, and there was no attempt to retain control in the hands of the original members; (3) interest on capital was fixed to encourage investment, but there was a limit on the amount of capital any one person could hold; (4) a dividend was paid based on purchases, an idea well established in Scottish co-operatives and probably brought to Rochdale by the ubiquitous Owenite 'missionary', Alexander Campbell; (5) trading was strictly for cash with no credit given, a recognition of the enormous pressure that any society would face in a working-class community if it did allow credit, and a product of hard-won lessons from earlier years, when many societies had crashed under the weight of bad debt; (6) the society sold only pure, unadulterated food, thus saving its members from the worst effects of constant poisoning from alum or arsenic; (7) there was an educational side to the society, concerned with propagating co-operative ideals; (8) again as a result of lessons well learned in the 1830s, the society was to be politically and religiously neutral.[21]

From the Rochdale system a new consumers' co-operative movement grew in the middle decades of the nineteenth century. Membership at Rochdale grew from 28 in 1844, to nearly 500 in 1864, to nearly 8000 in 1874 and to over 100,000 in 1878. More significant was the spread of co-operative stores throughout the north of England and Scotland: 39 new societies were formed between 1844 and 1853, and 346 in the following decade. By 1863 membership of co-ops was in the region of 100,000, with a turnover of £2·5 million, selling mostly groceries and provisions.[22]

1863 was a crucial year in the development of co-operative trading, for in that year the Co-operative Wholesale Society was founded. Most of the earlier co-operative societies had been linked with schemes for co-operative production, particularly of flour and bread. The Christian Socialists, that heterogeneous group of barristers, aristocrats and clergymen around Frederick Denison Maurice, had become deeply involved in schemes for co-operative production in the late 1840s and early 1850s. Shocked by the distress of the 1840s, frightened by the anger of Chartism, and inspired by Christian caring, J. N. Ludlow, Charles Kingsley, Thomas Hughes and others sought to create Christian fellowship and help the workers' plight by forming producers' co-operatives among distressed handworkers. It was the energetic Christian Socialist, Edward Vansittart Neale, and the former Owenite, Patrick Lloyd Jones, who sought to link co-operative production with the growing consumers' co-operative movement. Their Central Co-operative Agency supplied many of the early stores in the 1850s, and they sought, unsuccessfully at first, to create a federal supply system for co-operative stores. Their activities stimulated Lancashire societies to think in terms of a North of England Wholesale Society, but federal action between co-operative societies was blocked by the legislative provisions of the Industrial and Provident Societies' Act. Amendment to the law in 1862 opened the way to wholesale trading on a federal basis and the North of England Co-operative Wholesale Agency and Depot Society Ltd, was formed in Manchester in the following years, dealing in a limited range of groceries.[23] Five years later the Scottish societies set up their own S. C. W. S.[24]

Not all societies' management committees were enthusiastic about the new organisation. Managers and buyers of societies feared for their jobs. Others, trained in the private sector, favoured competition and believed in purchasing in the open market. Yet others, according to a correspondent in the *Co-operator*, were in 'bondage to the flattery and deception exercised by a certain class of adept travellers'.[25] The temptations open to buyers – in many cases members of the management committee – were obvious. James Duckworth, a Rochdale grocer who built up a chain of cheap grocery shops in Lancashire from 1868 onwards, found when he moved into wholesaling that co-operative management committees insisted on 'tipping' by the wholesalers. In other cases local societies were suspicious of any federal structure and clung to their local autonomy. In 1871 only one-eighth of goods sold in societies' shops were bought through the C. W. S.[26]

The advantages of centralised purchasing were fairly obvious, however, and the C. W. S. steadily extended its trading activities. Within a decade of its foundation the membership of the shareholding societies was 134,000. Five years later it was over a quarter of a million. The half-million mark was passed in 1885, one million in 1897 and the Society's diamond jubilee was celebrated with 2,160,000 members.[27] At first butter was their main commodity coming principally from Ireland and to a lesser extent from France and Holland; the first purchasing depot was opened in Tipperary in 1866. Ten years later the first overseas buying office opened in New York, concerned mainly with the purchase of cheese, bacon, lard and grain, and, in that same year, the first of what was to become a substantial fleet of ships was purchased. The SS. *Plover*, trading from Goole, was to carry loaf sugar, flour, apples and potatoes from Europe, which grew steadily in importance as a supplier. Depots were opened in France, Denmark, Germany and Spain, as well as in Canada and Australia, in the twenty years after 1876.

Until 1882 tea was purchased through the firm of Woodin, Jones & Company. In 1882, however, the C. W. S. set up its own tea-buying department to supply both the Scottish and English societies, and the first direct shipment from China arrived in July 1883. Between 1891 and 1913 almost 3000 acres of tea estates were purchased in Ceylon to ensure regular supplies, and, with its own blending warehouse in Leman Street, the Society was supplying co-operators with 25 million lb. of tea.[28]

The number of retailing societies continued to grow. In 1881 there were 971 registered societies and a peak was reached in 1903 with 1455, after which amalgamations reduced the number. Membership rose from 350,000 in 1873, to 1,169,000 in 1893, and to 2,878,000 in 1913.[29] Only in the depressed year of 1881 was there a decrease in membership. The strength of the movement continued to lie in the industrial Midlands and the north. Of the fourteen largest societies, each with membership of more than 5000 in 1880, six were in Lancashire, five were in Yorkshire, including the largest in Leeds, and the others were in Aberdeen, Leicester and Plymouth. Twenty years later, 25 per cent of the membership was in societies with a membership of over 11,000 and of these nine were in Lancashire, five in Yorkshire, four in Northumberland and Durham, three in Scotland and one each in Plymouth, London and Derby.[30]

This geographical distribution of the retailing societies reflected the working-class composition of the co-operative movement. In its areas of greatest strength it was more than merely a trading organisation.

Some of the idealism of the earlier co-operators persisted. The shops inspired a loyalty in their members that had nothing to do with their prices or their aesthetic appeal. Few had the faith of J. T. W. Mitchell, president of the C. W. S. from 1874 to 1895, that it would 'solve all social problems, destroy poverty, eradicate crime, and secure the greatest happiness to the greatest number',[31] and only 66 societies by 1871 devoted any of their resources to the early ideal of education. None the less at least some of the societies did perform a social and sometimes a political role. Co-operators tended to be members of the skilled working class, who could afford the cost of the initial share. Since most societies refused to give credit, in at least one working-class community the quarterly dividend was used as a means of paying off debts accumulated at the corner shop.[32] One exception to this no-credit rule was in that most calvinist of cities, Edinburgh. Soon after its formation in 1859 the St Cuthbert Society granted credit to the extent of 10s per £1 of share capital, much to the concern of a large number of the members, who withdrew their capital. Attempts by the leadership to overturn this ruling at various times over the next decades were blocked by the membership, and in 1871 the limit was in fact raised to 15s per £1 of share capital. It was, of course, the members of the general committee who had the 'undignified' task of acting as debt collectors.[33] How many other societies succumbed to the pressure to give credit is not clear, but certainly emergency credit arrangements at least would be made by a society if the workers in the area were badly hit by unemployment or an industrial dispute. Apparently in the Glasgow Co-op just before the First World War a system of weekly accounts was operated and 'no money changed hands until pay day'.[34]

Food sales made up 83 per cent of co-operative sales, reflecting the needs of a working-class membership. Butter was the main article sold in the summer or autumn, though it was less popular in spring, when it was likely to be highly salted and probably rancid. By the 1870s most shops sold cheese, bacon, eggs, lard, tea and bread. Most societies of any size started selling meat at an early stage in their career: by 1850 the Rochdale Society had a separate shop for meat. There was little attempt at centralisation of meat purchasing, and, like the private butcher, the co-operative butchery manager would buy his meat on the hoof and supervise the process from the slaughterhouse to the counter. The co-op butchers stuck to home-grown cattle, shunning frozen or chilled imported meat. A butcher of Edinburgh's St Cuth-bert's Society was duly censured by his management committee for purchasing some Canadian cattle, and 'was warned to keep clear of

foreign cattle in the future'.[35] The expansion of the butchery activity
of co-operative societies brought opposition from private butchers,
and in 1896 a boycott against the co-ops was organised throughout
Scotland. Salesmen who sold to co-operative butchers were boycotted
by the private ones, and co-operative buyers found their bids being
refused. When this happened at Glasgow's municpal market the Cor-
poration passed a bye-law keeping the market open to all bidders, a
law upheld by the House of Lords after appeal by the butchers' organisation. The butchers' response was to pull out of the municipal
market and to conduct their sales privately. It was this that forced the
S. C. W. S. to become a buyer, and by the end of the 1890s it was purchasing cattle for a number of retail societies on a commission basis,
importing cattle directly from Canada (this presumably being now
acceptable) and doing some slaughtering.[36]

There was nothing new in such boycotts. Merchants were under
pressure from retailers, who resented what they regarded as unfair
competition from dividend-paying co-ops, and frequently either
declined to sell to co-operators or sold only on condition that their
identity was kept secret. At the end of the 1860s the recently established *Grocer*, organ of the retail provision trade, began to organise a
boycott of merchants who dealt with co-operative societies. In 1872 a
list of eighty-four southern firms was published, with the announce-
ment that they would have no dealing with co-operators.[37] By that
time, however, societies were too well-established to be seriously
threatened by such action, and they had the ever-growing C. W. S. on
both sides of the border. Indeed such boycotts probably assisted the
growth of the wholesale societies.

Bread was, of course, a basic item in the working-class diet and
some of the earliest co-operative societies were centred on flour mills.
The second half of the nineteenth century brought an increase in the
number of co-operative mills and many retail societies utilised the
flour in their own bakeries. It had always been an important part of
the activities of the early Scottish societies, and in 1869 a number of
the Clydeside societies joined to form the United Co-operative
Bakery Society. Growth was fairly slow at first, but by 1900 turnover
had reached £332,000, nearly 10 per cent of all Scottish sales of bread,
biscuits and flour confectionery, and the U. C. B. S. began to open its
own shops as well as selling to retail societies.[38]

Signs of greater affluence were apparent when co-operative managers came under pressure from members to stock a wider range of
items. The Rochdale Society had made a cautious start in drapery in
1859, with plain, useful material, under instruction to avoid fancy

'bobby dazzlers' that would 'tempt working men's wives to indulge in unnecessary expense'.[39] Other societies followed, and by 1874 the C. W. S. was able to open a drapery section. The policy of shunning temptation was still followed, however, and the range offered was narrow. The C. W. S. entered the ready-made clothing industry with a boot firm in Leicester in 1886 and a clothing factory in Leeds in 1888. C. W. S. production tended to be scattered throughout the country, but in Scotland the S. C. W. S., under the guidance of the able William Maxwell, centralised production at Shieldhall in Glasgow's south side. There a shirt factory began production in 1881, tailoring started in 1882, cabinet-making in 1884, boot-making in 1885 and hosiery manufacture in 1886. By the 1890s factories on the site were producing leather goods, brushes, ham, confectionery, mantles, tobacco, coffee, tinware and pickle; there were printing and chemical works and engineering shops. Societies began to stock curtain material, bedding, beds, simple furniture and some rugs and carpets. But although co-operative cabinet-making was under way from the 1880s, expansion in this direction was very slow mainly because to stock furniture required a great deal of space, and few societies had room to display any great quantity of wardrobes or sideboards.[40]

By the first decade of the twentieth century co-operative societies could claim 9–11 per cent of all sales of food and household stores, 1–2·5 per cent of sales of confectionery, reading and writing materials and tobacco, 4·5–6 per cent of clothing and footwear sales, 7–8 per cent of all retail sales. It was a remarkable record of growth.[41] Sales per member stayed fairly stable, however.

1881–5	£28·4	1896–1900	£27·9	1910–14	28·7
1886–90	£27·1	1901–5	£28·9		
1891–5	£27·7	1906–10	£28·7		

Relating these figures to retail prices shows a substantial fall in sales from 1901 to 1914, with average sales per member, adjusted for changes in food prices, falling from £29·3 in 1901 to £24·7 in 1914. This decline was a measure of the decline in working-class real earnings in the early twentieth century, but it was also a product of the intensification of competition in retailing, as multiples battled for a declining market. Having said that, however, the co-operatives' share of the market did grow slightly in the first decade of the century.

The success of working-class co-operatives encouraged imitators among the middle classes. A group of civil servants, connected mainly with the Post Office, set up the Civil Service Supply Association in 1865. It was followed by a Civil Service Co-operative Society Ltd in 1866 and by the Army & Navy Co-operative Society Ltd in 1872. The restriction of membership to certain professional groups was a major difference between these co-operatives and those of the working class, but a more fundamental difference was that profits were distributed not to customers but were paid out in relation to shares held, with shares rising in capital value as profits rose.

The societies at first offered very little customer service, and customers were expected to queue. Overheads were kept to a minimum, prices were clearly marked and there was no haggling. The *Saturday Review* saw these middle-class co-ops as a reflection of 'a white heat of passion against the retailers', and, undoubtedly, many of those new people swelling the ranks of the lower middle class resented the traditional shopkeepers' practice of fitting the price to the customer. The range of foodstuffs, clothing and household goods sold in these stores grew steadily, and it was the advance of such societies which finally persuaded the *Grocer* to launch its onslaught on all co-operatives. By 1879 the Civil Service Assocation, with some 31,800 customers, had a turnover of over £1 million and the Army & Navy Society one of over £1·5 million. Naturally they were imitated in other towns, and similar societies appeared in Edinburgh, Liverpool and Manchester. In spite of the growth of competition in the 1880s and 1890s, which pushed the societies into improving their services, and therefore raising costs, turnover continued high and the Army & Navy's was over £3 million in 1898, easily surpassing its non-co-operative rivals. The co-operative stores also increased the range of goods which they held, in response to their members' pressure. They were in the vanguard of the development of department stores, yet another vital part of the retailing revolution.[42] Traditional shops, competing for a middle-class market, had to branch into other products if they were to fight off the challenge of co-operative trading.

The Department Store

The well-dressed lady in mid-century did her shopping for clothes in London, if at all possible. There she would find the latest fashions from France if she were flighty, from the Court if she were respectable. A carriage trip to Regent Street (its Nash pillars long since removed so as not to impede the flow of custom) preferably between two and four in the afternoon, the 'smart' time, would bring her to what Augustus Sala called 'an avenue of superfluities'. Here she would find the materials that were foremost in high fashion. Silk and shawls could be purchased from the leading silk mercers, Lewis & Allenby. Specialists in Paisley, Norwich and Indian shawls were to be found at J. J. Holmes, William C. Jay, Simpson & Co., Williams's Cloak and Shawl Warehouse and Farmer & Roger's Great Shawl and Cloak Emporium. The paraphernalia of death were catered for in a row of mourning warehouses, Jay's, Pugh's, Nicholson's and 'Black' Peter Robinson's. There were glovers, like Wheeler & Company, perfumers like the House of Piner, fan sellers like Jules Duvelleroy, milliners like Madame Parsons. For haberdashery and drapery there was Swan & Edgar, established on its prime site for nearly half a century.[43]

Regent Street was for the highly fashionable, but other streets were advancing their reputations. Peter Robinson had set up as a linen draper in Oxford Street in 1833, Marshall & Wilson in Vere Street in 1837 and Frederick Gamage opened in Buckingham Palace Road in 1858. They were also seeing the importance of a provincial market. Marshall & Wilson opened a branch in Society's favourite spa. Scarborough, in 1840 and another at Harrogate a little later. Debenham & Freebody opened their first branch in the equally fashionable Cheltenham, but also moved to Harrogate in the 1840s. These spa branches were at first open only during the season, in recognition that they were catering for a very limited clientele, but their establishment must have had an important impact on provincial taste. They offered a wider range of materials for the local dressmakers to work with and a variety of novel fashion hints.

There were, of course, provincial drapers, haberdashers, mercers and milliners, who also catered for the carriage trade. But in most towns the shopkeepers had to accept that, attractive as such business might be and useful as a row of carriages at the door was as an advertisement for the business, the bulk of their business was likely to be with the carriageless middle class and with artisans. As a result they kept a wide choice of materials.

Throughout the whole period from 1850 to 1914 a great deal of clothes for the middle as well as the working class were made at home. Housewives would make most of their own dresses, aprons, and underwear and those of their children. They would probably also produce their husbands' shirts and underwear. To supply the material for this was the function of the drapers, mercers and haberdashers. The introduction of the sewing machine encouraged home dressmaking, and paper patterns widened the choice and simplified the process. In some cases clothes could be bought partially made up, supplied from London by firms like Peter Robinson's, and the provincial shop or the local dressmaker would finish them off to the customer's exact specifications. Only in heavy cloaks and coats before the last quarter of the nineteenth century was there a substantial ready-made business in the high-class sections of the trade.

Fashion dictated that standardisation should be kept to a minimum in women's clothing, which in itself was a factor in delaying ready-made women's wear. It also meant that general drapers' shops had to maintain a large stock of materials and accessories needed for home clothes-making, and inevitably the divisions between drapers, haberdashers, merchants, glovers and milliners became blurred. Shops widened the range of dressmaking goods they held. As early as 1836, when three young men, Thomas Kendal, James Milne and Adam Faulkner took over the running of Watts' Bazaar in Manchester, they were buying an incipient department store with a wide variety of counters operating under one roof. By the end of the 1840s they offered materials (such as silk, satin, velvet, muslin, cashmere, linen, calico and gingham), ribbons, shawls, hosiery, gloves, lace, haberdashery, artificial flowers, umbrellas and parasols, bonnets, furs, cloaks and mantles, table linen, flannels, blankets, curtains, carpets and some furniture. They also ran a funeral service. In Newcastle Emerson Bainbridge was providing a similar service, with the addition of partly-made dresses bought from London.[44]

In London itself similar developments were taking place with the expansion of drapers' shops like Thomas Wallis's in Holborn, and Shoolbred's in Tottenham Court Road. In both cases the main extension was into furniture and carpeting. In Glasgow there was Anderson's Royal Polytechnic, and in Edinburgh, Duncan McLaren's. Presumably, it is evidence of the manner in which the Victorian wife – despite the stereotype to the contrary – was in fact master of her home that it was in women's shops, to catch the women customers, that a carpet and furniture trade developed.

These 'natural' developments of the department store were well under way in Britain before Aristide Boucicant took over Bon Marché in 1852 or before his techniques were copied by Macy's of New York in 1860. No doubt, however, knowledge of French and American experiments gave a spur to the more organic growth of the British store.

The department stores that developed in the decades after 1860 were aimed at midde-class customers. These were the middle classes who were spending on a much wider variety of goods than ever before, as they struggled to rig themselves out with the 'paraphernalia of gentility'. They had more money to spend, but it had to be spent on more things, and therefore they were cost-conscious. The stores sought to provide traditional carriage-trade services at lower prices. They offered rest-rooms and writing-rooms for the exhausted lady. Goods were delivered, carefully wrapped. Goods could be exchanged if they were later considered unsatisfactory. At the same time, however, goods were sold strictly for cash, prices were fixed and marked, profit margins were low and the aim was a large volume of business. Aggressive selling and advertising was another feature, and bargain sales played their part in this.[45]

The obvious success of many multi-department shops encouraged enterprising entrepreneurs to move into this new field. Best known of all was William Whiteley, a Yorkshireman, who in 1863 opened a store in London's Westbourne Grove. Whiteley's entrepreneurial skill was evident in his selection of a site, not in the West End, but in a recently built-up middle-class area. His store opened a few weeks after the underground railway, which ensured that while having a sound local base he was not confined to neighbourhood custom. It grew rapidly through the whole range of drapery and haberdashery, and, as he bought up adjoining property in Westbourne Grove in the 1870s, into new departments – books, household ironmongery, a house agency, a restaurant, a cleaning and dyeing department, hairdressing, and so the expansion went on. By the 1880s he was indeed 'the Universal Provider', as he claimed.[46]

The importance of the growing middle-class suburbs for the enterprising retailer was further illustrated by the development of stores in the Knightsbridge and Kensington areas, which had begun to be developed in the 1850s and 1860s. Traditional drapers like Harvey Nichols and William Hatch began to expand. Joseph Toms joined in partnership with Charles Derry, and they began to extend beyond toys and fancy goods. New entrepreneurs like John Barker, who had learned his trade at Whiteley's, began to move in with large glass-fronted stores on the now widened Kensington High Street. By the 1880s the grocery shop on the Brompton Road which Charles Digby Harrod had inherited from his father was selling additional goods such as carpets, furniture and household merchandise, and even later branched into drapery and fashion goods. Many other stores, while in no sense seeking to emulate William Whiteley as 'universal providers', none the less became at least partial department stores.

Most of the leading London stores were geared to the middle class, although showing an awareness that middle-class customers were price conscious. Outside London the new department stores at first looked to the working class as their main customers. David Lewis's multiplied from Liverpool in 1856 to Manchester in 1880 and Birmingham in 1885, as 'Lewis's, the Friends of the People' and in one of their early publications spelt out clearly their position:

> Lewis's have had the honour of being patronised by the Queen, the Princess of Wales, Princess Louise, the Duchess of Connaught, and many of the nobility of Europe. They have also supplied goods to the orders of the Duke of Wellington, the Earl of Derby, and other leading members of the British aristocracy; but they pride themselves upon the fact that their business is essentially with the masses.[47]

With the opening of their Manchester store in 1880, they adopted a deliberate policy of encouraging customers to come into the store and browse without any obvious pressure on them to buy. The policy proved so successful that it resulted in a court action against the firm for creating a nuisance by causing crowds to gather.

By the early twentieth century, perhaps as a recognition that working-class incomes had ceased to rise as fast as in the previous twenty years, most department stores were concentrating on the upper end of the market. Services like lifts, escalators, restaurants and rest-rooms were regarded as more important than low prices. Their main attraction, however, was in the wide selection of goods they stocked, particularly women's and children's clothes. The range of different kinds of goods no doubt had its attractions, but the selection of dresses, coats, blouses, materials, haberdashery and trimmings that they could stock was so much more extensive than that of the ordinary draper.

Part of the philosophy of department stores was that if people could be enticed into the store they could be tempted to buy. This was carried to its logical conclusion when Gordon Selfridge opened his Oxford Street store in 1909. Like traditional shops the early department stores laid great stress on the importance of the salesman. They had large staffs. By 1914 Whiteley's had a staff of 4000, and the service-conscious Harrod's one of 6000. The customer entering the shop would be approached by the shop-walker and directed to the department he or she required. The atmosphere was the traditional one of deference, with the aim, as Selfridge, an American, said, 'to reproduce the subdued and disciplined atmosphere of the gentleman's mansion'.[48]

Selfridge, who had served his apprenticeship at Marshall Field's great store in Chicago, opened the first brand-new store in the West End in a blaze of publicity. His policy was to attract customers into the shop and to let them browse through the various departments. He wanted them 'to enjoy the warmth and light, the colours and styles, the feel of fine fabrics'. There was no pressure to purchase: or rather, the pressure to purchase was through the eye, not through the ear, seduced by the smooth words of the salesman. His 'open-door' policy was a success and was quietly emulated by other leading stores.

The transformation of the distributive trades between 1850 and 1914, which (however over-used the word is) does amount to a 'revolution' in retailing, took many forms. First the hawker and the street-stall gave way to the fixed shop as the main centre of retail trading. The shop in turn was transformed by new techniques of selling. Clearly, marked prices which were fixed replaced prices based on the shop-keeper's judgement of what the customer would bear and on haggling. Reputation based on hearsay gave way to the creation of reputation by means of self-advertisement, particularly by means of window and front-of-shop displays. New forms of retailing unit began to appear and old-established trades gave way to new. Large-scale organisation came with the multiples, usually specialising in a small number of low cost items, and with the department stores, which offered an unprecedented range of goods under the same roof. ·

These developments came in response to major social and economic changes. Rising living standards among the working class produced a demand for relatively cheap goods, which the multiples and co-operatives sought to supply. A more self-confident working class was demanding better quality food, free from adulteration, than had previously been served up to them and this the multiples and the co-operatives offered. A growing middle class, conscious of price, none the less sought access to a greater choice of goods. Changes in demand were matched by technological changes in manufacturing and transport which allowed for cheaper and greater output. It was, it should be emphasised, a two-way process. Changes in retailing methods were possible because of economic and social changes, but the developments in retailing frequently forced change in production methods. When adequate supplies were not readily available it was often the retailers who went out and found them and created the new production units.

10. Advertising

'Keep the shops well lit.' Reputed to be the dying words of J. J. Sainsbury.

The usefulness and value of most things depend, not so much on their own nature as upon the number of people who can be persuaded to desire and use them.
An Advertisers' Guide to Publicity (1887).

The massive opportunity to catch the public eye which the Great Exhibition of 1851 provided was not missed. Sir John Bennett bought the space on the back wrapper of the catalogue to advertise clocks and watches, and in all fifty-three pages of the catalogue consisted of advertisements. But mass advertising still lacked the respectability usually associated with Prince Albert and his committee. Carlyle reflected the 'best' thinking in his disapproval of 'puffery'.

There is not a man or hat-maker born into the world but feels, or has felt, that he is degrading himself if he speaks of his excellences and prowesses, and supremacy in his craft; his inmost heart says to him, 'Leave thy friends to speak of these; if possible thy enemies to speak of these; but at all events, thy friends.'

Advertising was only for such as the Aberdeenshire 'hygeist', James Morrison, with his 'Universal Pills', or for the Devonport merchant, Thomas Holloway, with 'Holloway's Pills and Ointments'. From the 1840s to the 1870s the latter was the supreme advertiser: in 1855 his advertising budget exceeded £30,000 per year; twenty years later it was between £40,000 and £50,000. Joseph Beecham and many others were to learn well the techniques of such predecessors.

The main vehicle for 'puffery' was the wall poster. After 1848 improved printing processes could produce 10,000 sheets an hour at relatively low cost. W. D. & H. O. Wills paid only £150 in 1887 for

1(a) A middle-class parlour, *c.*1890. Fashion demanded that possessions be well-displayed.

1(b) A Scottish working-class living room, *c.*1880. Although possessions in this obviously 'respectable' home are few they are on show.

2 A daring lady bicyclist of the 1890s. New hobbies required new clothes.

3 The pawnshop in 1894, a vital source of credit for more than just the poorest.

4 A gable-end in Birmingham, 1868. Note the American challenge to Young's paraffin, which had reduced the incidence of exploding lamps.

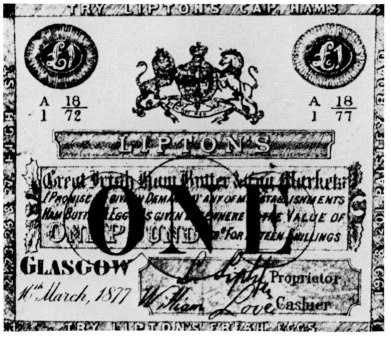

5 Thomas Lipton's 'pound note'. Four years after he opened his first shop he was showing a flair for self advertisement.

6(a) New Cut Market, Lambeth, 1895. Stalls were generally regarded as cheaper than shops.

6(b) A branch of the Home and Colonial in Barnstaple, in 1908.

7(a) Well-stocked windows in a Victorian 'shopping centre', *c.*1890.

7(b) The Department Store. This building at the junction of Oxford St and Vere St opened in 1876.

8(a) Larkhall Co-operative Society, 1910, displaying a wide range of goods mainly produced by the S.C.W.S.

8(b) Liverpool St Station bookstall, 1909. Since the 1840s such stalls had been a key outlet for cheap books and magazines.

9(b) Packing fish in Scarborough in the 1890s. The girls were probably Scots and followed the fleet round the coast.

9(a) Shop in working-class area of Glasgow, June 1900. The children's spades are ready for Glasgow 'fair holiday' and a trip to the seaside.

10(a) Packing soap at Lever Brothers, Port Sunlight.

10(b) Mass production at the Quinton Cycle Co., Coventry *c.* 1895.

11(a) Division of labour in a shoemaking garret, 1871.

11(b) Co-operative Wholesale Society Shoemaking Factory, Leicester.

12(a) The milkman at the turn of the century.

12(b) An ABC tearoom in 1900, offering clean, respectable service for the London commuter.

13 Traditional cattle market and fair combine to lure the Glasgow holidaymaker 'doon the water' to the Isle of Arran, c. 1890.

14 Bovril advertisement of 1900 playing on sentiment.

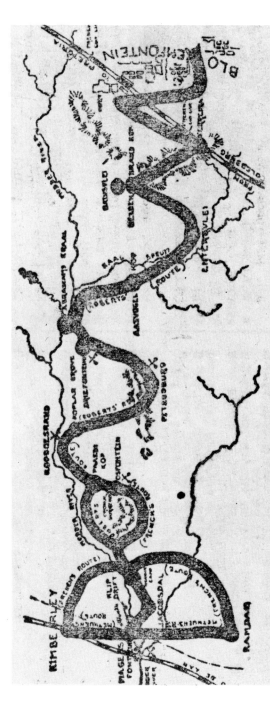

How Lord Roberts spells BOVRIL.

Careful examination of this Map will show that the route followed by Lord Roberts in his historical march to Kimberley and Bloemfontein has made an indelible imprint of the word Bovril on the face of the Orange Free State.

15 Bovril advertisement, 1900, displaying jingoism.

16 Weston-super-Mare, *c.* 1895. All kinds of enterprises were there to take advantage of a readiness to spend on holiday.

10,000 posters advertising their 'Black Jack' tobacco.[1] Every gable end, every naked wall, every unblemished railway carriage, every unspoilt station surface, indeed every surface exposed to the passing public gaze was hastily covered with posters extolling the virtues of some product or some service, (in a necrophiliac age undertakers were persistent advertisers) or the efficacy of some wonder pill. Battles between billposters were not uncommon as zealous paste and brush wielders plastered the few remaining spaces in rivalry with one another. Some attempt to regulate billposting came in the 1860s, when Edward Sheldon of Leeds initiated protected sites. Advertising contractors appeared in various towns, and in 1862 they formed the Billposters' Association to regulate their calling and to eliminate the worst excesses of competition. By 1885, 522 billposter firms were operating in 447 towns. There were still rivalries, and division within the Association produced a rift in 1886, but this was quickly closed when faced with mounting public criticism of advertisers and with a decision to charge rates on advertising hoardings. A United Billposters' Association was formed in 1890.[2]

All the best-known products used posters for advertising. G. J. Goschen even commented in one of his budget speeches that the consumption of cocoa and other non-alcoholic drinks had been created by mural advertising.[3] From the 1860s onwards Oxo had a prolific range of posters, as did Rowntree's from the 1870s and Bovril from the 1880s. Perhaps the most famous of advertisers was Thomas Barratt of A. & F. Pears Ltd, a London manager of the soap firm, who had taken the wise precaution of marrying Miss Pears. When he became a partner in the firm in 1865, its annual advertising bill was £80, ten years later he was spending between £100,000 and £130,000 per annum on such memorable coups as Millais's *Bubbles*, which he purchased from the *Illustrated London News*, or Lillie Langtry announcing, 'Since using Pears' Soap I have discarded all others.' To break into the American market he used Henry Ward Beecher's recommendation. Many of Barratt's creations were inspired: like his tramp's endorsement, 'I used your soap two years ago since when I have used no other'; and models of 'the dirty boy' about to get the back of his ears scrubbed by an irate mother left an indelible impression on the national consciousness. S. H. Benson, who became Bovril's advertising agent in 1893, did a similar exercise for that company with the famous Bull (which for some reason caused grave offence to the citizens of Cork) who was looking at a jar and remarking with a tear in its eye, 'Alas my poor Brother.' Captain Scott endorsed it for his Antarctic trip of 1904, and Shackleton's, 'It must be

Bovril', in 1909 became a national catch phrase.[4] The American, Sydney Gross, who joined Lever Bros in 1901, brought a range of imaginative techniques into the advertising of Lever's products.[5]

Poster painting began to attract reputable artists. Millais, unwittingly (at first, anyway), and Henry Stacy Marks (cruelly dubbed 'Trade Marks'), willingly, found their work gracing the hoardings, but it was men outside the portals of the Royal Academy who produced some of the classic posters. James Pryde and William Nicholson, the 'Beggarstaffs', provided Rowntree with numerous back-drops for 'Elect Cocoa for FLAVOUR'. W. H. Coffyn designed the Bovril Bull in 1896, and John Hassell's jovial fisherman convinced many railway travellers that Skegness was 'so bracing'. Tom Browne produced the first immortal red-coated Johnny Walker poster in 1906, and Phil May was the source of a tremendous variety of posters for Lever Bros.[6] With some justice the bill-posters could claim that they were providing the 'poor man's picture gallery'.

The spread of advertising at the end of the 1880s and in the early 1890s brought a middle-class backlash. The elements in it were a combination of puritanism, aestheticism, and that traditional British belief that nice as it was to have the fruits of an industrial revolution it should be allowed to impinge as little as possible on the graces of an essentially aristocratic sense of values. By 1890 enough psychology was known to show the value of linking a pretty girl with a product. John Player & Son had girls with cigarettes in their hands (not their mouths) in their advertisements of 1890. In the same year the London 'Aquarium' was advertised by a poster of a female acrobat, 'depicted in aerial flight on every hoarding in a position deemed by many to be indelicate'.[7] The National Vigilance Association opposed the renewal of the Aquarium's licence and a press campaign was stirred up. The *Standard* wrote of the 'Horrors of the Walls' and the *Daily Graphic*, no doubt hopeful that advertising would be switched to the newspapers, lamented for 'Our Streets and what they are coming to'. Undeterred, however, another hall's advertisement depicted a similar woman acrobat in flesh coloured tights. The public outcry encouraged the Billposters' Association to set up its own committee of censors to prevent undesirable or indelicate posters reaching the public. None the less abuses and protests continued. Hoardings along railway tracks and in many beauty spots blocked the view for the travelling public. Hoardings did nothing to enhance the appearance of Hyde Park, and when a gale in November 1891 blew down most of them there was an outcry against the danger to the public. A newspaper correspondence in *The Times* at the end of November 1892 resulted in the setting up in February 1893 of a National Society for Checking the Abuse of Public Advertising. Through campaigns in the press and through their publication, *A Beautiful World*, members of the Society sought 'to protect the picturesque simplicity of rural and river scenery and to promote a due regard to the dignity and propriety of aspect in towns', and 'to assert generally the national importance of maintaining the elements of interest and beauty of out-of-doors life'. They wanted local councils to have control over advertising, to have a special tax on advertisements and to have land and buildings protected. Finally they sought to organise a boycott of those commodities that were 'advertised in an offensive way' or those establishments that were 'exceptionally unscrupulous on advertising display'.[8]

A bill to prohibit advertisements in public places in rural districts failed to get a second reading in 1893, but in the following year, after magic lantern advertisements had been projected on Nelson's column and on the National Gallery and the billposting firm of Alexander Scott raised a hoarding in Trafalgar Square, an Act was passed giving county councils authority to issue bylaws regulating displays. The London County Council immediately banned sky-sign advertising, and control was gradually imposed on advertising, though the coming of electric lighting opened up a whole new range of vulgarity. In spite of controls, Bovril was advertised in lights at the corner of Trafalgar Square from 1896 onwards. Restriction on advertising was a slow process that came about only as a result of intense provocation, like the appearance in 1900 of Quaker Oats' billboards to greet the traveller steaming towards the white cliffs of Dover. After proposals to advertise meat extract along the open side of Princes Street had only just been blocked, Edinburgh and some other well-known towns of beauty pushed through local acts to allow them to regulate advertising within their boundaries, but it was not until 1903 that licensing of hoardings became general.[9]

The other great area for advertising was the press. From the eighteenth century until 1833 there was a tax of 3s 6d per newspaper advertisement, and after that it was 1s 6d until W. E. Gladstone repealed it in his great budget of 1853. As with so many of his moves towards free trade, Gladstone believed that the lost revenue would be quickly recouped by increased trade. In the case of advertising the Post Office would gain from posted replies to small advertisements. Two years later the tax on paper went, and the era of the cheap newspaper had arrived.

Newspaper editors showed little awareness of the opportunities that advertising offered their papers. Convention had it that nothing must break the regular columns, and there was a general agreement to ban large type. The only way to catch the eye was to repeat the firm's name endlessly or to use slogans, like Beecham's 'Worth a Guinea a Box', constantly. Not until the 1880s did papers like the *Daily News* begin to allow display advertisements to spread over more than one column, though the illustrated magazines were opening their pages to increasingly lavish pictorial advertisements. American methods, with eye-catching newspaper advertisements, came in very slowly, and a 1905 writer on advertising complained that 'in the main the newspaper advertisement is only read by the person who intends to read it'.[10] By that time, however, changes were already well under way. Advertising agencies had existed from the late eighteenth century, mainly organising the appearance of London advertisements in the provincial press. Agencies, like Samuel Deacon & Company, which dated from 1822, began publishing newspaper directories with claimed circulation figures and collected commissions from newspapers for the space sold. Some of the early directories were of doubtful accuracy, but by the 1840s and 1850s the agency of Charles Mitchell was bringing a new thoroughness to the checking of directory entries.

Significantly it was with the growth in the size of markets in the 1880s that agencies extended their functions. Now agents were selling space to advertisers which they had bought from newspapers. T. B. Browne Ltd, the Central London Agency, which had started in 1869 and, thanks to the Pears' soap commission, was probably the largest agency in the country by 1900, sold advertising space in *Answers* at £30 a page. Browne saw the function of his agency as being to find new markets for his clients and to develop old ones. No longer did the agencies see themselves merely as go-betweens. Another important London agent, Louis Collins, began to concern himself with copy-writing and lay-out in the 1880s. The Page Davis School of Advertising Methods, a branch of a school in Chicago, was established in London in the 1890s to teach the skill of copy-writing, and in 1899 S. H. Benson organised a highly successful Exhibition of Advertising, where businessmen were introduced to artists and lay-out experts, and to a variety of promotional ideas. Several hundred agencies were operating in London by the end of the century and were taking over the promotion of products: Benson's were used by Bovril, Smith's by Crosfields, Street's by many others.[11]

Led by the *Daily Mail*, Harmsworth's most dynamic innovation, newspapers became aware of the importance of advertising as a main source of income. The *Mail* showed no reticence about disclosing its rapidly growing circulation figures. Advertising managers, like

Wareham Smith, worked to attract new advertising and showed a readiness to experiment with more exciting lay-outs. Whole pages were being taken by advertisers, such as Bovril's in the *Daily Mail* of 1900, which explained 'Bovril's part in the South African War'. Philips's 'Guinea Gold' took four pages in the *Star* as part of the great battle between American and British tobacco manufacturers. As many as ten of the *Daily Telegraph*'s sixteen large pages were devoted to advertising in 1904, and the first newspaper photographs in the *Daily Mirror*, in the same year, opened up a whole new range of possibilities for the press advertiser.[12] It was again the *Mail* which realised the importance of expanding advertising opportunities and in 1908 launched the Ideal Home Exhibition at Olympia. Up until then there was almost no general advertising of paints, wall-paper, fireplaces and other materials for the home. Advertisements for these were confined largely to the trade papers, and builders followed the recommendations of the architect. The annual exhibition created a whole new range of potential customers for Wareham Smith and his team of advertising managers.

Many people looked on aspects of press advertising with considerable distaste. There was certainly an element of *lèse majesté* in cartoons of the Prince of Wales offering Bushmill's whiskey to the Shah of Persia, or the Pope sipping his Bovril under the caption 'The Two Infallible Powers'.[13] There could have been little enthusiasm at Hawarden at the drawings of Mr Gladstone chopping down trees wearing his 'Electropathic Belt'.[14] Unpleasant as much of this was for the great, what caused greatest concern was the mass advertising in the press of patent medicines, secret remedies and medicated wines. In 1914 the Select Committee on Patent Medicines reported that £2 million per annum was spent on advertising secret remedies, and that for many provincial papers and for the sundry religious papers, all of which were suffering from declining circulations, such advertisements were their life blood. It was a vast market, for a first priority of the working class's increased purchasing power had been medicines, sales of which rose by 400 per cent between 1850 and 1914. Such advertisements were in the tradition of Holloway and Morrison and were equally successful. George Taylor Fulford, the proprietor of 'Dr Williams' Pink Pills for Pale People' left a fortune of £1,111,0000. From 1891 onwards the St Helens' millionaire, Joseph Beecham, spent £120,000 a year on advertising his pills and making far-reaching claims for their efficacy. For many years Beecham's Pills claimed a 'remarkable curative influence ... in cases of Bright's disease' and even syphilis was not safe from their assault. Although by 1914 advertisements were making it clear that in all cases of the disease skilled medical advice should be sought, they were still claiming:

> But the process of eradicating the poison from the system will be materially assisted by the aid of a perfectly safe, but reliable searching, cleansing, purgative medicine; and nothing better for that purpose can be used than Beecham's Pills.[15]

Others made even more far-reaching claims, such as Fenning's Fever Cure, 'for the prevention and cure of typhus, ... cholera, diptheria, scarlet fever, ... yellow fever, ... influenza ... low spirits ... smallpox &c'. 'Mother Seigal's Syrup' one of the most widely advertised secret remedies and one of many made by A. J. White Ltd of Farringdon Road, London, was offered as 'a cure for impurities in the blood', for dyspepsia and liver complaints and for anaemia.

In many ways more concern was shown for the nation's morals than for its health, and the temperance movement had for a long time been troubled by the expansion of the market for medical wines. Messrs Colman & Company spent £50,000 per annum on advertising 'Wincarnis', a wine with 19.6 per cent alcoholic strength, as 'the world's greatest tonic, restorative, blood-maker and nerve food', and in some cases, manufacturers of such wines paid the licences of retailers, the assumption being that it would lead on to a wider range of alcoholic consumption. There was also concern at the extensive advertising of abortifacients. Again Beecham's were one of the offenders. In a pamphlet accompanying their pills, headed 'Advice to Females', women suffering from 'any unusual delay' were recommended to take five pills a day. Sir Joseph Beecham admitted to the Select Committee of 1914 that the most common cause of delay was pregnancy.[16] Other manufacturers were more specific. There was a great deal of deceptive advertising, with paid testimonials from doctors and false claims. Vogeler & Company manufacturers of 'Vogeler's Curative Compound', 'a positive cure for every form of Dyspepsia, Liver Complaints, Kidney Diseases, Indigestion, Acidity, Sleeplessness, Nervousness, Weakness, Languor, Debility, Melancholia, Hysteria, Anaemia, Headache, Heartburn, Dizziness, Ringing noises in the Head, Eczema', ran a series of advertisements for a threepenny booklet called 'Do You Know How to Cook Fish?' that gave no indication that it would have information on drugs in it.

Just as the United States pioneered the most extravagant aspects of the advertisement, so it was from there that there came efforts to curb the worst excesses. The attacks were focused on the insidious pushing of patent medicines. H. G. Wells satirised the process in *Tono-Bungay*, where the hero and his uncle peddled their 'slightly injurious rubbish at one-and three-halfpence and two-and nine a bottle', in a variety of forms as hair-stimulant, lozenges, chocolate, mouthwash and a Thistle Brand with 11 per cent alcohol for north of the Cheviots.[17] He helped to arouse concern in Britain, as did the British Medical Association's publications *Secret Remedies* (1909) and *More Secret Remedies* (1912), though no newspaper allowed any discussion of these pamphlets, and most, including the most respectable, declined advertisements for the pamphlets. So much had advertising revenue come to govern the thinking of the press! The revelations did, however, lead on to the damning Select Committee on Patent Medicines. Like the B.M.A., the Committee organised analyses of some well-known remedies. Fenning's Fever Cure which retailed at $1s$ $1½d$ for 8 fl. oz., consisted of a dilute solution of nitric acid and peppermint: the estimated cost of the ingredients was $½d$. The 'Daisy' Company of Leeds sold its headache powders in five-grain packets at $1d$ a piece. They contained acetanilide and phenacetin, which cost only $9d$ and $2s$ $11d$ per lb. Sir Joseph Beecham informed the committee that there used to be morphia in Beecham's cough pills, and when this had to be labelled as a poison it was removed, then later a tiny 'comparatively innocuous or perfectly innocuous' quantity was put in, not enough to bring it under the Poison Acts.[18] The Report issued was a scathing indictment of patent drug companies and a record of greed, fraud, irresponsibility and deceit. Newspaper editors were not, however, faced with the moral dilemma of whether or not to publicise the Report and thus harm their advertising revenue. The Report was issued on 4 August 1914, a day when other matters monopolised the headlines, and it was not for another quarter of a century that action was taken to ban 'cures' for cancer and consumption, for palpitations, paralysis and pregnancy.

The remunerative value of advertising meant that most publications, maps, guide-books, catalogues and paperback novels had their advertisements. Bird's custard and baking powder had been on calendars from as early as the 1840s. The sides of trams and omnibuses provided another hoarding again, in the case of the latter, dating from the 1840s. There was a *fin de siècle* extravagance in much of the advertising, which inevitably brought hostility both from rivals and from the bombarded public. Salmon & Gluckstein, the tobacconists, had five burnished silver omnibuses running between Liverpool Street and Olympia in 1892, charging only $½d$ a ride and providing passengers with a coupon that could be exchanged at any of the firm's branches.

Enraged protests were heard from other tobacconists as well as from those who felt that there was enough gaudiness in the blues, yellows, whites and golds of the competing omnibus companies.[19] Other cities had similar gimmicks and grievances. One of the issues that brought about the municipalisation of tramways in Glasgow in 1894 was the garish and unsightly advertisements on the trams of the private company, which were banned when the city's own 'cars' were introduced.

At the end of the century there was much talk of a 'science of advertising'. George P. Rowell of New York's most important agency gave due warning in 1895 that 'when we are a little more enlightened, the advertising writer, like the teacher, will study psychology'.[20] In fact, many of the best-known advertisers did not need to be taught much about the workings of the human mind. Lever's soap advertisement 'Why Does a Woman Look Older Sooner than a Man?', which he bought from a Philadelphia soapmaker, may not have been particularly subtle, but it must have struck home to many a harassed housewife. Association of products with the Queen and the Prince of Wales showed an awareness of the deference towards and interest in royalty, particularly in the decade between the two jubilees. On the other hand, forty years before, biscuit-makers had grasped this with their range of Osbornes, Alberts, Balmorals and Victorias. There was a great deal of identification with the Empire, and the Boer War gave copy-writers a field day. Perhaps the most original discovery was that (with a bit of imagination) the route of Lord Roberts's march from Kimberley to Bloemfontein spelled out 'Bovril' across the map of South Africa. Advertisers were quick to grasp the importance of influencing the young and the major social revolution which had been created by the 1870 Education Act. Copies of Lever's *Sunlight Year Book* were sent to all masters and mistresses in Board Schools, an advertising idea that was adopted by Beecham's Pills and Watson's Matchless Cleaner, among others. When Ladysmith was relieved during the South African War, Bovril wired the news to headmasters of all the country's schools. Thus a connection was made in many an innocent mind between victory, Bovril and a half-holiday from school.[21] When the appeal of patriotism waned, as it did for a short time after 1902, social conscience was appealed to, as in Bryant & May's 1905 advertisement for their new patent safety matches – 'Afford protection from fire, do not contain Phosphorus, and are quite harmless to all employed in their manufacture.'[22] As the advertising agents became more professional, they grew more aware of the importance of display and colour. Alfred Harmsworth selected yellow and blue as the colour of the *Mail* hoardings after experiments had shown that these two colours were least susceptible to changes in light during the length of a day.

The nature of advertising changed according to its purpose. At first many firms needed to create their market. When, for example, William Hesketh Lever launched his Sunlight soap in 1875 he concentrated for twenty years on persuading the working-man's wife to use more soap. There was a guide, *Sunlight Soap and How to Use It*, which, written by Lever himself, spelled out in the most simple terms what could be done by the working-class woman. He wrote:

> The only point where I went beyond this was with instructions for cleaning pampas grass, feather and so on, but I view these as to be found in many working men's houses, the pampas grass in a jar on the Bible, in the sitting room, and the feathers in the hats of the daughters.[23]

Having built a market, the next stage was to drive off rivals, and this brought some of the more spectacular stunts. Soap wrappers that could be exchanged for gifts were introduced in 1887 – another American idea – and when Lever made an attempt to withdraw them a decade later they found that their rivals, Crosfield & Sons and other members of the Northern Soap Makers' Association, took it up. It was their rivals' gaily coloured vans that sped through suburban streets delivering their gifts of cheap jewellery and china.

Another highly competitive area was the tea trade, where competition went wild at the end of the century. Nelson & Company offered widows' pensions of 10*s* a week to purchasers of relatively small quantities of tea. 19,000 widows all looking for £25 per annum for life soon bankrupted the company. Less ambitious were the gifts with every pound of tea, as Lipton's, Brooke Bond, Vey's Kardomah and Libby's Mazawattee and others battled for a slowly growing market. Competition between newspapers brought some of the most bitter advertising wars, with prize competitions to catch the public eye. *Answers* offered 'a pound a week for life' to anyone who could guess the amount of gold coinage in the Bank of England banking department on 4 December 1889. Nearly three-quarters of a million postcards were sent in, and since each had to be witnessed by five witnesses nearly three million people must have had occasion to talk about the paper. A low point was reached by Alfred Newnes's offer of £100 to the next of kin of anyone killed in a railway accident who had been carrying a copy of *Tit-Bits* in his pocket.[24]

Techniques with a more modern ring were also tried. In 1886 newspaper advertisements by Ripley's Oval Blue were making direct comparisons between that product and Reckitt's Paris Blue. It was claimed that after three times as much water was added to the Oval Blue, it had 'even then a richer and stronger hue than its competitors'.[25]

It was not enough for a manufacturer to get his products' names across to the public: he had to ensure that the retailing outlets were available. At the beginning of the period this was usually left in the hands of commission agents, and some firms, like Alfred Bird & Company, used such agents till as late as 1912.[26] Agents were usually on a 10 per cent commission.[27] But by the 1870s many leading firms were coming to depend on their own commercial travellers, 'the aristocrats of business employees in Victorian England', as Charles Wilson has called them, with their dress of top-hat and frock coat *de rigueur* into this century. £4 per week seems to have been a common remuneration for them in the 1870s,[28] though Wills were paying their senior men this as early as the 1850s. By the mid-1890s, Wills's travellers were paid £400 per annum and their senior travellers £800 per annum plus expenses.[29]

By the end of the century American techniques of salesmanship were having their influence, particularly in those areas where competition was fiercest. Salesman were urged to ever greater efforts in their door-to-door sales, by such maxims as Lever's 'Ding-Dong every day, every hour, every minute – the way to success and happiness.' From an American director came advice to district agents (D.A.s):

a D.A. should never give up until he has focused the woman's attention. It is the writer's experience that a woman will take the sample and then hastily beat a retreat and close the door. The D.A. should hold the sample in his hand and never let go, either of that or the booklet that he gives to her, until he has completed his story'.[30]

After the 1890s the bicycle allowed the traveller to cover more ground more speedily, and the provision of a De Dion Bouton motor car in 1905 to McVitie & Price's chief salesman heralded the arrival of the familiar modern 'rep'. By the early twentieth century, however, there were suggestions that the status of the commercial traveller had declined. Expenses were less generous, and 'many men are driven from the fine old Commercial Hotels to cheap Temperance Houses,'[31] though death from alcoholism or diseases of the liver was still a major hazard in the profession.

The traveller could offer a range of discounts to the shopkeeper, though the amount of competition in the field of discounts varied a great deal. By the last quarter of the nineteenth century there appears to have been little difference, for example, in the biscuit trade, with Huntley & Palmer (a firm that disdained mass advertising) and Peek Frean (a particularly dynamic advertiser) working closely on price lists and discounts.[32] For this reason the salesman's skill and devotion to duty was vital, catching the extra order, reaching a customer before a rival, guaranteeing rapid delivery. The Crawford biscuit firm had cut the time from order to delivery down to two days at the beginning of the twentieth century, though three weeks was generally regarded as good.

In the tobacco industry, on the other hand, this was an area of bitter competition. The attempt by Wills to maintain control over the prices charged by retailers lasted for a mere three years from 1889 to 1892. They were opposed by the retailers Salmon & Gluckstein, who went in for price-cutting in a big way. Once retail price maintenance had been abandoned, competition intensified. It came to a head in 1901–2, when James Buchanan Duke of the American Tobacco Company bought the Liverpool firm of Ogden's. He made no secret of his intention to take over or drive out of business the other British tobacco firms. Price cutting began immediately, and in defence the firms of Wills, Player, Lambert & Butler, Stephen Mitchell & Company and Hignett Bros joined together to form the Imperial Tobacco Company. There followed a battle for the retailers, with both sides often selling at a loss.

When price cutting had only limited success, the next stage was to seek exclusive outlets. This was not an entirely new idea. Wills, for example, had made an exclusive agreement in 1886 with Speirs & Pond, who ran the refreshment rooms on the Midland Railway, and in 1898 with the Cyclists' Chalet Company to distribute cigarettes to its forty chalets. The Imperial Tobacco Company was the first to offer a share in its profits and a bonus of £50,000 to those retailers who would bind themselves exclusively to the company. Ogden's responded by offering to distribute their entire net profits, plus an annual sum of £200,000 for four years among those retailers who traded only with them.[33] In spite of this, the victory went to the Imperial Tobacco Company. In October 1902 Duke pulled out, transferring Ogden's to the Imperial Tobacco Company, who put it into voluntary liquidation. Those retailers who had contracted to Ogden's were left with little but four years of litigation and scant comfort from the fact that their fees helped to elevate the Birkenhead lawyer F. E. Smith to a style of life to which he rapidly became accustomed.[34]

Such competition over discounts was probably the exception and travellers generally had to rely on the reputations of their product and their firm and their own selling ability. The importance of reputation as a selling factor was reflected in the use of brand names, registered under the Trade Marks Act of 1875. The customer came to depend on the label as a guide to quality rather than on the gustatory and olfactory skills of the Victorian shop keeper. The most successful firms generally pioneered branding and wrapping. Wills led the way in branding tobacco and they devoted a great deal of attention to the presentation of their product, concerning themselves with the pattern of the cartons. They packed the cigarettes in metal foil and included the first of generations of cigarette cards in 1887. Lever immediately registered their first soap 'Sunlight' under the Trade Marks Act and introduced wrapped tablets in the mid-1880s – until then soap had been cut from a huge slab by the shopkeeper. Wrapping had a particular appeal to the growing chains of multiple shops, who wanted to keep labour costs to a minimum and increase the speed of customer through-put.

The success of advertising in creating demand for a product is impossible to assess, but by the last decades of the nineteenth century it had become essential for any firm seeking to break into a market, to move from a local into a national market, or, in many cases, to hold on to its existing market. The intensity of advertising competition in many areas between 1890 and 1914 probably proves that demand was not rising as rapidly as supply. Too many firms were caught up in this competition, which made it difficult for any firm to be the first to pull out. By the turn of the century advertising had become well established as an industry, and an ever-growing number of workers in advertising industry were committed to its continued growth. The pressure to advertise became too intense for even the most conservative of firms to resist.

Part III

Demand Satisfied

11. The Nation Fed

The sort of man who had bread and cheese for his dinner forty years ago now demands a chop.

F. A. Graham, *The Revival of English Agriculture* (1899).

In spite of the fears of British farmers, the repeal of the Corn Laws in 1846 – a crucial victory for the manufacturing class – did not usher in the destruction of British farming. Overseas supplies of grain did not yet exist in sufficient quantity to swamp the British market. In addition growth in demand could consume what came in from abroad and a growing home supply. For a quarter of a century farming had time to adjust, and to a great extent it took the opportunities offered to it.

The preaching of the farmer-journalist, James Caird, that the best substitute for protection was high farming, began to be heeded. The period between 1846 and the early 1870s saw a reaffirmation of faith by the landed classes in the value of land, with massive investment in the new techniques of intensive farming. Poor land was drained and new land brought into cultivation; artificial fertilisers were used to produce more grass and grain from better quality seed, which in turn could feed better quality stock. Machinery was used increasingly, although the actual machines had existed for decades. Only after 1846 did the horse-drawn reaper begin to replace the scythe and sickle (Cyrus McCormick's machines at the 1851 Exhibition gave a considerable impetus to this development) and horse-pulled hoes, drills and harrows became commonplace.

The extent to which a conservative rural community adjusted in a quarter of a century should not be exaggerated. By no means all farmers adopted the new methods: many still preferred farmyard muck to superphosphate or lime; many did not feel the need to mechanise when farm labour was relatively cheap. There were farmers in Sussex, Wiltshire, Devon and elsewhere who, even in 1878, still used ox-teams.[1] The extent to which farms had been consolidated was

149

limited and patchy, and not always sufficient to take full advantage of mechanisation. None the less changes were taking place.

In another matter attention was being paid to Caird's diagnosis. He wrote,

> in the manufacturing districts where wages are good, the use of butcher's meat and cheese is enormously on the increase; and even in the agricultural districts the labourer does now occasionally indulge himself in a meat dinner, or seasons his dry bread with a morsel of cheese ... the great mass of the consumers, as their circumstances improve, will follow the same rule... Every intelligent farmer ought to keep this steadily in view. Let him produce as much as he can of the articles which show a gradual tendency to increase in value.[2]

Those areas near the growing industrial towns of the north and Midlands switched from arable to pastoral farming. An increasing number of farms became mixed arable and dairy, a change that was to save many from the worst disasters of the later depression. Price changes encouraged this tendency. While grain prices remained fairly stable, wholesale prices of meat and dairy produce rose by probably 40 per cent between 1850 and 1867.[3] The rinderpest of the mid-1860s pushed prices up still further and strengthened the trend towards livestock rearing.

The wisdom of following this trend was amply borne out in the last quarter of the century, when grain prices began to fall. By the mid-1890s wheat was down to less than 30s per quarter (22s 10d at one point in 1894), a level that had not been touched in a century and a half. After a quarter of a century the seed sown in 1846 was being harvested, and for some it proved a bitter harvest.

Imports of foreign grain had gone up substantially in the 1850s and 1860s from around 14 million cwt. to around 32 million cwt. The main suppliers were France and southern Russia. In both countries there was a growth in domestic demand, but, in addition, the international disarrangement caused by the Crimean War, continuing Russian–Turkish hostility and other lesser conflicts had given the British farmer some temporary protection. The United States was another supplier, but there too bloody civil war had delayed the impact in the 1860s. By 1870, however, 60 per cent of British grain imports were coming from countries outside the traditional European supply areas, mainly from North America.

Shipping freight rates had begun a decline that was to continue till

1910.[4] Nearly 60,000 miles of railroad now chequered the North American continent and a further 100,000 miles were to be built in the next twenty years. Chicago had become the railhead for the opened prairies, and from there the grain was carried to Europe, where prices slumped. Five years of disastrous home harvests – 1873, 1875, 1876, 1877 and 1879 – meant even more grain was imported, 15 million cwt. in 1870, 60 million cwt. in 1900. There was little sign of a substantial recovery in domestic output before 1914. The acreage given over to wheat production fell from 2,564,237 acres in 1888 to 1,375,284 acres in 1904, a 43·3 per cent decline. High rail-freight rates did not help. As a witness told the Royal Commission on Agriculture in 1881, he could get grain from San Francisco to his flour mills in Barrow for 17s 6d–20s a ton, the same as he had to pay the railways to carry grain from Lincolnshire.[5]

Faced with American competition, some wheat farmers found a road to recovery in market gardening. A growing public taste for fruit encouraged the conversion of former wheat lands in Kent, Middlesex, Worcestershire and Cambridgeshire to fruit-growing. The acreage of orchards rose from 148,221 acres in 1873 to 243,000 acres in 1904, a 64 per cent increase in 31 years, with the greatest increase in the decade from 1878 to 1888.[6] But most market gardens remained small: from two to twenty acres was the standard small-holding in the Vale of Evesham. Many market gardens around Sale and Bagley in Cheshire at the end of the century, although an important area of supply, were little more than one acre in extent. Few had hot-houses and the tenants made an income of about £50 per acre per annum, little more than an unskilled labourer.[7] Soft-fruit merchants regularly complained that such small units could not provide the same uniformity and consistency of product as their European competitors nor could they ensure regularity of supply.'[8]

A substantial quantity of the more common vegetables would come from farmers and market gardeners around most of the main cities. Small producers would generally dispose of their product themselves at the market, though larger producers might consign them to a salesman to be sold on commission. The fast railway network allowed rapid transit, and surplus from London's Covent Garden, which closed at 9 a.m., often found its way by the afternoon to Manchester's Smithfield fruit and vegetable market, which was open twenty-four hours a day.[9] Although home supplies were increasing, ever larger amounts of vegetables came from abroad by the 1890s. Onions, which in the 1850s had mainly been grown in Bedfordshire, now came principally from France. New potatoes were more or less available all the year round, as Canary Isles, and French supplies replaced the former Scottish ones. The carrot season was extended, with French and Dutch supplies being imported via Hull and Grimsby.[10] A wider range of vegetables became available.

Surprisingly, there seems to have been no serious attempt to diversify into poultry rearing, although demand for eggs and poultry always exceeded supply. In 1873, 766,708,000 eggs were imported, and by 1908 this had risen to 2,185,208,400, not including 801,070,880 eggs from Ireland. Most egg imports were from Germany, but France, Russia, Denmark and Canada were also major suppliers, as was Italy, from where eggs went to Belgium to be pickled for winter use in Britain.[11] Yet large farmers showed no interest in the possibilities of poultry farming. There was a widespread and persistent belief that it could not really pay, so the poultry was left to the farm women, who pottered around with antiquated methods selling to the local market or the travelling grocers' vans.[12] It was quite common for eggs to be sent to the market only weekly or even fortnightly, because there was no regular system for collection.[13]

Meat

All was not conservatism and disaster, however. For the livestock farmer cheap grain meant cheap feeding, which encouraged more farmers to switch to livestock. Barley prices fell less sharply than wheat prices, so it was those heavy soil areas which concentrated on wheat growing that suffered most. The once rich grain lands of Essex became the pastures for Scottish cattle. In all 2·5 million acres were switched from arable land to grass between 1872 and 1900.[14] Such was the demand for meat, however, that beef and mutton prices continued high. Again, the British farmer was naturally protected because of meat's tendency to deteriorate over time, and only in pork was there an extensive trade between Britain and the United States. In 1868 John Bell & Sons of Glasgow imported live cattle from the United States, but not until 1873 did this trade become a regular one.

With developments in refrigeration, the first chilled meat began to arrive in 1874 at Glasgow and Liverpool, via the Anchor and White Star lines. By the end of the decade more than 0·5 million cwt. were being imported, and ten years later the figure was more than 1·25 million cwt. The introduction of the chilled beef trade did not kill the imports of live cattle, because there were still many problems to be overcome. Difficulties of storage at the ports meant that rapid dispersal was essential, and if a number of beef-carrying ships arrived at the same port at the same time this could have a disastrous effect on prices.

Major improvements were made in refrigeration in the 1870s, largely by the Bell-Coleman Mechanical Refrigeration Company. In 1877 Charles Tellier shipped meat from Buenos Aires to Rouen, overcoming the barrier of the tropics, which allowed Australian meat to find its way to the British market. The arrival of the *Strathleven* on 2 February 1880, with its cargo of frozen meat from Australia, opened a new era in the southern hemisphere. Refrigeration allowed Australian production to grow in a way that would never have been achieved with the rather obnoxious boiled mutton in cans which had been coming from Australia since the late 1860s.

New Zealand gained even more. By 1886, 30,000 tons of frozen mutton, almost two-thirds of it from New Zealand, were arriving at British ports, together with 1000 tons of frozen beef, more than half of it from New Zealand. By 1913 the comparable figures were 250,000 tons of mutton and 70,000 tons of beef, two-fifths of it from New Zealand. The same innovations helped South America. In 1847 Baron Justus von Liebig had published details of a method of reducing meat to a concentrate, and in 1863 a German engineer, G. C. Giebart, set up a factory in Uruguay to make and ship meat extract. Two years later the British became involved, and began to exploit the Liebig process at Fray Bentos, the initial expansion being largely financed by British investment. As the historian of the Argentinian meat industry wrote:

In the River Plate region livestock improved by the continued heavy import of British-blooded animals, moved on British-owned railroads to British equipped and financed plants, from which the finished product was shipped on British steamships to England.[15]

In the late 1870s compressed cooked meats brought a further expansion, and then in the 1880s freezing transformed the situation once again. The really spectacular expansion in the South American trade came at the turn of the century, when South America gained from drought in Australia, war in South Africa and from a combination of industrial unrest and fast-rising domestic demand in the United States. In 1900 more than 770,000 cwt. of frozen South American beef was being imported, and a decade later it was over 5 million cwt.[16]

By the end of the century the imported beef and cattle trade was in the hands of a small number of giant firms. The trade from North

America was largly controlled by the 'Trust Companies', Armour & Company, Swift & Company, Morris & Company and the National Packing Company (the latter being a subsidiary of the Armour, Swift and Morris Companies and with directors from all three firms). All of these operated in Britain under a variety of names. The National Packing Company, for example, went under the name of the Hammond Beef Company, while Morris & Company operated as the English Products Company. Two other American firms, loosely tied to the 'trust', Cuchahy & Company and Schwarzschild & Sulzberger also operated in Britain, the latter under the name of Archer & Sulzberger. These firms were accused of controlling the trade in both live cattle and chilled meat from North America by monopolising space on the cattle steamers, getting preferential terms from the railway companies, controlling supplies coming on to the market to keep up prices, and generally seeking to divide up the market.

A Government enquiry into the meat trade in 1909 accepted that there was a meat trust or 'combination' in operation in the United Kingdom, though it did not find evidence that the trust companies were seeking to drive out their rivals. By the nature of the organisation details were difficult to come by, but the enquiry revealed that of the 344 shops at the central markets at Smithfield, Armour owned four, Morris three, Archer & Sulzberger three, and Hammond three, plus one operating under the name of H. S. Scott, the company's secretary. J. W. Curry owned five, which operated in close connection with the Trust. Outside London, they operated through independent wholesalers. Fletcher's of Newcastle, Hull, Leeds and Sheffield, one of the largest of the northern wholesalers, operated as commission agents for Armour at a commission of 2·5 per cent.[17]

The main shippers from South America were James Nelson & Sons, operating in the Argentine. In 1909 seven companies in the Argentine were slaughtering and exporting frozen and chilled meat, and the London managers of these companies met weekly to fix prices.[18] Most of the capital in these companies was English, though in 1907 the American Swift & Company bought out two of the largest Argentinian companies.

One-sixth of Britain's meat supply had been imported in 1880. When the century closed Britain was dependent on foreign sources for one-third of her beef and mutton and for over half her pig meat. By 1914 the proportion of beef and mutton imported was around half. Whereas in 1869 98 per cent of meat sold at Smithfield was killed in England, by 1910 only 30 per cent was. None the less, domestic production also increased, since there was a marked difference in quality between home and imported meats. The estimated number of cattle in the United Kingdom rose from 9,731,000 in 1877 to 11,732,000 in 1908. In spite of disasters like liver-rot, which decimated the sheep flocks as the 1870s moved into the 1880s, home output of mutton also rose by about 10 per cent in the last quarter of the nineteenth century, but decline in this had started before the First World War. Consumption of bacon and ham, however, grew from the 1860s onwards. Up until that time there was a relatively small trade, in Irish imports and home-cured meat, largely supplied by the local pork butchers. When the packing-houses of Chicago were opened, large shipments of bacon made their way to the United Kingdom. At the beginning of the 1880s, the Danes started to build factories to cure bacon on the English Wiltshire principle and there was an extraordinarily rapid progress in Danish imports.

Dairy Produce

The demand for dairy produce brought a similar growth of overseas and domestic production. As in other areas of British agriculture, the picture was not uniform nationally. The most profitable area was liquid-milk production, which could not be affected by foreign competition, and this was the fastest growing of the major agricultural sectors, expanding by about one-third between 1867 and the end of the century.[19] The dairy industry switched its concentration from cheese and butter to liquid milk.

Some 70 per cent of milk in the 1860s was used to make cheese and butter; by the first decade of the twentieth century the proportion was little more than 25 per cent.[20] In half a century cheese and butter production had been abandoned in those areas of the country near enough to urban centres to make the liquid-milk trade attractive. American competition was once again a crucial factor. Cheese was being made in factories in the United States from the 1850s onwards, and by the 1870s it was being exported to Britain in ever greater quantities. Attempts to face the challenge of foreign competition were slight. By 1874 there were at least six cheese-making factories in Derbyshire organised by the Derbyshire Agricultural Society,[21] but generally farmers found it easier to switch to milk supplying than to make the necessary technical improvements or price adjustments. Butter producers faced competition from margarine and Danish and Irish butter, and their response was the same, to switch wherever possible to liquid-milk supplying. 6d–8d a gallon in summer and 8d–9d a gallon in winter was more remunerative than cheese- and butter-making.

Distribution of milk to the cities was aided by the rapid transport system provided by the railways and by the possibilities of refrigeration. Coolers, such as the Lawrence cooler, which were cheap and efficient, were coming into use in the late 1870s and were certainly common by the end of the century. Many wholesalers began to set up their own cooling depots at country railway stations.[22] Milk could be carried over distances of 100 to 150 miles to urban markets, though there were difficulties in devising an adequate milk can which could be easily handled and which would not churn the milk. Severe shortages still occurred when summers were exceptionally hot, as in 1893 and 1911, when the milk turned sour before it reached the consumer.[23]

Because of these early difficulties of preserving and handling, the best quality milk in the 1850s and 1860s was still thought to come from urban dairies. But cattle plague, sanitary regulations and the increasing price advantage of rural diaries took their toll of those in the towns. In 1866 7 million gallons of milk were brought into London by train; fourteen years later the figure was around 20 million gallons. None the less, even in 1891, there were 673 licensed cowkeepers in London (predominantly Welshmen), though ever-tightening L.C.C. regulations had reduced these to 491 by 1894. In 1910 half of Liverpool's milk was supplied by cows left within the city.[24] The dairy farmer would consign the milk to one of a number of wholesalers, who would then sell the milk to retailers at the railway station. Wholesale dairy companies grew in size and numbers. There were eight in London in 1870, such as the Express County Milk Company and the Amalgamated Dairies Company, both of which were owned by old-established urban dairy families. By 1880 there were fourteen such wholesalers, who were in many cases taking control of retailing. Large companies like the Great Western Farm Dairies Company (owned by the Price family) Wiltshire United Dairies (owned by the Maggs and Butler families), the Surrey Farm Dairy Company and the Dairy Supply Company (the wholesaling subsidiary of Express Dairy owned by the Barnham family), took over smaller family dairies.[25] Attempts by farmers' co-operatives to break the hold of these wholesalers met with little success, and the distribution side of the trade was, by the end of the century, dominated by four or five large firms. Only these had the capital necessary to cope with fluctuations in production. Trends in this direction were apparent in most other cities, but in country and town there was still much direct selling by farmers or by retailers purchasing directly from the farmers, as well as an elaborate system of middle-men. Only in this century did the co-operative movement branch out into the milk industry.

In spite of the tendency towards larger wholesalers and dairies, the conditions of milk supply were quite notorious. No food stuff was more frequently adulterated, mainly by adding water but more harmfully by adding boric acid, salicylic acid or formalin to 'preserve' the milk. With milk passing through the hands of several middlemen, the quantity of those additives could be alarming. On summer Sundays in Clerkenwell in 1896 the inspectors (not expected on Sundays) found that 47·5 per cent of the milk sampled was adulterated.[26] While inspection could keep some check in towns there was little control over country dairies, where conditions could be horrific. A writer in the *British Medical Journal* in March 1903 described a visit to one farm near a large town

> The operation of milking was in full swing, three dirty-looking boys being hidden away behind their respective cows... The clothes which the boys wore were equally dirty, and the stalls, which were supposed to have been cleared out while I was waiting, were several inches deep in manure and foul-smelling straw... The hindquarters of the cows were coated with filth... I was horrified to see the filthy state of the milk as it flowed out of the pail. It was discoloured with grit, hair and manure. 'Look at that,' I said, pointing to a specially large bit of manure. I regretted my zeal, for Tom dipped his whole hand into the pail, and, as he brought it out, said, 'Oh that ain't nothing; its only off the cow.'[27]

Tuberculosis scares did bring some awareness of the dangers of contaminated milk, but the quality of milk available varied greatly from area to area. The Aylesbury Dairy Company in London and Sorensen's White Rose Dairy near York were both particularly recommended for their cleanliness and for their use of modern methods,[28] but elsewhere the old patterns continued for a long time, and it was significant that a great deal of milk was still sold by price rather than by measure. There were no standard fixed measures until bottles were introduced, and before 1914 diarymen were on the whole hostile to bottles. Cost was no doubt an important influence, but because of the problems of sterilisation many regarded them as a failure. Recently invented paraffin-coated paper bottles seemed to indicate a hopeful future development.[29]

Many of the larger firms also produced condensed milk, which solved the problems of preservation and handling, and was a cheap alternative to fresh milk. From the farmers' point of view it provided an outlet for skimmed milk. The Anglo-Swiss Condensed Milk Company, which had begun operations at Cham on Lake Zug in Switzerland in 1866, had a factory at Chippenham in 1873 and by 1881 had another two in operation. In 1904 Anglo-Swiss amalgamated with another successful manufacturer at Vevey on Lake Geneva, Nestlé. There were other much smaller firms. The factories diversified into baby food and calf food to stabilise the use of surplus milk. Processes devised by Just in the United States and Hatmaker in England allowed the production of powdered milk after 1902.[30] Before 1914 the New Zealand firm of Joseph Nathan & Company was operating in England, producing dried milk for babies under the name 'Glaxo', while the former West Surrey Central Dairy Company, run by the Gales family, was advertising 'Cow & Gate Dried Pure English Milk' from 1908.[31]

By the first decade of the twentieth century only 13 per cent of the butter and 24 per cent of the cheese consumed was home produced. 85 per cent of cheese imports consisted of factory-made cheddar, with 71 per cent of the total being imported from Canada, 8 per cent from New Zealand and 6 per cent from the United States. The remaining 15 per cent of imports consisted of fancy and soft cheeses from Italy and the Netherlands.[32] Ireland was the main source of supply for butter, followed by France and Holland, though by the 1890s these last two were being surpassed by Denmark, which provided a quality and consistency of butter that was markedly lacking in the notoriously variable Irish product.[33] Butter itself had to face competition from 'butterine' or 'bosch butter', two of the names give to margarine. The French food-research chemist Mège Mouriés sold his patent for producing a nutrient fat made from beef tallow and skimmed milk to the Dutch butter wholesale firm of Jurgens in 1871. They were quickly followed into the new product by the neighbouring firm of Van den Bergh. Other factories were set up in Germany, Austria and Norway by the end of the decade. Something of a breakthrough came in 1878–9 when petroleum discoveries reduced the demand for tallow and stearine, and brought the price down steadily from 43s per ton in 1876 to 24s in 1886, so that butterine could sell at half the price of butter. By 1886, 869,000 cwt. of 'butterine' were being imported and the *Grocer* magazine was pressing for the use of the term 'margarine' as opposed to 'butterine'. The result was the Margarine Act of 1887, which clearly defined the terms butter and margarine.[34] None the less, adulteration still went on, sometimes at source and sometimes at the retailers. Many tons of margarine were imported into Limerick, the centre of the Irish butter industry.[35] In Manchester, where there was an active vigilance committee among grocers and provision dealers to guard against adulteration, ten years after the Act 17·8 per cent of the butter samples taken contained margarine.[36]

The first margarine factory in England was built by the largest Danish manufacturer, Otto Monsted, in 1889 at Godley in Cheshire, particularly to supply the Maypole Dairy Company. The two main manufacturers were the Dutch firms of Van den Bergh and Jurgens, and there were very few British firms involved in manufacturing. Of twenty-five margarine manufacturers listed in the London Directory of 1895 less than half a dozen had English names. The main retailing outlets for margarine were the great multiple grocers, and there was intense rivalry between the leading margarine manufacturers to get the rights of exclusive supply to as many outlets as possible. A bitter struggle took place in the early years of this century between Van den Bergh and Jurgens. They bought their way into some companies, for example Van den Bergh had shares in the Meadow Dairy, and Jurgens bought an interest in Scottish chains like the Grove Dairy and the Golden Crown Dairy Company, and in other cases they lent money for expansion or for advertising. Monsted still remained the main supplier of Maypole, while Van den Bergh succeeded in getting long-term contracts with Lipton and Jurgens won the Home & Colonial contract. Some 56,000 tons of margarine were imported into Britain in 1910, but increasing amounts were being manufactured in Britain; some 84,000 tons in 1913 (compared with Holland's 88,000 tons and the United States' 69,000 tons), two-fifths of German output.

In 1902 the German chemist, Wilhelm Normann, patented a method of hardening vegetable oils, which opened up a new source of raw materials. It was this that was to bring Lever Bros, with plantations in the Pacific, West Africa and the Belgian Congo, into the margarine industry, though the decision to start manufacturing margarine themselves was not taken until the war years, and they were mainly concerned before then with supplying raw materials to Van den Bergh and other large firms.

Fish

The smell of fish, which, according to Mayhew in the 1850s, pervaded the rooms of the neediest of London's population was that of herring, probably lying in a salting barrel in the corner. Its source would have

been one of the fishing ports of north east Scotland. By the early nineteenth century the Scots had learned from two centuries of Dutch experience how to catch and cure herring. With Government help at the
beginning of the century, adequate harbours had been built from
Wick down to Eyemouth. Although Wick had been the most important harbour at first, by the second half of the century Fraserburgh,
Peterhead, Aberdeen and the Moray Firth ports had passed it in
numbers of registered boats. Starting from Shetland in May, the Scottish herring fleet followed the shoals down the coast, ending in East
Anglia just before Christmas. To the ports went the wives, daughters
and widows of the fishermen, the 'fish girls', who gutted and packed
the fish at a rate of one every five seconds.[37] It was an industry run on
a small scale by families and it persisted on this basis in spite of a great
expansion in production.

Further south small boats, small harbours and small markets were
the pattern for the provision of fresh white fish in the early nineteenth
century, providing what was essentially a luxury food. Preservation
was a major difficulty and most of the fishing was line fishing, where
the fish could be kept alive and transported as near to the market as
possible in 'wells'. Fish would be landed wherever there was a likely
market, or where there was the possibility of quick transport to a
market, but an unfavourable wind or tide which meant missing the
daily fish wagon could mean the loss of a whole catch. London, with
its great Billingsgate market, was a vital centre which took the bulk of
the catch.

After 1815 the two most dynamic fishing communities in the south
were Brixham and Barking. Brixham trawlers had made their way
along the south coast and into the North Sea in search of sole, turbot
and other flat fish. In 1832 they were landing at the herring port of
Yarmouth, where they could make use of the carting service that the
Barking firm of Samuel Hewitt's had developed to carry the catch live
to Billingsgate in twelve hours. By 1835 Brixham men were supplying
the fashionable clientèle of Scarborough in the spa season from Whit-
suntide to October, and it was they who reputedly located the 'Great
Silver Pits', sixty miles off the mouth of the Humber. This shifted the
industry's focus to the Humber ports, since Scarborough could not
offer the necessary resources and repair facilities, while those dependent on the high-class holiday trade objected to carts of fish rumbling
through the streets from quay to station. In the 1840s a number of
Brixham crews had settled in Hull, which had extensive repair and
fitting services for its whaling industry (though no fish market), and
others were moving to Grimsby, a fishing port whose fish until then

had generally ended on the fields of Lincolnshire as a fertiliser.

The expansion of a readily available supply of a range of white fish coincided with the development of railways, which provided the necessary speed of transportation to the markets. The railway companies were generally quick to seize the opportunities offered, actually seeking new markets by giving fish merchants free railway tickets for the purpose of obtaining orders inland, though there were constant, largely justifiable complaints at the high freight rates charged.[38] In Grimsby the Manchester, Sheffield and Lincoln Railway joined with the Great Northern Railway Company to form the Deep Sea Fishing Company in 1854, with a fleet of thirteen smacks. Harbour and transporting facilities were rapidly extended. Within thirty years landings at Grimsby had grown from 453 tons to 60,000 tons. Shipment by rail remained relatively expensive, and much fish still made its way to Billingsgate by cutter. It is usually Samuel Hewitt of Barking who is credited with the use of fast cutters to get the fish to market, a process that encouraged the use of 'fleeting', with smacks staying at the grounds for a month or more. Most of the smacks would be skipper-owned and Hewitt's encouraged this, while the firm provided the necessary maintenance services and gave the use of their cutters.

If the railway helped to produce the market, ice helped to transform the supply side. As always, Samuel Hewitt was at the forefront. Early in the nineteenth century he had persuaded Essex farmers to flood their fields in winter and to 'farm' ice, which was stored in his underground ice-house. From the end of the 1850s onwards, however, most ice was coming from Norway, from where Robert Hellyer first imported ice to Hull. The use of ice brought an end to the 'well-smacks' and allowed vessels to develop the trawl, whose use in the past had been limited by the fact that it landed the fish dead on the deck. Now the trawl made catching much faster: the fish could be loaded into baskets (from the late 1870s boxes), and from there into cutters (steam-powered from the 1860s), arriving at the market relatively fresh. Trawling made a range of fish part of the diet of the metropolitan common people for the first time. The use of ice allowed trawlers to extend their range to the coasts of Norway and northwards, an important consideration as some grounds became fished out.

Important changes in consumption habits produced what seemed an insatiable demand for fish. Plaice and haddock, once thrown back as 'offal', now became as acceptable as the cod, sole, turbot and brill of earlier decades. The market for fish now became national. Sheffield, for example, opened a new wholesale fish market in the 1870s to exploit its rail link with Grimsby, and became the main distribution centre for the markets of the West Riding and Lancashire. Thirteen fish trains a day carried Grimsby's fish throughout the country. The electric telegraph and the railway facilitated speedy communication between wholesaler and retailer, and allowed the trade to become more geared to market supplies, which in turn brought an expansion in overall turnover.[39] In spite of this, there were undoubtedly areas where supply remained inadequate. Parts of Lancashire, important industrial centres like Preston, Bolton, Wigan and Warrington, were very poorly supplied with fresh fish even at the turn of the century, either as a result of failings in distribution or because of lack of demand. Perhaps taste had been artificially restricted by the well-known Lancashire enthusiasm for fried fish and chips. By 1913 it was estimated that over 25,000 fish-and-chip shops in the country consumed at least a quarter of all fish landed.[40]

A further transformation of the fishing industry began in the 1870s with the introduction of steam power, first used in the cutters. The Grimsby Ice Company, formed by leading smack-owners in 1863 to import Norwegian ice, bought its first steam cutter in 1878. The concentration of ownership into a few hands intensified with the coming of steam trawlers. These seem to have appeared first in the more recently developed ports of the Firth of Forth. Leith and Granton on the Forth had twenty-one steam trawlers registered by 1883, while Hull, with 400 or so boats, had none that went by steam except the carriers and cutters. The first in Grimsby was registered in 1882, when the Great Grimsby and North Sea Steam Trawling Company Ltd registered two vessels, built at Hull and costing £3,500 each. Hull, with greater experience in steam and better credit facilities, then took up the challenge of steam, and by 1895 had 215 registered steam trawlers to Grimsby's 188. When the March gale of 1895 seriously reduced the Grimsby fleet, however, no further sailing smacks were built and investment in steam accelerated. In 1913, 625 were registered at Grimsby compared with 397 at Hull.[41]

Steam power allowed the supply of fish to expand: nets could be heavier, trawling deeper and much greater distances could be travelled. As the North Sea grounds became depleted – a process hastened by the steam-trawler fleets – trawlers moved further afield. Steam line-fishers were to be found off the Faroes at the end of the 1880s, and the first Grimsby trawler visited Iceland in 1891 for plaice and haddock. By 1903 one-third of the fish landed at Hull came from Icelandic waters: over 0·5 million cwt mainly of cod, and intrepid fishermen were following whalers into the furthest Arctic.

Ports such as Fleetwood and Milford Haven expanded with the development of new grounds in the north and west, and the railway companies again acted as the principal innovators. By 1902, 24,000 tons of fish were being despatched by rail from Milford Haven, and the town's population had almost doubled in a decade.[42] The catch at the most important northern port, Aberdeen, rose from a mere 9000 tons in 1887 to 63,000 tons in 1902 and to 112,000 tons in 1911.

Because more capital was needed to purchase steam vessels and finance long-distance voyages, one-man companies and owner-skippers gradually disappeared. The multitude of small fishing villages along the coast declined as the industry concentrated on the larger ports, which could provide the required ancillary services of boxes, nets, stores and ice. However as late as the mid-1880s, it was still fairly typical for a single man to buy his own boat at about £1600 on a mortgage. Some, in the prosperity of the third quarter of the century, had enlarged their fleets. Henry Smethurst, Grimsby's largest owner, had 50 smacks in 1882 and, although Hull had nothing comparable, John Holmes had 17 in 1878 and A. W. Answell had 11. With the coming of steam the more percipient smack-owners formed limited companies to raise the £4–5000 required for a steam trawler. Some huge companies appeared, like the Hull Steam Fishing & Ice Company Ltd, with an authorised capital of £200,000 in 1890 and Hellyer's Steam Fishing Company, founded in 1891 from the firm created by Robert Hellyer, one of the Brixham smack-owners who had settled in Hull in the 1850s. The company was worth £0·25 million in 1906. Many firms still bought on mortgages from the local banks and London finance houses, and it was on mortgages – at as low as 3 per cent interest in 1891 – that the industry was transformed. It became a source of investment for many connected with the sea.

Landings continued to increase. At Hull and Grimsby over 0·25 million tons, worth more than £3·5 million, were the average annual landings in the first decade of the century and Hull still sent an additional 50,000 tons to London by cutter. At the smaller ports along the East Coast, nearly half a million tons of herring were landed at the turn of the century, three-quarters of them to be exported. By 1913 Britain's annual catch of fish was over one million tons.

Canned Foods

Fish had always been a good food for canning. Since the 1820s there had been a domestic industry around Aberdeen canning grilse, lobster, trout, crab and salmon. Messrs Moir & Son were the main firm involved. They moved from fish to meat, poultry and vegetables, and by the 1870s were exporting canned strawberries, a particular delicacy in Australia. Another Scottish firm, Gillon & Company of Leith, had started food preserving in 1829, and by 1876 was offering Scotch broth, cocky-leeky, hotch-potch, sheep's head and trotters and haggis, 'so that Scotchmen of every clime can be gastronomically reminded of the culinary delicacies of their native land'.[43] Nor were English palates neglected – Gillon's were the first to preserve plum puddings.

In 1849 Crosse & Blackwell established a salmon-canning factory at Cork and Mayhew reported that the firm was canning 180,000 lb. of anchovies, 50,000 lb. of preserved Labrador salmon and 70,000 lb. of Scotch salmon.[44] By this time the salmon-canning industry was developing on the Pacific coast of North America, and the tinned salmon that caused such delight in Boot's shop of the 1880s probably came from the Pacific canneries, which were sending 2500 tons of salmon to Britain in 1880, double the quantity of five years previously. Other canned fish such as sardines were generally imported from France, but in 1903 a former employee of Lever, Angus Wilson, set up a canning business in Newcastle to pack Norwegian fish under the trade name 'Skippers' and these rapidly made an impact. At first they were sold as sardines, but after French producers successfully contested the use of the name from 1912 they were identified as brisling.[45]

Not much meat, fish or vegetables were preserved in England in the 1850s. What canning of meat there was was generally for victualling the army and navy, and the product had a most unsavoury reputation. Scandals over the quality of tinned meat, particularly that from the Goldner factory in Moldavia, resulted in the Admiralty setting up its own canning factory at Deptford in 1856. Although there is little doubt that the quality of the meat was better from this factory, some scepticism persisted among sailors, who referred to the meat as 'Sweet Fanny Adams', after the unfortunate victim of an early mass murderer. The meat shortage resulting from the cattle plague in the late 1860s encouraged importation of tinned beef and mutton from Australia. John McCall & Company of Houndsditch was the major importer, acting as agent for the Melbourne Meat Preserving Company, whose tinned rabbit was renowned. It was McCall's who, in the summer of 1876, introduced pressed corned beef from the United States.[46] The only attraction of such products to the public was their cheapness, since suspicion of the contents persisted and there were enough scandals on conditions in meat factories for this suspicion to be justified. Olive Malvery, visiting a meat-packing factory in the East End early in this century, found heavily seasoned potted tongues, and savouries were still being produced from sometimes putrid sheep's hearts and livers imported from Serbia. They were known among the workers as 'Bulgarian atrocities'.[47] It took a long time for suspicion of tinned meats to die away.

Bread

The extent to which Britain became dependent upon overseas wheat and flour (80 per cent was imported by 1914) encouraged the trend against domestic baking. Even by the mid-nineteenth century there were reports that the art of bread-making was dying out in urban areas, and this pattern soon spread to rural areas. In his survey of 1867 Dr Edward Smith found that 80 per cent of farm labourers bought some of their bread, and 30 per cent bought it all.[48] Home baking was still prevalent in the 1870s in some Midland and northern manufacturing towns, but often, while the dough was made up at home, it was taken to the bakers' ovens to be cooked.[49] By the end of the century part of the 'servant problem' for the middle class was the impossibility of finding servants who could bake bread.

In 1914, as in 1850, most people had their bread supplied from small bakehouses. None the less, in the second half of the period the industry went through a revolution. When G. Dodd wrote *The Food of London* in the 1850s there was no large bread factory in the metropolis, though Carr's of Carlisle were producing bread in large quantities.[50] However, the number of small bakehouses grew rapidly: for example, in 1862 there were 3000 master bakers in London.[51] Fourteen years later there were reputedly 3500 master bakers within a fifteen-mile radius of Charing Cross, 1200 of whom were their own foremen and took a share of the daily work.[52] Less than half a dozen of them used over 100 sacks of flour per week, and the great majority used only eight to twelve sacks. Such bakehouses were notorious for their lack of cleanliness and their intolerable working conditions. Even in the 1890s Charles Booth knew of underground bakeries in East London, 'so low that a tall man cannot stand upright in them, and so small that the three men have hardly room to turn about'.[53] When the L. C. C.'s Medical Officer of Health reported on the 'Sanitary Condition of Bakehouses' in February 1894, he found that 118 of the 200 visited were below or partially below ground.[54] Pressure from

Medical Officers of Health, public analysts, and trade unions slowly improved problems of hygiene, and technological advances led to better conditions. Such changes came slowly: new ovens and power-driven machinery were expensive, and many bakers could not raise the capital to buy them. Only a small number of firms were extensively mechanised before 1914. None the less, the trend towards factory-baked bread was marked. Firms were fewer and larger. The number of bakers in London was down to under 2000 by the end of the nineteenth century, and in Edinburgh the average bakery labour force increased from four in 1871 to sixteen in 1901.[55] There was some resistance to big bread-making companies in England. A number, like the League Bread Company in the 1850s, and Stephen's Machine Bread Making Company, which was formed in 1860, collapsed after a few years. Even co-operative bakeries in Birmingham and elsewhere were not a success, and those bakeries supplying institutions generally 'farmed out' work to small bakers. There were a dozen wholesale bakeries in London by the turn of the century, the largest of which were E. H. Nevill, J. & B. Stevenson, Wm Hill & Son, the Civil Service Bread Company and the Golden Grain Bread Company. In Glasgow, from the early 1870s, the Bilsland brothers had expanded the branches of their bakery until, by 1882, they were producing 17,000 dozen loaves per week in the winter months and 10,000 in the summer months from five branches, each using more than 200 sacks of flour. In 1880 they decided to centralise production in a custom-built bakery, using the latest power-driven dough mixers and most advanced ovens.

The product was standardised, and 22,400 standard 2 lb. white loaves were being produced each week at the Hyde Park Street factory by 1900. The firm continued to grow, as motorised transport opened up markets outside Glasgow.[56] The Bilsland loaf was a white loaf made from flour refined in the new roller mills, which had been spreading since the first one was built in Glasgow in 1872. Joseph Rank opened his first roller mill in Hull in 1885, expanding to London and South Wales from about 1904. However, there was a reaction against high milling, led by medical men like T. R. Allinson and the Bread Reform League. The result was the appearance of patent breads, such as the well-advertised Hovis loaf. Richard Smith of Staffordshire produced wheatgerm flour in 1887, having solved the problem of fermentation which the germ caused by the use of steam treatment. He joined with Fitton & Sons, millers from Macclesfield, to produce the flour. In 1898 the Hovis Bread Flour Company Ltd was launched with a capital of £225,000 and, in 1906, production was switched to Trafford Park, conveniently near the Manchester Ship Canal.

Hovis launched a massive advertising campaign to win the public and bakers to their product, and the use of baking tins with the Hovis imprint was the first attempt at branding bread. By 1914 *Hovis* was a household word, and, significantly, the main advertising had switched from journals like the *Illustrated London News* to the more popular *Daily Mail*.[57]

It took time for the market for patent breads to move beyond the middle class. The same is true of biscuits. Although local bakers might well produce some of their own biscuits or confections, biscuit production was quickly dominated by a small number of firms. J. D. Carr had founded a milling and biscuit-making firm in Carlisle in 1831, and within twenty years had opened an outlet on the Strand in London. In Reading, George Palmer, baker, miller and mechanical engineer, had joined Thomas Huntley, a confectioner, to form Huntley & Palmer in 1857. That same year George H. Frean and James Peek went into partnership in London, to be joined five years later by John Carr, a younger member of the Carr Family of Carlisle.

Technology boosted production: Carr's first biscuit-cutting machine to make 'alphabet biscuits' was introduced in the 1840s. Demand was also growing. Railway travellers needed biscuits to sustain them on their journeys, and ladies needed biscuits to sustain them through a long idle afternoon. Biscuit-makers moved into factories. William Meredith, the London baker, had a factory in Commercial Road in 1840; in Edinburgh, William Crawford turned to factory production in 1860. Huntley & Palmer's growth in the late 1850s was rapid. By 1860 they had 500 employees in their Reading factory. Seven years later they had nearly a thousand, and six years after that there were about 2500, as the working class, which was experiencing unprecedented prosperity, learned the delights of the Osborne, the Abernethy or the Ginger Nut.[58]

Several major new producers made their appearance in the 1880s. Jacob's who had been in Dublin since 1851, moved across St George's Channel in the 1880s in time to launch the Cream Cracker on the world. At about the same time an Edinburgh baker, Robert McVitie, began biscuit-making, joining in 1889 with C. E. Price, a Quaker confectioner who had learned his trade at Cadbury's and had come to Edinburgh as a salesman. Not until 1911, however, did they devise their first chocolate biscuit. Macfarlane Lang, another Scottish firm, moved from bread into fancy biscuit-making in 1886, with the opening of their Victorian biscuit works in Glasgow.

As the biscuit habit spread to the working class, the multiples began to incorporate them in their range of items and to produce their own brands. By the end of the century, Lipton had a biscuit-making plant of his own and the C. W. S. was producing a cheap brand. Bilsland Bros found themselves with biscuit-making capacity when they bought an interest in Gray & Dunn & Company in 1890.

Most biscuit firms started off as small local bakeries, concentrating on their own area and engaged in cash trading from vans. By the 1880s they were expanding into the national market. For some time even the largest firms remained private, and the traditions of the small family firm persisted. At McVitie's, for example, no mixing of the new Digestive biscuit introduced in the 1890s could be undertaken without the presence of the chief baker, Alexander Grant, and even when McVitie's opened a factory in London, Grant would commute between the two capitals to supervise the process.[59] Towards the end of the century family firms were giving way to limited companies. Estate and death duties took their toll, but generally the need to expand pushed firms to raise more capital. Jacob's went public in 1883, Carr's in 1894, Peek Frean's in 1901 and McFarlane Lang in 1904. These were the giants. Huntley & Palmer, 'the Seventh Wonder of the Commercial World', as the *Daily Telegraph* called them, was employing 6000 people in 1906, twice as many as their nearest rival Peek Frean's and four times McVitie & Price, Macfarlane Lang or Carr's. Jacob's had 2000 employees.[60]

Jam and Sugar

Jam became increasingly popular with bread in the second half of the nineteenth century. It was often produced in the most unpleasant circumstances in small factories. Visiting one such factory in East London at the turn of the century, Olive Malvery was struck by the dirt and total lack of sanitation. The women workers on 7s a week started work dressed as they came in from the streets. The fruit used was second or degenerating fruit from Covent Garden, though there were recurring stories of orange peel swept from the streets being used in marmalade. 'Grape' sugar, made from beetroot, potatoes and other sugar-yielding plants, was used rather than cane.

Such places were no doubt common, but larger firms did begin to appear. Crosse & Blackwell, who since 1706 had been sauce and pickle manufacturers in Soho Square began to produce jam in the 1840s. By the 1860s they were using 450 tons of fruit for jam-making.

Growth was held back by the high duty on sugar. It was to avoid this that Alex Keiller had set up his factory in the duty-free Channel Isles, and for twenty years his product dominated the market. The abolition of sugar duty in 1874 brought in rivals. W. P. Hartley began to manufacture jam, first at Colne and then at Bootle in the early 1870s, and later opened factories in Liverpool and London. Stephen Chivers, the third generation of the fruit growers selling to Covent Garden, started jam-making as an alternative to fruit distribution in Cambridgeshire in about 1873. In Scotland James Keiller & Sons of Dundee, who specialised in marmalade, was the largest confectionery firm in Britain at the end of the 1860s with 300 employees. They opened a branch near London's Albert Dock in 1879. As with biscuits, the growth of the popularity of jam was signalled by the entry of the multiples. Lipton embarked on jam manufacture at a factory in Bermondsey, with 250 employees in 1892, and, with the kind of vertical integration that came to be expected from Thomas Lipton, he then moved into Kent fruit farms. The C. W. S. opened a jam factory in Oldham in 1897, having started fruit preserving at Crumpsall twelve years earlier.[61]

The jam industry was greatly aided by the cheapness of sugar. From 1842 the duty on imported sugar fell steadily until it was abolished in 1874. Sugar remained duty free until 1901, when a modest duty was added to refined sugar to help meet the cost of the Boer War. Imported sugar was very cheap since it was aided by the subsidising policies of beet-sugar-producing nations. The price of raw sugar in London fell from 25s 6d per cwt. in 1872 to 8s 6d in 1903. Not surprisingly, it was sugar refiners and cane producers who were most active in opposition to subsidised foreign beet imports through the 'fair trade', anti-bounty movement which made some impact in the 1880s.

The main sugar firm was Henry Tate & Company, established in 1859 in Liverpool, where their large modern refinery was opened in Love Lane in 1872. They opened a factory in North Woolwich Road in London in 1878 to develop the production of cube sugar by the Langon process. Up till then sugar had been sold in larger conical loaves, which each grocer cut up for his customers. Cube sugar replaced this, and by 1907 output in West Ham was 3000 tons of cube sugar per week. Other leading firms were John Walker & Company of Greenock, where at the end of the 1860s there were ten refineries in operation, and Abram Lyle & Sons, also from Greenock, who moved into the London area, near the Tate factory, in 1881, concentrating on the popular 'golden syrup' of which they sold 100 tons per week in 1889.[62] Lyle had previously worked with the Globe Sugar Refining Company of Greenock. Other family firms such as James Fairlie &

Sons and Robert McFie, also expanded from their Greenock base to Liverpool and London.

Henry Tate, who had a thriving grocery business in Liverpool with a chain of six shops, had moved into sugar refining in 1859, first as a partner in the firm of John Wright & Company and then, in 1862, had opened his own refinery. There were at least half a dozen other refiners in Liverpool, but it was Tate's decision to purchase the patent rights to the Boivin and Louiseau method of purifying the raw sugar liquor, and to adapt his Love Lane refinery to this, that ensured the survival of his firm when most others disappeared. Increased importation of European beet sugar, and a bounty war between France and Germany, brought prices often below the cost of production and had a disastrous effect on British sugar refining. In 1864 there were more than fifty refiners in Great Britain, by 1882 there were thirty three, and by 1900 only sixteen. Quite large firms closed, such as Duncan, Bell & Scott, another Greenock firm which had opened a refinery in Silvertown, Essex in 1860, and David Martineau & Sons, which had been operating in London since the end of the eighteenth century.[63] Manchester, Plymouth, Glasgow and Leith all ceased to be sugar-refining centres and the industry became concentrated in London, Liverpool and Greenock.[64]

Tea, Coffee, Cocoa

Until 1833 tea had been the monopoly of the East India Company, but in the 1850s it came mainly from China, carried in such famous Aberdeen-built clippers as the *Reindeer* and the *John Bunyan*. In 1865 only 3 per cent of the total came from India. By 1900 India's share of the market was 55 per cent, with Ceylon providing 30 per cent and China only 7·5 per cent.[65] It was sold by the brokers of Mincing Lane, where such retailers as John Horniman, who was the first to introduce tea packets, and Arthur Brooke (there never was a Bond), who opened his shop in Manchester in 1869, did their purchasing. Brooke moved from retailing into wholesaling and then into production. Brooke Bond & Company went public in 1892. Ceylon tea began to be produced in 1878, and the first auctions were held in 1883. Thomas Lipton went to Ceylon in 1889 when he decided to by-pass Mincing Lane and import directly from his own estates. By 1890 Ceylon was supplying half of Lipton's tea (though only a small proportion came from the 7000 acres he had bought). He had buying agents in India and Mincing Lane, and the tea was blended and packed in handy pound, half-pound and quarter-pound packets in London's City Road, where he employed 600 girls. Within a year or two he was one of the largest wholesale suppliers in the world.[66] Rival retailers were not too enthusiastic about stocking their shelves with well-marked Lipton packets, and this gave other companies, such as Brooke Bond, the opportunity to supply their own brands or to supply loose tea to the grocer, so he could blend his own.

C. W. S. remained another important supplier. It broke its connection with Woodin, the Mincing Lane broker, in 1882, and set up its own tea-buying department, with direct shipments from China beginning in 1883. Within a year there was a turnover of £4·5 million. The Mazawattee Tea Company was another market leader. Founded as Densham & Sons in 1869 it led the market in introducing Ceylon tea after 1878. It came to grief in 1905 with a disastrous decision to enter retailing.

Cocoa gained steadily in popularity, with *per capita* consumption rising from 0·4 lb. in the mid-1880s to over 1 lb. in the first decade of the twentieth century. Although cocoa had been first introduced in 1656 and had been something of a fashionable craze in the late 1720s, demand had grown little subsequently. When George and Henry Cadbury took over in 1861 the firm of chocolate, cocoa and chicory-makers which the Quaker, John Cadbury, had formed from the tea and coffee shop that he opened in Birmingham in the 1820s, they found that the 'business was rapidly vanishing' and only eleven girls were employed.[67] The introduction of a new process, developed by the Dutch firm of Van Houten in 1828, which involved the extracting of fats from the cocoa as opposed to the traditional method of adding farina and sugar to counteract the fats, brought a change of fortune, as Cadbury's marketed their 'absolutely pure' cocoa, in contrast to the notoriously adulterated product. (However, demand for the older traditional cocoa persisted, so Cadbury continued to produce it until the 1890s.) The removed fat or cocoa butter could then be used for chocolate slab-making.[68] The firm gained from its reputation for purity after the passing of the Adulteration of Food Act, and by 1879, when they moved to their new premises at Bournville, they were employing 230 people, and had abandoned the tea and coffee side of the business to concentrate on chocolate and cocoa.[69] The 1880s was a period of exceptional growth, particularly on the chocolate side, and the number of employees increased five-fold at Bournville within the decade. In 1910 the firm had nearly 5000 people on its staff.

The older Quaker firms of Rowntree's and Fry', based in York and Bristol, followed a not dissimilar pattern of growth, and by the early twentieth century the three firms dominated the market. Rowntree'. who employed 100 people in 1879, was employing 4066 in 1909. The chocolate industry moved into factories at a very early stage (Fry's had installed a Boulton and Watt steam engine in 1795), but at the same time it remained in many cases small-scale, with a slow diffusion of new techniques. The Dutch firm, Van Houten, had agencies in London, Leeds, Liverpool, Edinburgh, Glasgow and Dublin in the 1870s, before the main British firms had effectively established a national network. A similar situation existed in the upper-class chocolate market, where the market leaders until the turn of the century were the French firm of Menier.

New Foods

There had always been a ready market for food additives of all kinds, presumably to give taste to the tasteless or to overcome too strong a flavour. Crosse & Blackwell were best known in the 1860s for the 27,000 gallons of catsup (a word not yet replaced by what Mahew regarded as the 'vulgar barbarism', ketchup) it was producing annually. The firm of sauce and pickle manufacturers had existed in Soho Square since 1706, though as late as 1830 it had only been employing six full-time workers. By the 1860s, however, it was producing 200,000 gallons of pickles and turning 450 tons of fruit into jam. They were also in the business of preserving anchovies and Scotch salmon and, since 1850, had been producing table jellies.[70] Although there were many small pickle manufacturers satisfying particular local tastes, it was not until the 1890s that Crosse & Blackwell faced a serious national challenge from the Pittsburgh firm of H. J. Heinz, who offered an increasing range of sauces and pickles, which seems to have attracted the British palate very quickly.[71] In a slightly different corner of the market the firm of J. J. Colman, which had moved from Stoke to the Carrow works in Norwich in 1856, expanded on the strength of their mustard. By 1910, 2600 workers were employed at Carrow, making mustard, blue, starch, chocolate, vinegar, beer and patent wine.[72]

There were always new convenience foods coming on to the market, though the pressure for this was less intense in a servant-hiring society than it was to be later. The Birmingham experimental chemist, Alfred Bird, had perfected a fermenting powder or baking powder as it came to be called, as a substitute for yeast in 1843. Soon after came his eggless custard powder, and both of these products were distributed nationally by 1850. Other items were gradually added. The firm's blancmange powder, with a choice of fourteen flavours, was a big success during the 1870s and jelly crystals followed in the 1890s.[73] Quick breakfast foods stemmed from the dietary concerns of American mid-west Seventh Day Adventists and of sanatorium director, John Harvey Kellogg. By the 1890s there was a boom in a variety of instant breakfasts. In the United States the Kellogg Company quickly became the market leader, but it does not appear to have broken into the British market, where the main rivals were the American Cereal Company (later Quaker Oats), which opened a London agency in 1893 and the Shredded Wheat Company of Canada, which set up a U.K. subsidiary around 1908. There were also some short-lived British products like Falona and John Bull. It is not clear how far these products penetrated beyond a small section of the middle class before 1914. Presumably they lacked the 'filling power' that many of the working class would have thought essential. There is evidence, however, of Quaker Oats being popular with agricultural labourers, at any rate in good times.[74] Most of the working class and middle class probably still believed in the value of a more hearty cooked breakfast.

Although the development of farming and of the food industries offered the population a much wider range of food stuffs, some of the advantages were perhaps off-set by other problems. There were gains in hygiene as bakeries moved into larger units, but much nutritional value was lost by the use of highly-refined flours. The great increases in the consumption of sugar, while indications of a rising standard of living, brought in their train an ever-growing problem of tooth decay, so that a substantial proportion of the working class, by their twenties, were physically incapable of eating some of the foodstuffs available: four out of five conscripts in 1916 had such bad teeth that they could not eat properly.[75] Greatly increased consumption of dairy products and meat, while generally taken as a sign of improvement in standards of living and while undoubtedly making a contribution to a more balanced diet for much of the population, brought with it other long-term health hazards.

The nation was fed mainly by the products of other countries. The changes that took place in British agriculture largely came about in order for it to survive, and were changes forced upon farmers by developments elsewhere. A process of gradual adaptation to changing home demand had been taking place at a fairly leisurely pace from the 1840s to the 1870s. From the 1870s onwards time for leisurely change was not allowed. Adjustments from arable farming to animal products and market gardening did take place, but on nothing like the scale possible or necessary to meet growing demand. Farmers in other countries were quicker to grasp the opportunities offered. There was a failure to find where the openings were and to seek out the best techniques, and although output continued to rise throughout the period there seems little doubt that much more could have been achieved.

12. *The Nation Clothed*

What end does it serve? It enables Messrs. Parnell, Lynch, Moses & Son, Samuel Brothers, Nicolls and others, to undersell honest and respectable tradesmen, and supply garments in a style and at a figure which no employer with a conscience could approach. It enables the engineer, the builder and the clerk who have from 30*s* to £3 a week for eight to ten hours a day, to support their figure in stylish garments at two-thirds of their value, at the expense of poor wretches who work eighteen hours a day for a bare existence. John Williamson, editor of *The Tailor*, writing on the 'sweating' system of East London in 1866.

According to the 1861 census, just under 7 per cent of all workers in England and Wales were engaged in the manufacture of clothing. Almost a quarter of these were in London, and it is for the industrial pattern in London that most information exists, but the system of production was not so very different in other major industrial centres.

The second half of the nineteenth century saw a revolution in the clothing industry, associated particularly with the development of the ready-made clothing trade. This was the side of the industry that 'Parson Lot' (Charles Kingsley) observed at the end of the 1840s – 'the "dishonourable" trade of the show-shops and slop shops – the plate-glass palaces, where gents – and, alas! those who would be indignant of that name – buy their cheap-and-nasty clothes'.[1] This was a side of the industry which Mayhew found in sharp contrast to the West End bespoke trade:

The quiet house of the honourable tailor, with the name inscribed on the window blinds, or on the brass-plate on the door, tells you that the proprietor has no wish to compete with or undersell his neighbour. But at the show and slop-shops every art and trick that scheming can devise or avarice suggest, is displayed to attract the notice of the passer-by, and filch the customer from another. The quiet, unobtrusive place of business of the old-fashioned tailor is transformed into the flashy palace of the grasping tradesman. Every article in the window is ticketed – the price cut down *to the quick* – books of crude, bold verses are thrust in your hands, or thrown into your carriage window – the panels of every omnibus are plastered with showy placards, telling you how Messrs —— defy competition.[2]

The firm of Elias Moses of Aldgate was already selling ready-made clothing in the 1840s, in response to a demand for alternatives to the old-clothes market, and generally claimed to have pioneered ready-made clothing. However, the Colchester firm of Hyams seems to have predated Moses, who had been one of Hyams's employees. Hyams moved into Cheapside in the 1840s and grew to become, as Messrs M. & S. Hyams, the largest wholesaler of ready-made clothing.[3] It was the technological developments of the 1850s – the sewing machine and the band-saw – which allowed great expansion to take place; an expansion accomplished within the existing small-scale organisation. Generally a wholesale clothier would do the cutting at the warehouse and then give out the pieces to tailors, who would sew them up at home and return them to the warehouse. In time, middlemen came between the wholesalers and the workers, and there was even more sub-contracting.

One of the remarkable features of the industry was the extent of its specialisation and sub-division. When Beatrice Potter (not quite yet the formidable Mrs Webb) was engaged in her investigations for Charles Booth in the mid-1880s, she found the coat-making sector largely confined to Whitechapel and organised by Jews. Most employers were small: 76 per cent of those surveyed by Beatrice Potter were in workshops employing less than ten and only 1·6 per cent (fifteen) employed over twenty-five workers. The bigger employers would provide a workshop, perhaps the floor of a large house or even a custom-built shed in the backyard, but the typical small employer would know little 'distinction between a workshop and a living-room'. The small master would work himself, having probably bought his presser's table and sewing machine by hire purchase. The Singer Sewing Machine Company had thirty collectors operating in the East End, calling for the weekly instalments.[4] The master tailor would have working with him men and women of varying degrees of skill, engaged in the numerous sub-divisions of coat-making:

the same man may baste out and 'press off' the 1s coat; a mere machinist may pick 5*d* jackets from off the heap by his side, run up the seams and round the edges, the garment flying backward and forward to the general hand who will do all the soaping, felling, and buttoning that is required.[5]

Trouser-making, vest-making and juvenile suit-making in London operated in a similar manner, but here the workers were generally non-Jewish women workers, in many cases the wives and daughters of unskilled and casual workers. They would work either directly for the wholesale house or for a distributing contractor who would have women home-workers to do the machining, others to do the finishing and would themselves attend to the pressing. By the end of the century there were signs that such middlemen or women were disappearing, and an increasing number of wholesalers were establishing their own workshops or directly employing home-workers.

This kind of pattern was to be found in other cities. Manchester, Birmingham, Bristol, Glasgow and Leeds all had their Jewish coat-making communities, operating the 'sweating system'. However, in Leeds a factory-based industry gradually developed. Leeds had the advantage of nearness to supply of worsted, wool, engineers and labour. John Barron operated two workshops in the 1840s, producing bespoke garments in addition to some ready-made smocks, moleskin trousers, breeches and children's wear (sailor suits were a speciality). He opened his first factory in Alfred Street, Leeds in the 1850s, with twenty to thirty machines producing ready-to-wear garments. He also sub-contracted to outworkers, who were mostly Jewish. In 1858 Barron introduced the band-knife, which had been developed from the wood-cutting band-saw, and in 1867 moved to larger premises, with ready-made stock to the value of £10,000. By now almost all the work was ready-made, with travellers sent out to sell the stock. A decade later continuing growth necessitated Barron's first custom-built factory. Each decade saw moves to larger premises, and by 1904, just after the firm went public, 3000 employees were housed under one roof.[6]

In 1871 the factory inspectors listed fifty-eight tailoring and clothing factories in Britain, but the growth of the factory system in the clothing industry was relatively slow. The invention of the oscillating shuttle in 1879 allowed the replacement of hand and foot treadle machines with powered ones – steam and gas powered before there were adequate public electricity supplies – and American developments of blind-stitching machines, of new cutting techniques and, by 1914, of button-holing and buttoning machines all encouraged the trend into factories. Against this could be set a seemingly endless flow of labour willing to work in the industry, and because of fluctuating seasonal demand it was cheaper for the large-scale manufacturer to use outworkers at peak times than to have an enlarged factory standing idle. However, the Aliens' Immigration Restriction Act of 1911 cut off an important source of such outworkers.

At first manufacturers like Barron retailed through existing drapers' shops, but by the end of the century others such as Hepworth and Blackburn, both of whom had established factories in Leeds in 1867, were opening their own retailing outlets. In 1905 Hepworth had 143 branch shops. It was in Sheffield, in 1906, however that Montague Burton opened his first shop, where made to measure clothes could be ordered, to be made up in his Sheffield factory. Soon he moved to Leeds and opened retailing outlets throughout the north, successfully combining some of the advantages of the traditional bespoke trade with the cheapness and mass-production of ready to wear. Burton was not the first: there had been wholesale bespoke tailoring earlier, with 'special orders', but Burton was operating on a larger scale than anything that had gone before. Perhaps his timing was opportune. The trade paper, *Men's Wear*, had commented a few years before that just as the depression of the 1880s had turned many a middle-class gentleman from his accustomed cigars to the pipe, so the recession of the early 1900s might persuade 'some men who ... very properly get their clothes made for them by a tailor, [to] be tempted by a really good cloth made into ready-made clothing in a large and detailed number of fittings...'.[7]

In other cases distribution was arranged through wholesale warehouses, and these in turn sometimes moved back to manufacturing. One such was the Glasgow firm of Stewart & MacDonald, wholesalers, who set up a factory in Strabane in Northern Ireland for the manufacture of white shirts, collars and cuffs, and ladies' and children's underclothing. Another factory in Glasgow produced ladies' mantles, children's dresses, men's shirts, hats and caps. Youths' and men's ready-made clothing were produced in their Leeds factory.

By the turn of the century complaints were growing about foreign competition at the lower end of the market. *Men's Wear* in 1902 was reporting that German-made trousers were being 'dumped' at a mere 18*s* 6*d* per dozen, and the United States' ready-made clothing industry, which had experience dating from the 1830s, was in a position to take advantage of the growing acceptance of ready-made clothes. American producers were very successful with the fashionable 'shirtwaists' or blouses, so loved by the 'typewriters', and the British blouse industry seems to have been slow to face up to this competition.

The ready-made industry for women's clothing developed more slowly than for men's and children's wear. Dressmaking was in the hands of the small dressmakers and tailors with which every town and village abounded. They would make clothes to order. Toward the end of the century, some of the department stores began to keep their workroom staff employed in producing a few ready-to-wear items. The C. W. S., which had begun to manufacture woollen cloth at Batley in 1887, quickly expanded into the manufacture of cloaks and children's wear in the 1890s, and, at the turn of the century, caps, bonnets, blouses, overalls and aprons were being produced in the Society's Holbeck factories. In 1912, with twenty workers, factory dress-making was pioneered by Dean & Thompson of Shipley. Messrs W. Pretty of Ipswich were probably the main stay-making firm, and here again the application of power to the sewing machine and cutting equipment had brought most of the industry into factories by the turn of the century. However, up until the first World War only a tiny proportion of the supply of women's clothes was ready-made.

A great deal of clothes-making was still done at home by mothers and daughters, and the continuance of this was made possible by the sewing machine. The industry was largely a product of American ingenuity and of a partnership in the early 1850s between Isaac Merrit Singer and Edward Clarke. Singer & Company commenced their British business with premises in Buchanan Street, Glasgow, which were opened in 1856 – the agency had to be in Scotland because of patent difficulties in England. Two years later, it was reported, there were 900 machines operating in Glasgow, 'chiefly employed on portions of skirts, chemises, stays and other underclothing, on caps, on shoes and boots and on portions of men's and women's outer garments'.[8] Other firms came into the market, and by 1880 five sewing-machine companies were selling their wares in Britain, but the Singer Manufacturing Company quickly dominated the market. It had begun its European expansion in 1864 when the American market was being squeezed as a result of the Civil War. George Woodruff, the London agent, built around him a band of local sales representatives who could make 25 per cent commission, or more, on their sales. A small assembly plant was opened in High John Street, Glasgow, in 1867, to produce thirty machines per week. Glasgow offered the advantage of good shipping, low labour costs and, despite a later reputation, a surprisingly docile labour force. In 1871 the factory moved to Bridgeton in the east end of the city, and by 1876 output was in the region of 3000 machines per week. Only six years later work was begun on an even larger plant at Clydebank, which when it opened in 1885 employed 5000 people to produce 10,000 machines per week.[9] Sales in Britain and Ireland amounted to 150,000 in 1890.

There were many other manufacturers: the *London Post Office Directory* listed over fifty in 1895, many of whom had a well-established trade. The Jones Sewing Machine Company and the Wheeler & Wilson Manufacturing Company were the best known after Singer, and there were also importers of American and German machines, such as the Willcox & Gibbs Sewing Machine Company and Joseph Wertheim, but Singer continued to lead the market.

Boot and Shoemaking

Like the clothes-making industry, boot and shoemaking moved from being a domestic to a factory-based industry in the years between 1850 and 1914.

In the 1850s the traditional method of shoemaking still operated in small towns and rural areas, with the cordwainer making a complete shoe. In the cities, however, since the eighteenth century, the labour had been divided into the three processes of 'clicking', 'closing', and 'making'. The 'clicker' was a man of considerable skill who cut out the leather for the uppers. His work complete, it was passed to the 'closer' who would sew the various sections of the upper together and hand over to the 'maker', who would attach the sole and heel. The 'clicker' was likely to work on the premises of the shopkeeper, but the other workers would be outworkers, working in their own homes assisted by their family.

As in tailoring, there were two sides to the trade, the high-class, bespoke side where the well-to-do paid for a perfect fit and a carefully sewn finish, and the ready-made side, where cheapness was the prime consideration. From the middle of the eighteenth century the ready-made market in London, the colonial market and the army and navy contracts had been largely supplied from Northamptonshire and Staffordshire. These were the great wholesaling areas where large manufacturers organised a vast army of outworkers in the towns and surrounding villages. A firm like Horton & Company of Stafford was employing nearly a thousand such outworkers – men, women and children – at the beginning of the nineteenth century,[10] and some London firms were sending cut-out pieces to the 'closers' and 'makers' of

Northamptonshire from about 1809 onwards, because of the cheapness of the work. Shoes could be made there for half the London price. The London shoemakers complained to Mayhew that every child in Northampton had a leather apron.[11]

A factory system developed in Northamptonshire for the 'clicking' stage, but for the other processes outworking persisted well into the second half of the century. Again, as in tailoring, change came to the shoemaking industry with the coming of the Singer sewing machine: a machine for sewing leather was available in 1855. It was sold for £30 and appears to have been heavy, clumsy and not particularly efficient. It was suitable only for closing the uppers, but, by 1857 and 1858, was posing a great enough threat to the 'closers' of Staffordshire and Northamptonshire for strikes against its introduction to be widespread. These were often accompanied by machine smashing. It was the prolonged opposition to sewing machines in the traditional areas that from the end of the 1850s contributed to the rapid rise of Leicester as a centre of wholesale manufacture. In some cases the coming of the machines brought 'closers' into factories, but since no power was involved the most common pattern was for wholesalers to rent machines to outworking 'closers'.

Other American inventions were imported soon after, products of a society where imagination and initiative were encouraged and rewarded and where skilled labour was scarce. An American sole-cutting machine was in operation in the high-class shoe firm of C. & J. Clark at Street in Somerset in 1858, and in the following year the Blake sewer was imported, which for the first time, allowed uppers to be machine-sewn to soles. There were initial problems, because the Blake machine could not work with waxed needles and could only do chain stitch. By the mid-1860s, however, these problems had been satisfactorily overcome and the machine was in widespread use, generally under a system of leasing whereby boot-makers paid a premium of about £100 and a royalty equal to about a penny on every pair of shoes sewn.[12] This system encouraged the growth of specialist firms concentrating on sole-sewing, just as there were specialist machine closers.

A further contemporary development was the re-introduction of riveting as a method of attaching soles to uppers. I. K. Brunel had devised such a method for producing army boots, but it had not been widely adopted. At the end of the 1850s the Leicester firm of Thomas Crick revived the method, and it spread rapidly in the 1860s, being quicker, cheaper and requiring less skill than sewing. The Nottingham leather merchant, G. A. Royce, and the Mansfield shoemaker, J. J.

Gascoine, were one example of a partnership launched in the late 1860s to produce riveted women's boots. In 1875 they opened a factory in Leicester, producing boots mainly for the export market.[13] A machine for riveting was available, but it took thirty years for hand-riveting to be replaced by the machine.[14]

These technical changes transformed the industry. Both outworking and factory production increased. New men came into the industry, both as workers and employers. In Leicester, for example, traditional hat manufacturers turned to shoe manufacture and the trade journal was complaining in 1888 of 'capitalists and adventurers with no knowledge of the technicalities' crowding into the industry.[15]

Elsewhere change came very slowly. In London in the late 1880s the bespoke trade still operated in the traditional manner. As Booth and his observers in East London found, however, ready-made uppers were used increasingly, coming, in most cases, from the factories of Wellingborough and Northampton, but in a few cases from London closing factories.[16] Bethnal Green had a considerable number of riveting shops, producing boots for women and children.

The increasing number of middlemen was remarked upon everywhere. There were distributors selling to retailers, who would themselves be purchasing from wholesalers. In some cases these might be manufacturers, but in others they might just operate as middlemen. There were also 'factors' who co-ordinated the many small part-manufacturers. Only in a few cases were retailers directly linked to manufacturers: Lilley & Skinner Ltd was one such in London; as was Manfield & Son, of Northampton, who had by the end of the century branches in Liverpool, Glasgow, Manchester, Birmingham, Leeds, Bradford, Sheffield, Hull, Newcastle and Nottingham.

Further important changes took place in the 1890s largely as a result of the 'American invasion', with its system of carefully worked-out sizes and half-sizes and fittings for machine-made footwear. Mechanisation, until 1895 confined to a progressive minority of manufacturers, now became essential for survival. Many American finishing machines were adopted, and Goodyear welting machines replaced the old Blake machines. Even more sophisticated upper-sewing machines also came in. By the late 1890s, apparently, the latest Goodyear machine could do in eighteen seconds what had formerly taken an hour. The process of innovation was eased, from the employers' point of view, by the weakness of a trade union crippled financially and in spirit by a major lock-out in 1895.[17]

As a result of these changes firms grew larger, with outworkers disappearing and almost all processes now being undertaken under one roof. A typical 'large' factory at the turn of the century might employ two hundred workers, though there were giant firms like John Cooper & Son, in Leicester, Walker, Kempton & Stevens (who were among the first to specialise in rugby and football boots), Joseph Dawson & Sons, William Hickson & Sons, or Manfield & Son in Northampton. C. & J. Clark of Street, which had become a private limited company in 1903, employing about 1400 workers, produced nearly one million pairs of shoes in 1910. However, a remarkable number of relatively small firms survived. They were helped by the policy of the American machine-making companies and their British subsidiaries, who leased, rather than sold, their machines. New men with small amounts of capital could still break into the industry. American machines dominated. Companies like the Union Boot and Shoe Company and the American Special Machine Company had agencies in Leicester and Northampton from the 1870s onwards. The C. W. S. factories in Leicester were supplied by the American Campbell Machine Company and, in spite of the name, the British United Shoe Machinery Company, formed from a series of amalgamations in 1899, was firmly controlled from the United States. This last grew from the partnership of Charles Bennion and H. Peason with the United Shoe Machinery Company of America. There was a long struggle between this company, which rented its machines, and the Gimson Shoe Machinery Company which sold theirs.[18]

Local specialisation still remained a feature of the industry before the First World War. Stafford was the centre of women's high quality shoes. Edwin Bostock & Company of Staffordshire was the principal firm out of which Lotus Ltd grew after 1903. Medium-quality women's shoes centred in the city of Leicester and the lower quality in the country areas. Norwich was a centre for lightweight women's shoes, with, among others, the firm of Howlett & White, which began using the name Norvic around 1910. In men's wear, the high-quality centre was the town of Northampton, with the lower quality in the country districts. Bristol and Kingswood were centres for heavy working boots, and the Rossendale valley in Lancashire had developed, from the 1880s and 1890s, as an important area of slipper manufacture.[19] London still had firms producing goods of all qualities and the Clarks in Street, who had started off as slipper-makers back in the 1820s, had eighty years later a range of nearly 500 items of good quality, plain footwear.[20]

Although some boots and shoes had always been imported from Europe, the quantity was always very small. However, from the mid-1890s onwards, American manufacturers launched a sustained effort

to break into the British market. 86,000 dozen pairs of American footwear reached the British market in 1902 at a value of over £400,000.
Twelve years before United States shoe exports had been worth £532.[21]
The American industry had been producing standardised products from
its factories since the 1840s and 1850s, and was in a position to expand
in competition with a British industry where small workshops and small
partnerships remained quite typical. In terms of price, fashion,
appearance and finish the American product was increasingly regarded as superior by the turn of the century, while there were criticisms
that British manufacturers showed a comparative lack of taste and
attention to detail, and produced goods that were poor in fit, poor in
appearance and poor in finish.[22] Well into this century the speciality of
the British ready-made industry was still a rather ill-fitting, black,
elastic-sided or hobnailed boot. If anything beyond that was required
the customer was wise to look to the United States or the bespoke
shoemaker.[23]

However, unlike many other industries, the British footwear
industry responded to this competition, by paying much greater attention to style and appearance, and by 1914 was standing up to foreign
competition well – there was much (premature) talk of the 'victory of
the British Boot'.

Hosiery

Similar patterns of development were to be found in the hosiery and
underwear industry. Well-established as a domestic industry in Nottinghamshire, with cotton wear, and in Leicestershire, with worsteds,
for at least two centuries, it began the process of transformation
around the mid-nineteenth century. The application of steam power
to circular knitting frames seems to have been first applied at the firm
of Paget of Loughborough in about 1844, and Warner & Cartwright,
also of Loughborough, had a power-driven factory for shirt-making at
about the same time. Hine & Mundella established a factory in Nottingham in 1850, taking advantage of a rapid expansion there when
common land was made available for building development. Their
aim was to break the hold on the market which hosiery imports from
Saxony had. The firm searched for new patents which would allow
them to mechanise most of the processes. By the end of the 1850s, in
association with Luke Barton, the firm was producing stockings on a
new round frame which could make the process a hundred times faster
than hand-knitting and which allowed the stocking to be fully

fashioned by automatic action. The Crimean War boosted demand for stockings and underwear by the military authorities, and by 1857 Hine & Mundella were employing 4000 workers, both inside and outside their 'model' factory.[24]

In Leicester the firm of Nathaniel Corah also made the transition (though on a smaller scale) to factory production, and at the Great Exhibition showed a wide range of their knitted goods – 'hose, wool vests and drawers, cuffs and sleeves, hoods, hats, bonnets and ladies' wool paletots'.[25] But many other firms were slow to change. I. & R. Morley of Nottingham did not start factory production until 1866. All these were well-established merchant hosiers, but it seems fairly clear that the new opportunities in the industry attracted new entrepreneurs who were quicker to take advantage of innovatory possibilities than those who had for decades relied on hand workers scattered in the cottages of the East Midlands. As long as labour remained relatively cheap, there was not the same incentive to mechanise, and in the mid-1870s the total number of factory workers in 129 factories in the industry was only a small proportion of the total workforce. A bewildering variety of middlemen organised the domestic industry, coming between the knitters in the villages and the warehousemen in Leicester or Nottingham. Rising wages in the 1870s, thanks both to increased demand and to trade-union activity, pushed more workers into factories. This was helped by the abolition of the frame rent in 1874, and the introduction of compulsory education, which deprived the industry of its cheap child labour.

I. & R. Morley, sharing in Barton's patents, acquired six factories between 1875 and 1890,[26] and Messrs Corah & Sons opened their St Margaret's works, employing 1000 workers, in 1886. Other well-established merchant hosiers like Allen Solley at Arnold, near Nottingham, and J. B. Lewis & Sons in Nottingham itself, began factory production in the 1880s, so that by 1890 there were less than 5000 framework knitters left in Nottinghamshire. Not all the new factories were successful, and many of the new enterprises went bankrupt as competition produced intensive price-cutting. Small manufacturers still sought to compete with the new giants. Also, German firms, mainly from Saxony, were able to compete very successfully at the cheap end of the market both in Britain and the United States. New tariffs in the United States and a flooding of the market by German goods in the 1890s more or less destroyed the Nottinghamshire cotton hose industry, though Jaeger's wool movement and falling Australian wool prices helped maintain the demand for woollen goods. By 1910 cotton hosiery goods worth over £1.25 million were being imported.

Hats

For gentlemen the beaver had given way to the silk hat in the 1830s and 1840s. Fifty years later felt replaced silk. The silk-hat industry was concentrated in small factories in the major cities. In London, for example, Blackfriars Road was the main area for manufacturers, using silk plush imported mostly from Metz. The manufacturers would supply to order or to their own retail outlets. From the outset felt hatting was concentrated in factories, with Stockport, Hyde and Denton in Lancashire as the main centres. A domestic-based finishing trade remained in London and other towns. Cap-making was also pulled towards the supply of raw material, and Manchester became an important centre, but there was still a domestic industry in London's East End Jewish workshops; and, as Booth remarked, 'Even caps bearing the names of well-known hatters are made in Whitechapel.'[27]

Straw bonnets for ladies and straw boaters for men retained a remarkable popularity, though subject always to the inexplicable vagaries of fashion. The industry was firmly based in rural Bedfordshire, Hertfordshire, Buckinghamshire and Northamptonshire. Originally local straw was used, and there were sweat shops masquerading as 'plaiting schools' throughout these counties, where the art of straw-plaiting was taught; but as the century progressed local supplies had largely given way to imported straw plait from China, Japan and Europe. There was a complicated search for cheap supply. Many hats and bonnets at the end of the century were constructed from black cotton bought in Manchester. This was made into plait in Germany and Austria, which was in turn despatched to Luton to be made into hats and bonnets, in some cases in factories, but more often by home-workers. There was also Japanese plait, which was sent to Italy to have green straw run through it and then sold to Luton.[28]

Textiles

Increased demand for clothes produced changes at the earlier stage of cloth production. Up until 1860 cotton clothing predominated, but fashion and the cotton famine of the 1860s caused a movement to other textiles. Cotton and worsted, for example, proved a popular combination for ladies' dresses. By 1880 only about 15 per cent of the value of cotton cloth produced went to the home market; this rose to

21 per cent at the end of the century, only to fall to a level around 17 per cent in the decade before the war.[29] Although the cotton industry expanded rapidly in countries like the United States, France, India and Japan, it affected British exports only, and foreign cotton imports did not make a real impact before 1914, except for a few specialist items like high-quality French muslins. With so high a proportion of output being exported, the industry tended to develop in response to overseas stimuli, rather than to domestic demand.

The industry's response was to improve its efficiency, and in less efficient areas like the west of Scotland it had nearly died out by the 1870s. It had become concentrated in Lancashire and Cheshire, with a high degree of specialisation in particular towns. Oldham was the spinning centre of the coarse trade, and Bolton and Manchester were for fine yarn. In Preston and Chorley these would be woven into fancy cloth, in Colne and Nelson into coloured fabrics and in Blackburn and Bury into shirtings.[30] The process of mechanisation had been largely completed by the 1880s with the development of combing machinery. In spinning, the hand mule was still important, because of doubts about the ability of the self-acting machine to handle the finest yarn: a problem that also affected the ring spindle, which came into use in the United States during the 1870s, but was adopted in Britain only very slowly. It was a similar tale with the automatic loom, which, although made in England, had hardly found its way into Lancashire mills by 1914.

There was little increase in the number of cotton firms. Clapham calculated that there were about 1700 to 1800 between the late 1880s and 1904. After that there was an increase to 2011 in 1914. Weaving firms grew only slowly: the typical firm had less than 500 looms in 1914; but there was a faster and more significant growth in spinning mills. The dark tenements of the industrial revolution gave way to 'light and almost beautiful' mills in the twentieth century, with 60,000 spindles a typical number in 1911, compared with 25,000 in 1884.[31]

While cotton had little to worry about in the home market, across the Pennines in Yorkshire the woollen and worsted industries faced growing competition from France, but overall demand was affected from at least the 1880s onwards by changes in women's fashions. Demand for alpaca and mohair gave way to a demand for all-wool fabrics. It took time before it was fully realised that this was no short-lived fickle fashion, but a long-lived change, which justified the necessary investment and re-equipment, because all-wool fabrics required very different processes from mixed worsteds. Even in the first decade of the twentieth century, Bradford manufacturers were still trying to make do with modified old-fashioned equipment.[32]

Firms in the woollen industry were mainly small family concerns. In 1870 the West Riding had 1572 firms and only two had adopted limited liability. By 1912 there were only 439 firms, of which 153 were limited companies.

New materials appeared on the market. Messrs Courtauld opened their artificial silk factory at Coventry in 1905, though the pioneering work in this had been done by Waddle & Davenport Ltd, first in their factory in Tubize in Belgium and then at Leek in Derbyshire. However, it was Courtauld's who undertook most of the new development, and by the outbreak of the First World War they were employing 3000 people at Coventry.[33] As Sir John Clapham remarks, this was a rare example of an old, well-established business, for Courtauld's had been producing crape since the 1820s, anticipating competition from a revolutionary new material by itself becoming an innovator. When demands for black mourning crape fell rapidly in the late 1880s and early 1890s, Courtauld's had been quick to introduce new processes for the production of coloured gauzes, crêpon *crêpe-de-chine*, chiffon, and *mousseline-de-soie*, and their interest in artifical silk was a continuation of this entrepreneurial expertise. There was competition with German output, but trade agreements between the leading firms kept competition in the home market to a minimum and allowed the new process to become well established.

Accessories

The amount of additional ornamentation in clothes varied very much with fashion, but from the 1840 to the 1880s trimming was used increasingly. Lace was particularly popular. There were lace veils for bonnets, close-fitting lace caps for indoor wear, cascades of lace to be worn over bustle skirts – up to eight yards of trimming might be used on one skirt – and few dresses were without their frills and ruffles, their collars and chemisettes.

From the end of the eighteenth century lace was made mainly around Nottingham. Like hosiery and shoemaking in the same area, lace-making was going through a slow transition from outworking to factory production. In 1858 for example, Thomas Adams, one of the largest of the Nottingham firms, employed 500 people in a factory *cum* warehouse and another 500 outworkers.[34] In 1903 there were still 2282 outworkers employed in the industry in Nottingham. There was a tendency towards factory production, but since lace-making machines could be hired rather than bought many small, independent lace-makers continued to survive, to the general detriment of the industry. There was much conservatism and a slowness to produce new designs which could compete with French, German and Swiss products. The ribbon industry too had succumbed in the face of imports. In Coventry it collapsed soon after the Cobden Treaty of 1860. Those ribbon-makers who were left moved into factories.

Buttons came from Birmingham, which had started as a centre for metal buttons, but by the 1850s was mainly producing mother-of-pearl buttons and covered and linen buttons. Between 5000 and 6000 people were employed in the industry in 1851. There was some factory production of metal and linen buttons, twenty button factories each employed 150 people or more in the 1870s,[35] but pearl and vegetable-ivory buttons were made on a domestic system or in small workshops. Anyone could hire the necessary tools for four shillings per week, buy his shell on credit and sell to the factors, who were the middlemen who organised the industry. Even when particular sections of the industry became factory-based, the task of sewing the buttons on cards was still sub-contracted.[36]

From the 1860s onwards the Birmingham industry felt the effects of the growth of industry in other countries. It stagnated in the face of German and French competition in the vegetable-ivory section, while world demand produced shortages of raw materials. This competition intensified in the following decades, and made severe inroads into the Birmingham industry. Germany, Italy, Austria and the United States were suppliers of cheaper buttons than could be produced in Birmingham, which was far from any of the raw materials. Even the pearl-button industry, which had for long been the most important section in Birmingham, was squeezed out by Japanese manufacture of cheap mother-of-pearl substitute. In the 1880s pearl button-making had employed 2500 people; in 1914 there were only 500 workers left.

Fashion also affected the industry. When the butterfly tie and the fancy waistcoat went out in the 1890s only cheap buttons were needed under the long tie. It is true that there was a considerable demand for buttons for women's clothes, but it was a much less steady demand than for men's and much more subject to the foibles of fashion. As a result, the Birmingham button industry in the early twentieth century was left catering largely for a small high-class trade or for government orders for metal buttons. The growing market for cheap vegetable-ivory buttons for ready-made clothes was going elsewhere. In an effort to meet competition the industry attempted to rationalise itself, when the firms of Thomas Carlyle, Plant, Green & Manton and Harrison & Smith came together in Buttons Ltd in 1907. By 1914 this firm employed half the workers in the trade in Birmingham.[37]

More buttons presumably meant a steadily increased demand for needles, and here again the Black Country was the main supplier. Up until the 1880s needles were mostly made by outworkers in Worcestershire and Warwickshire villages, like Alcester, Studley, Redditch and Henley-in-Arden. Over the next thirty years the industry became concentrated in factories, principally in Redditch. While little threatened, this highly concentrated industry did have to face some German competition. The German industry had shown a much greater readiness to mechanise than had the Worcestershire men.[38]

Lancashire cotton firms, like Edmund Ashworth & Sons and James Chadwick & Bros, both of Bolton, produced sewing thread, but by the last decade of the nineteenth century the industry was dominated by the Paisley firms of J. & J. Clark and J. & P. Coats. Clarks was the first to introduce spool-cotton sewing thread to replace hanks and skeins, and to ensure a guaranteed length. They catered, with their 'Anchor' brand, mainly for the home market, though to avoid American tariffs they had mills at Newark, New Jersey. The other main Paisley firm, J. & P. Coats, had long had a substantial export trade. In 1840 three-quarters of the firm's trade was with America.[39] Coats too erected mills in the United States, at Pawtucket in Rhode Island, between 1870 and 1883, and later moved into Russia, Germany, Austria, Hungary and Spain.

It was on the distribution side that a tendency to monopoly first began to develop. In 1889 Clarks and Coats combined their selling in the Sewing Cotton Agency, which later became the Central Agency when Jonas Brook & Bros of Meltham, near Huddersfield, joined.[40] In 1890, Messrs Coats went public and Clark & Company followed in 1896. When in 1895–6 J. & P. Coats Ltd bought up five other firms in Paisley and in Lancashire, they controlled 80 per cent of the industry and their monopolistic challenge was only partially met by fourteen other, mainly Lancashire, firms combining in the English Sewing Cotton Company in 1897. These included some of the oldest names in the industry, like Sir George Askwith & Company, Edmund Ashworth & Sons, John Dewhurst & Sons, W. G. & J. Strutt. Their share of the industry was relatively small compared with Coats's. After a few years the two combines did not seriously compete, and, indeed, it was agreed that the two should 'preserve, maintain, and have protection for the trade they have done in the recent past, not interfering with each other's business'.[41] Both companies distributed through the

Central Agency and any firms outside the Agency found efforts to undercut Agency prices blocked. An agreement in 1912 with the Drapers' Chamber of Commerce prevented retailers selling other than Central Agency cotton thread, unless they received the same margin of absolute profit on non-Central Agency thread. What competition there was was confined to new foreign markets.[42]

At the start of the period, any jewellery accompaniment to clothes was likely to be expensive and made in one of the many Birmingham jewellery shops. 7500 workers were employed in the Birmingham jewellery trade in 1866, just as the industry was expanding following the silver discoveries in Nevada. The price of silver fell rapidly, as did the quality of much of the work produced, but it opened up a much wider market. Gilt and imitation jewels were made in increasing numbers following improvements in electro-plating. In both areas, silver work and the cheaper section, machine-made items principally from the United States, offered sharp competition. The Birmingham Jewellers' and Silversmiths' Association of 1887 made an early attempt to ease the competitive pressure through price-fixing agreements, though the Association also encouraged a greater awareness of design through technical education. Small factories did develop, but most work was done in small workshops, and wedding rings were still made by outworkers in 1914.[43]

The coming of the railways and the standardising of time on Greenwich increased demand for watches and clocks. This was largely met by Swiss watches and American clocks, 'low in price, and with little pretence to accuracy'.[44] Cheap factory-produced watches had been pioneered by Aaron L. Denison and the Waltham Watch Company of Roxbury, Massachusetts in the 1850s, when he produced a watch mechanism of standardised parts and reduced the time to produce a watch from twenty-one man-days in 1853 to four in 1859. It was, however, after 1870 that Swiss (Swiss manufacturers were also producing interchangeable parts) and American watches seriously came to threaten the position of London, Coventry and Liverpool watches, made by hand in small workshops, where there was total sub-division of the multiplicity of part-making and fitting. Up until 1870 demand generally exceeded supply, but with Swiss and American watches prices fell to 15s–20s by the 1890s.[45] A measure of factory production came to Britain in 1866 when John Wycherley of Prescot in Lancashire started producing machine-made movements with steam-powered machinery. Others followed in the area, such as T. P. Hewitt, who established works for making keyless movements by machinery in the 1870s. By 1876 total production of the Prescot, St

Helens, Rainhill, Cronton, and Widnes district was 100,000 to 120,000 movements per annum. Some hands were made in Lancashire, but most of the rest of the watch was made and assembled in the small workshops of Clerkenwell, Coventry, Liverpool and Birmingham. In 1882 Wycherley and Hewitt combined to produce complete watches, becoming in 1888 the Lancashire Watch Company Ltd, with a capital of £50,000, and most of the existing Prescot manufacturers merged into the company. By 1901, 2777 men and 444 women were employed by them.[46]

There was, however, wide resistance to the introduction of new methods of production in watch-making. The Anglo-American Watch Company, established in Birmingham in 1879 to produce watches on the American system, collapsed within a few years, apparently because of hostility from the workers. According to Booth in the 1890s, the London watch-makers were still refusing to adapt to the changed situation and persisted with the old hand methods. None the less, they were able to survive because the demand for watches grew so enormously, though there was really no attempt to compete in the low- and medium-priced watch market.[47]

The clothing industry made some of the most far-reaching adjustments to meet the rise in demand for its products. Initially there was clearly some leeway for expansion of output by traditional methods and outwork persisted as an important part of the industry into the twentieth century. From the 1870s, however, a factory system developed. At first it made most progress in boot and shoemaking where, by 1897, nearly 70 per cent of those employed in the industry worked in factories. In tailoring on the other hand, only about one-third of the labour force were working in factories in 1897. A decade later the position there was transformed, with 73 per cent of tailors working in factories and 86 per cent of shoemakers. The machinery used, which developed rapidly to bring about a widely acceptable level of quality in ready-made clothing by the end of the century, was largely a product of American inventiveness, but British industry learned to use it and to keep a firm hold of the home market as well as to push up exports.

13. The Nation Furnished

> In the beginning of those evil days the graceful furniture of Chippendale and Sheraton were pushed away and consigned to attics, or sold cheaply at country auctions to fit up inn parlours or rooms behind shops; and the heavy 'handsome' furniture of mahogany and damask bore down upon us, and made us for a time the most depressed people, heavy with our ugly furnishings, and the mock of all nations that had better taste and lighter hearts than we were possessed of.
>
> J. E. Panton, *From Kitchen to Garret* (1890).

One only needs to look at photographs of interiors from the mid-Victorian to the Edwardian period to see the huge market for furnishings that existed. Fashion dictated that more would be spent on house furnishing and fittings than ever before. Rooms were expected to be laden with furniture and ornaments. Varieties of tables, chairs, sideboards, chiffoniers, escritoires, pianos and 'what-nots', were covered with tasselled velvet or velveteen cloths, runners or antimacassars, bedecked with stoneware toby jugs, Staffordshire figurines, Doulton china bowls, brass candlesticks, *papier maché* models, japanned tea-trays, enamelled tea caddies, electro-plated fruit bowls, innumerable inlaid boxes, glass vases, wax fruit and stuffed birds. Looking down on them were walls covered with paintings, photographs, plates, samplers, wall lamps and clocks, unless William Morris's efforts to improve taste had persuaded the occupants to display some of the more attractive wall-papers. The general impression was one of darkness and dullness: paint, wallpapers, woodwork and carpeting were all a dark brown. With yards of heavy draped velvet or rep curtains hanging from great brass rings together with lace curtains and probably an aspidistra in the window, little sunlight penetrated either to relieve the gloom or to endanger the colours of the furnishings or the complexion of the ladies of the house. Although from the 1860s and 1870s the moulders of taste had been urging a greater simplicity, reacting against overcrowding and excessive ornamentation, the impact of their didacticism was very limited before 1914.

> On the whole, the average middle-class home in 1914 was still over-burdened with furniture and ornaments, still had dark-brown paint, a whitewashed over-decorated plaster ceiling, and a fierce carpet in blues, reds, greens and purples in a complicated all-over pattern. The mantelpiece would still be surmounted by a massive and intricate erection of cupboards, shelves and mirrors, hung with velvet drapery, fringe and tassels, and decorated with innumerable photographs and ornaments.[1]

In a middle-class home some of the paraphernalia was the accumulation of more than one generation, and even in a working-class cottage the process of furnishing was cumulative. But everyone setting up house needed a bare minimum.

The wise young man marrying the loved daughter of some secure upper-middle-class gentleman could reasonably expect to have his furniture bought by his future father-in-law. £150–£200 spent at Shoolbred's, Maple's or Whiteley's could produce a very reasonable standard of comfort in the 1890s. Plain mahogany dining-room chairs at 32s–42s each, or with padded seats and backs in ebonised New Zealand pine, upholstered in dull-brown morocco at £3 10s each, could impress any guests, but it was possible to get rush-seated, black-framed chairs for as little as 3s 6d. Wickerwork armchairs could be bought for 5s to 6s or, at the other end, a Maple's mahogany and horsehair sofa for £8 8s, which could be carefully protected by a muslin cover when not in use.[2]

For the floor, carpet squares started at about 35s 6d, or a fitted Kidderminster at 4s 6d–5s 6d per yard. For the kitchen stairs, Dutch carpeting at 1s 6d per yard would suffice. For the windows, velveteen curtains came at 2s 3d–2s 6d per yard, but there might be old ones that could be re-dyed at Pullar's. Foreign competition had pushed down the price of china and glass, and a plain-white china dinner-set from Maple's could be purchased for a mere 2s a dozen for plates and dishes.[3]

The working-class couple would start with much less. They too would probably be helped by family and friends. They would no doubt purchase many items from the second-hand market, but, like their middle-class counterparts, the working-class couple believed that what they had ought to be well-displayed and this must have encouraged spending on newer items, whenever possible.

Faced with an empty room, cottage, flat or house to furnish, the covering of walls and floors was a priority. For the woodwork of doors and skirtings, and for the almost inevitable dado around the bottom half of walls, dark-brown varnish was necessary, and at least around the edges of floors there would be dark varnish and stain. For the walls and ceilings a white or coloured distemper was popular, though these too could be covered by a heavy patterned lincrusta paper and painted or varnished over.

The paint industry developed very little, in terms of technology, throughout the nineteenth century. In 1900 the same formulae for the production of varnishes were being used as had been described in the 1770s. Only in the twentieth century did innovations begin to revolutionise the industry. Only gradually was white lead in paint replaced by zinc oxide, but this produced cracking and flaking. New dyes from Germany gave an increased colour range. But well into the twentieth century most house paints were made of white lead, linseed oil and various driers and thinners. Anything else added or the colours offered depended largely on the knowledge and experience of the painting contractors. Fairly quickly paint darkened and yellowed to give that pervading gloomy brownness. Only a very limited range of ready-mixed paints was available by 1914, and almost all mixing was done by the skilled painter. The drysalter or colourman could generally offer advice to those who wanted to do it themselves.

Paint manufacturers seem, on the whole, to have been small and, in some cases, spin-offs from other industries such as lead-pipe making or the chemical industry. Some of the colour manufacturers were probably associated with the textile dyeing industry. Glasgow and Liverpool were both important centres for paint manufacture, encouraged no doubt by the demands of their ship-building industries. Alexander, Ferguson & Company, Blacklock & Macarthur, Archibald Eadie & Company, and James & John G. Scott Ltd were all leading Glasgow manufacturers who were supplying a national (indeed international) market by the 1890s. In Liverpool, Goodlass, Wall & Company Ltd and John Matthews & Company were important. Among the leading London firms were Lewis Berger & Sons Ltd, who had been established since the eighteenth century, Denton & Jutsum of Bow, who were advertising ready-mixed paint in tins by 1895, and Wilkinson, Heywood & Clark in the Caledonian Road.[4]

The better-off would certainly use wall-paper and by the mid-nineteenth century an increasing range of paper-hangings was available. The great calico printers of Darwen in Lancashire, C. H. & E. Potter, had modified their cloth-printing rollers for paper in time for the 1851 Exhibition, thus allowing machine wall-paper to replace the expensive hand-printed variety. Prices also came down with the reduction in paper duty, which had held back expansion until 1861. Output increased from nineteen million pieces in 1860 to thirty-two million pieces in 1874.[5] The designs of William Morris, Walter Crane and others helped to improve the general standard of appearance and craftsmanship, but most designs still tended to consist of large patterns of rather gloomy colour for downstairs and strongly patterned flower or fruit designs for the bedrooms. The industry was concentrated in a relatively small part of Lancashire around Darwen and Heywood in a variety of firms, but at the end of the century five Darwen firms, plus six other Lancashire firms, amalgamated to form the Wallpaper Manufacturers Ltd, with a capital of £4,200,000, and the new giant soon absorbed many more firms and attained a near monopoly. Quite rapidly it achieved a notoriety for its maintenance of a fixed minimum price and for cutting off supplies to any merchants who sold other than trust paper.

Rugs and carpeting for the homes of the middle class could be supplied from a variety of centres, with the names providing little guide. 'Brussels' carpet was mostly made at Glasgow, Kidderminster, Halifax and Durham; 'Kidderminster' carpets were mostly produced at Dewsbury, Kilmarnock and Bannockburn; and 'Axminster' had long ceased to have any connection with the town of that name and came mainly from Kidderminster. Even before power looms came into the industry in the mid-nineteenth century a number of carpet firms were large by the standards of British industry. With the coming of the power loom this trend continued. A cheaper form of 'Brussels', known as 'Tapestry', was devised by an Edinburgh manufacturer, Richard Whytlock, at his factory at Lasswade, and by the last half of the nineteenth century most Brussels carpets were probably produced on this patent. Messrs John Crossley & Sons of Halifax, the largest carpet firm in the country in 1850 which produced 30 per cent of the nation's output in 1863, and the Kidderminster firms of Pardoe, Hoomans & Pardoe, James Holmes and Henry Brinton & Sons all operated under licence from Whytlock. Gradually mechanisation, and with it cheaper quality, came to the other standard makes. Over half the Scottish carpet weavers were probably employed on Kilmarnock Kidderminster or 'Scotch' as they were sometimes called. In the development of the more expensive Axminster the leading firm was James Templeton & Company of Glasgow, which pioneered imitations of Persian and Turkish fabrics and generally helped to reduce the price of the product.[6] Although in the last half of the nineteenth century there was a substantial reduction in the price of carpeting, it was still only brought within the range of a wider section of the middle class. Fashion also helped cheapness, when from the 1880s the fitted carpet gave way to the carpet square with polished or stained surround. The working class would rely on the occasional cast-out piece of carpeting, the home-made rug with scraps of material pulled through sacking and the gradually cheapening floor-cloth and linoleum.

Scotland was also an important centre for floor-cloth, an alternative to carpeting. The firm of M. B. Nairn & Company of Kirkcaldy, founded by Michael Nairn in 1847, with the first partnership set up in 1858, produced floor-cloth 'with all the richness, the minuteness and the finish of a velvet pile carpet', according to the *Art Journal* of 1862, though most oil cloth probably remained crude in colour and execrable in design long after that date.[7] Nairn's inventive genius devised a printing process that gave any number of colours and tints, and in a quarter of the time it had formerly taken. When Nairn started in 1847, making and maturing oil cloth had taken a year, by 1864 it was ready for the market in three months. Until 1873 the firm had marketed through agents, but in that year a warehouse was opened in London, followed soon by others in Manchester and Glasgow. 1876 brought a move away from oil cloth to the cheaper linoleum production, which Frederick Walton of Staines had devised, and Nairn's began producing this in quantity in 1877. By the mid-1880s they were among the best-known linoleum producers in the world, with branches in the United States.[8] However, Mrs Peel in 1898 was advising the new house-buyer that American imported oil cloth was still cheaper than home-produced linoleum.[9]

For furniture the householder was offered a wide range of quality and prices. Furniture-making was another craft which only gradually moved from domestic to factory labour from the 1850s to 1914. Twenty years before Mayhew was writing, the typical pattern had been for the small cabinet-maker to have a workshop behind his shop selling directly to the public, with most goods made to order. In the 1830s, however, wholesale furniture warehouses made their appearance, and by Mayhew's time, the 'garret-masters' in the cabinet trade were building 'on spec' and selling their goods at the warehouses. Other cabinet-makers and upholsterers might specialise in supplying additional goods to the great furniture stores, such as Maple's, Gillow's, Jackson's and Graham's, goods of a slightly cheaper quality than might be made in their own workshops. By the end of the 1850s these stores were now either making their own goods or buying from the warehouses. The cabinet-maker who had formerly supplied the trade was squeezed out. As one told Mayhew, the business was 'not fit for honest men – it is now only fit for scamps and scamping masters'.[10]

The advent of the wholesale middleman had pushed down prices. With 3s 3½d one of Mayhew's informants could buy all that was necessary to make a desk. After four hours work he could sell this to the warehouse for 3s 6d and get the capital to purchase more wood. Twenty-eight hours work on a chest-of-drawers could bring a profit of 5s 5d: 19s 7d for the materials and the finished article selling at 25s. By 1850 three-fifths of the working cabinet-makers in London supplied warehouses.

Like all crafts, the furniture trade had a geographical concentration. The East End trade in London largely concentrated near Curtain Road, where most of the wholesale dealers were, and spread north and east into Hoxton, Shoreditch and Bethnal Green. Another concentration of a slightly better class was to be found around Tottenham Court Road, which was also the centre for mattress-making. Further west some high-class specialists remained. A few large workshops remained, employing perhaps twenty or more journeymen, and here there would be division of labour, with some concentrating on ornamental work, some on tables, some on clock cases and so on. The system, as Booth pointed out, forced specialisation on the 52,000 craftsmen employed in the trade in the 1890s.

> The existence of a market in which any finished article can be sold at some price – even late on Saturday to provide Sunday's dinner, or early on Monday to furnish money for more wood – the competition amongst themselves of small employers, whose numbers are for ever recruited by the ease with which under such conditions a 'man' becomes a 'master'; and the necessity, pressing on such men of finding some sort of livelihood from week to week; all those causes taken together have led to highly specialised work, both masters and men employing such skill as they possess, in making as rapidly as possible these articles after which there is a sure sale, even though at prices leaving continually a smaller margin for profit, rather than those from which a larger but less immediate return might be anticipated.[11]

Booth did see a few factories in London in the 1890s, such as the Lebus one in Tabernacle Road. Ambrose Heal moved into the family business in 1893, and began producing machine-made furniture of

good design at moderate cost; Maple's had East End factories supplying their West End stores by the end of the century, but it was mainly
after 1900, with the spread of electrification, that a factory system developed. It grew, not in London, but in the traditional chair-building
area of Buckinghamshire, around High Wycombe. This had long been
a centre for chair-making, with firms like Gomme's, Still's, Birch's
and Jones's, who had been producing the common Windsor chair and
cane and rush-seated chairs in many cases since the previous century.
The industry was organised on an outwork basis, with various tasks
sub-divided and chair-legs coming from the beech woods of the Chil-
terns to be assembled at Wycombe. Local publicans frequently acted
as 'chair masters'. The High Wycombe manufacturers provided the
8000 chairs for the 1851 Exhibition and the 19,000 required for the
Moody and Sankey evangelistic campaigns in 1873. In 1860 it was
claimed that High Wycombe turned out a chair a minute all the year
round, 1800 dozen per week. In 1885 there were about fifty chair-
making factories in Wycombe; twenty years later there were nearly a
hundred. Although the reputation of High Wycombe chair-makers
had been based on cheap, plain country chairs, by the 1880s leading
firms were branching into quality furniture.[12]

Towards the end of the century some of the more successful
London firms, looking for ways to expand, but finding London land
prices prohibitive, turned to High Wycombe with its plentiful, skilled
labour force. Frederick Parker & Sons, for example, who had been at
St Pancras since the 1850s, moved to High Wycombe at the end of the
century. Similarly, in Scotland the main factory development took
place, not in Glasgow, where traditional cabinet-making went on, but
in Beith in Ayrshire.

Old and new patterns of production continued side by side. *The Victoria County History* of Buckinghamshire in 1908 identified three
classes of manufacturers in the area around High Wycombe: those
who had their own steam mills and produced the finished article;
those who sent wood to the public saw mill and then assembled the
chairs; and, finally, the smaller men in the surrounding villages, the
'bodgers' working in the woods who supplied 'turned stuff', forelegs,
stretchers and chairs according to pattern, so that in many cases only
the backs, hind-legs and seats were made in the factory proper. These
last would in many cases be independent, self-employed men working
alone or in pairs, buying the timber, cutting it up in the woods and
then shaping the chair-legs and the stretcher pieces, which would then
be transported for sale by the gross to the High Wycombe factories. In
other cases, the trees would be bought by a local farmer, who would

then employ 'bodgers' who worked on a part-time basis. Before 1914 a 'bodger' could expect to receive five shillings for a gross of chair-legs and three-quarters of a gross of stretcher parts, rarely providing an income of more than twelve shillings per week.[13]

Sometime during the late 1830s the large wooden bed had given way, with remarkable suddenness, to the brass and iron bedstead, and for these the centre of production was Birmingham. In 1847 there were only five metal-bedstead makers in the city; by 1862 there were twenty, employing about 2000 workers. Between five and six thousand bedsteads a week were being produced by 1865, about half of which were exported. Twenty years later output had risen to over 20,000 per week. It became a highly unionised occupation, and in the 1880s and 1890s employers and unions were engaged in price-fixing operations which ensured that excess competition did not push down prices or wages. The feather mattress would probably have been stuffed in a 'sweat-shop' or by a domestic worker, though by the end of the century factory production was developing with the use of wire-springs.[14] The blankets would probably be from Yorkshire, perhaps with Dewsbury 'shoddy', though imports were increasing.

Tables were likely to be protected from sun and scratches by coverings, probably of plush or velveteen to match the heavy, draped curtains and the valance covering the mantel. The material would be a product of a Lancashire firm, such as Jones Brothers of Leigh, Middleton, Jones & Company Ltd, or the Tootal Broadhurst Lee Company Ltd of Manchester. For other tables there would be table baize or oil cloth. This had been produced from the 1840s by the firms of William Storey and James Williamson, both of Lancaster. For a time these two had a monopoly, but in 1868 Nairn's of Kirkcaldy began to produce table covering and in the 1880s the three firms were involved in a fierce price war which brought baize within the reach of the poorest.[15]

The range of dishes, plates, bowls, basins and jugs available was immense. Josiah Wedgwood had been one of the first in Britain to discover a mass market with his cheap and elegant earthenware. Until the appearance of Wedgwood most British pottery came from Holland at the cheap end, and from Germany and France for quality goods. A hundred years later Wedgwood and other British manufacturers were supplying the world.

The five towns of the Staffordshire pottery district were the main centres of the industry. By the second half of the nineteenth century firms like George L. Ashworth & Bros and J. & G. Meakin had built up a flourishing trade in cheap, durable, white earthenware. The latter, in particular, had a firm hold on the American market. Finer, more decorative work came from firms like Minton and Wedgwood, but generally there was not much originality or imagination in this area and a tendency to rely upon imitation of traditional or foreign designs. The willow pattern, which Thomas Minton had engraved for Spode, seemed to hold an unremitting fascination.[16]

Major firms were to be found outside the Potteries: J. & M. P. Bell & Company, for example, in Glasgow, employed 800 people in the 1860s, and the great firm of Doulton's originated in Lambeth. From 1815 to 1858, as Doulton & Watts, Henry Doulton, a pioneer in the use of steam-driven wheels, built up the firm with a mixture of frivolities, like the Toby jug and the practical and vital stoneware pipes which made the public health work of Edwin Chadwick and his successors possible. Employment by the firm at Lambeth grew from around 100 people in 1850 to 600 in 1878 and to around 4500 in 1905. Even such a well-established firm as this, however, felt the pull of the skills of the five towns and it opened a branch in Burslem in 1877.

A major area of expansion in the industry in the last quarter of the century was in sanitary ware. Thomas Twyford of an old Hanley pottery firm invented the all-earthenware water closet, which gradually replaced Bramah's eighteenth-century invention, the earth-closet, and, from then on, many of the firms developed in this area. Ashworth & Bros, Doulton & Company, J. & M. P. Bell all became major producers of lavatory fittings.[17] Just before 1914 fitted baths were becoming more commonplace, at least in new houses, and with them wash-basins and various other bathroom fittings. In most bedrooms, however, the traditional wash-stand with its ewer and basin remained.[18]

In 1850 the glass industry had only recently been freed from excise duties on glass which had held back its development. Birmingham was an important centre, with the firm of R. L. Chance, which had taken over the British Crown Glass Company of Smethwick in 1824. They concentrated on sheet, plate and optical glass, as well as on quality flint glass, while the cheaper, pressed-glass trade, producing tableware, became centred in Newcastle-upon-Tyne by the end of the 1850s. However, from the 1870s onwards, British glass companies found it very difficult to compete with foreign imports. An influx of Belgian tumblers and wine glasses badly hit the flint-glass trade between 1875 and 1886. Similar competition from Germany and Bohemia affected those manufacturers who sought a market for the ugly, fancy coloured glass vases and bowls that became so popular in the 1870s. By the 1890s large quantities of pressed-glass from the United States were reaching the market, followed by German and

Austrian wares. As a result several flint-glass manufacturers gave up the struggle, and abandoned the making of glass to become glass-cutters and finishers for foreign glass imported in a rough state.[19]

By the turn of the century the best glass chimneys for paraffin lamps came from Bohemia, but the lamps themselves were likely to be Birmingham-made, as were most brass candlesticks and gas fittings. Paraffin-lamp manufacturers had appeared there in the 1860s. William Gammon employed between 150 and 200 people in the 1870s, making table lamps and other tableware.[20] Among the largest by the end of the century, were Burroughes & Watts Ltd, who had branches in Manchester, London and Newcastle, as well as in Birmingham; Evered & Company Ltd, of Smethwick; Hodge & Company, and Joseph Lucas & Son, who were in Little King Street, Birmingham, and already specialised in cycle lamps. In addition there were numerous small firms specialising in some particular patent lamp. Joseph Lucas had first moved from cheap hollow-ware-making into lamp-making with the 'Tom Bowling' ship lamp in 1875. He produced his first cycle lamp in 1878.[21] Although the industry appears to have been, on the whole, relatively successful, there was considerable American competition.

In spite of the development of paraffin and gas, candles remained of considerable importance throughout the nineteenth century. Thanks to the French chemist Chevreul, candles had replaced the tallow dip by around 1830; he had pioneered methods in the decomposition of oils and fats. It was for the separation of coconut oil that William Wilson and a Mr Lancaster established the firm of Edward Price & Company in 1830 in Battersea. The company began producing stearic candles with a plaited wick (another French patent) in 1833. J. P. Wilson, one of the Company's chemists, made the major techno-logical breakthrough in the 1840s by discovering how to harden stearine, thus allowing candle-makers to draw on a whole variety of new raw materials – bone fats, skin fats, fish oils, greases recovered from other processes and palm oil.

American refinements of the candle-moulding machine encour-aged a trend towards large-scale factory production and Price's Patent Candle Company, as the firm had become in 1847 with a capital of £500,000, continued to dominate the field, and had its own cocoa-nut oil plantation in Ceylon. Until nearly the end of the century the firm was run by William and James Wilson.[22] After 1871 paraffin candles were introduced, and firms associated with the West Lothian shale oil industry, such as the Broxburn Oil Company and Young's Paraffin Light & Mineral Oil Company Ltd moved into candle-making.

Because paraffin wax was unstable, however, it did not suddenly, or entirely, replace stearine. In addition, since most candle firms were also involved in the manufacture of soap and lubricating oil, they were able to withstand the fall in demand, and in the early twentieth century Price's were still employing over 2000 workers in Battersea. There were forty London candle-makers listed in the Post Office Directory of 1895.

Pots and Pans

Birmingham, Wolverhampton and places between supplied most of the nation's jugs, kettles, pots, pans and baths in tinplate. Between 1850 and 1880 the amount of tinplate used, largely for cheap domestic utensils, increased sevenfold. The industry remained small scale: small tinplate-makers, few owning more than three or four mills, supplied small fabricators. Not until 1890 was ownership in tinplate production concentrated, when Richard Thomas & Company bought up cheaply many firms who were facing financial difficulties because of the United States' McKinlay tariff.[23] On the fabricating side, from the 1840s onwards, the replacement of handcutting and soldering by fly presses encouraged larger firms, and by 1860 there were some fourteen factories in Wolverhampton, employing about 1600 workers in all. Ryton & Walton was the largest firm in the trade; many of the other firms were established by craftsmen who had served their time with Ryton & Walton, for example Richard Perry and Henry Fearncombe.[24]

From the 1850s the making of tea and coffee pots from tin was being challenged by the development of the electro-plating process. Messrs Elkington's of Birmingham first applied the process of electro-deposit commercially, and their factory employed 1000 workers in 1860. But, as with so much of Black Country industry, the typical pattern was the small workshop with 'factors' acting as middle men and wholesalers, and indeed, largely organising the production among the small employers and 'garret-masters'.[25]

The industry in cast-iron hollow-ware – kettles, saucepans, pans – was centred on West Bromwich and Bilston. A. Kenrick & Sons, the most important firm, made use of the enamelling process which Thomas & Charles Clark of Wolverhampton had patented in 1839.[26] Demand grew steadily until the 1890s, when a number of factors began to affect the industry. The introduction of gas stoves required lighter and less substantial pans of wrought iron, most of which were supplied from Germany. Cheap enamelled hollow-ware from Germany was displacing both tinplate and cast-iron Black Country products from the 1890s onwards, and German aluminium hollow-ware followed hard on its heels.

For cutlery the consumer looked to Sheffield, even if the knife blade might be stamped with a London name, and here again the small workshop proliferated. To hand-forge knives two men would work together, the maker and his 'butty' who operated a heavy double-handed hammer. From the forger's workshop the table knife would go to the grinder's shop, where a number of grinders would probably be hiring power and wheels from the workshop owner. From there the knife blade went to the handler, who used horn, ivory or pearl. Developments in machinery pushed more of the cutlery industry into factories in the second half of the nineteenth century, though Messrs Greaves' Sheaf Works had been the first factory in 1823 in which the whole process, from steel-making to the finished article, was undertaken.[27] Most of the largest firms grew from work-shops established in the late eighteenth century or even earlier, for example Messrs Joseph Rodgers & Sons could be dated back to John Rodgers's workshop of 1724, but traditional hand-making of cutlery persisted up to the First World War. The average 'factory' probably had no more than half-a-dozen workers at the turn of the century. Horn and ivory handles were giving way to factory-made substitutes, and the American innovation of the trip hammer had increased the output of table knives by two men twenty-fold.[28] Factors played a crucial role in organising the numerous 'little masters', supplying the steel, purchasing the finished goods and probably providing credit, though some cutlers would sell directly to the market, undercutting larger manufacturers. Even with the growth of a factory system sub-contracting continued to 'small masters', who employed their own men, and provided them with tools and paid for the power.

Large firms were increasingly significant by the early twentieth century: Messrs Joseph Rodgers & Sons, Messrs Harrison Bros & Hounson, Messrs James Dixon & Son, Messrs Walker & Hall and Messrs Mappin & Webb were among the best known. All of them, however, faced a big threat from German competition in the domestic market. In Germany better organisation and the more rapid replace-ment of handworking by machine methods meant a steady rise in their exports of cheap cutlery. Imports of German cutlery to the United Kingdom rose in value from £78,000 in 1907 to £120,000 five years later.[29]

Fenders and fire irons were likely to come from the Black Country around Dudley and Wolverhampton, with many ornamental fire-places and stoves coming from central Scotland. The Carron Iron Company, along with other companies in the Falkirk area, specialised in these. That indefatigable adviser of the young, Mrs C. S. Peel, however, particularly recommended Leeds grates, from Messrs Teale.[30]

Cleaning

To keep clothes, house and self clean an increasing choice of soap products was available. In the thirty years after 1853, when the excise duty of 3d per lb. was repealed, the soap industry was transformed. The change came not so much on the technical side, but in marketing, though early in the nineteenth century chemical discoveries by Leblanc and Chevreul had revolutionised production techniques. At the beginning of the period the striking feature of the industry was the limited, local nature of its markets. Wm. George & Sons of Widnes, established in 1855, did not sell their product much beyond Lancashire. R. C. Hudson, established in West Bromwich since 1837, would not sell Hudson's Dry Soap Powder beyond the Midlands. John Knight, who had been in Silvertown since 1817, and A. & F. Pears, established in 1789, who set up a factory in Isleworth in 1862, served the south east, with others. Joseph Watson & Son of Leeds, which developed from the trade in fat and home-made tallow, and moved into candles and then tallow soap, had a major part of the Yorkshire market.

The man who changed all this was William Hesketh Lever, who determined to make his well-advertised, wrapped and branded Sunlight soap a national product. Unlike most contemporary soap, it was made largely from tallow, which gave a good lather. His output of 3000 tons of soap in 1886 from his small factory in Warrington had risen to over 15,000 tons by the time the firm moved to Port Sunlight in 1889. Thereafter, output rose by 3–5000 tons per annum. Five years later in 1894, when Lifebuoy soap was introduced, Lever Bros Ltd was set up, with authorised capital of £1,500,000. Their competitors had to follow this pattern. A. & F. Pears had become a limited liability company in 1892 to facilitate expansion, with capital of £810,000.

Competition between companies battling for a national market, by breaking into new areas, became fierce and bitter, with massive sums spent on advertising, singing the miraculous powers of Perfection, produced by Joseph Crosfield & Sons of Warrington or of Watson's

Matchless Cleaner. To rival Lever's Lifebuoy soap Crosfield's had their own brand, Eureka. When Lever brought in Vim in 1904, Crosfield's Clitto followed, though less successfully, as did their Feather Flakes to match Lux. Another response to a falling home market and to what was seen as excessive competition was to seek to eliminate the competition. Lever Bros attempted to form a soap trust linking Gossage of Widnes, Watson of Leeds, Crosfield of Warrington, Hodgson & Simpson of Wakefield, Ogston & Tennant of Glasgow, Jones of Liverpool, Thomas Bros of Bristol, Barrington of Dublin and two London companies, Cook and Vinolia, with Lever. The public outcry at the creation of this monopoly was such that the 1906 attempt had to be publicly abandoned. However, within five years a controlling interest had been obtained by Lever in all these firms, bar Gossage and Crosfield, and even in these last two cases an arrangement was worked out with Brunner Mond, who bought their firms in 1911. By 1914 another twenty firms had been absorbed by Lever Bros.

Soap powder, with its much improved cleaning action, made its appearance at the end of the century, and in 1907 Crosfield & Sons obtained the patent rights to the German invention of powder with a bleaching agent, with the registered name of Persil. It had already been rejected by the Hull firm of Reckitt & Sons, and took time to become accepted.[31] Isaac Reckitt & Sons were, however, the source of many other accessories for cleaning and finishing. This Quaker partnership had grown as a spin-off from Hull's corn trade in the early 1840s, and by 1854 the firm's range included various starches, essential for stiff table linen and even stiffer collars, potato flour or Farina, arrowroot for invalids, laundry blue, black lead imported from Germany, and a not very successful washing paste. For a time the firm owned a biscuit works, but they sold this side of the business, which included the Osborne label, to Peek Frean & Company in 1866.[32] By the time the firm went public in 1888, as Reckitt & Sons Ltd, it had capital of £450,000 and entered a decade of rapid growth firmly based on starch, blue and black lead. In 1897 they purchased the patent for Heinrich Mach's starch, which was easier to iron on than their own product, and this led to the production of the long-lived and popular Robin brand. The well-advertised Zebra grate polish was introduced in 1890, when it replaced their older Diamond lead. American competition, which had always been a problem in this area, with Rising Sun stove polish and Sun Paste stove polish from Morse Bros, was eliminated by buying out the British agency of H. G. Chancellor.[33]

Despite their rejection of Persil, like so many of the most successful companies, an openness to new ideas and products was a feature of

Reckitt & Sons. They brought a new liquid metal polish from Australia to replace older pastes, and early in the twentieth century Brasso
was manufactured to ease the lot of the lamp polishers. To ensure
success, rival firms like the Bluebell Polish Company of Fulham, the
Shinio Polish Company of Liverpool and the Mepo Manufacturing
Company of Newcastle were bought out. Reckitt's did the same with
washing blue, and in 1912 moved into boot and furniture polish with
Cherry Blossom and Mansion, which were produced by the Chiswick
Polish Company, which Reckitt's owned jointly with Mason Bros of
Chiswick. The company's response to competition was to buy up
rivals, and between 1903 and 1912 at least eleven major firms were
bought out, together with other smaller ones.

A major rival was the Norwich firm of Jeremiah Colman, another
Quaker establishment. In the 1850s Francis Reckitt had been complaining of competition: 'Colman had brought out his Rice Starch. He
is offering it at 40/- a cwt. He braggs [sic] a great deal of it.'[34] Colman's
strongest line was, of course, mustard, but they had other related products. In 1898 Reckitt's, Colman's and a third firm, Keen, Robinson
& Company, considered amalgamation. Nothing came of the proposals, though Colman's bought Keen, Robinson's in 1903, and from that
year Reckitt's and Colman's co-operated in joint trading ventures
abroad.

To satisfy the demands of the possession-conscious Victorians many
small firms up and down the country flourished in the last half of the
nineteenth century. Since the working-class parlour, whenever possible, modelled itself on the middle-class drawing-room, a great range
in quality and price was needed. Although the remembered firms and
the survivors tended to be those which kept quality as part of their
business as well as widening their range at the cheaper end of the
market, there were many small, local firms, rarely looking beyond
their narrow regional market. Neither furniture nor other fittings
became dominated by a few large firms, for alongside these firms that
were growing rapidly and developing into household names were
numerous, often short-lived, workshops and factories ever-conscious
of a fickle, popular taste. None the less, here too the long-term trend
was towards factory production. Three-quarters of those working in
the furniture trades were in factories by 1907. In the Sheffield cutlery
trades the small workshop had all but disappeared by the 1890s, and
by 1907 some 95 per cent of the labour force worked in factories.

14. The Nation Entertained

The cheap press, with its ubiquitous correspondents and historians of all contemporary ranks and occurrences in the body politic, has transformed the severely domesticated Briton of both sexes, of all ages, who belonged to a bygone generation, into an eager, actively enquiring, socially omniscient citizen of the world, ever on the outlook for new excitements, habitally demanding social pleasure in fresh forms.

T. H. S. Escott, *Social Transformations of the Victorian Age* (1897).

The sixty years after 1850 saw a flourishing of museums, art galleries, public libraries, of temperance cafés and of halls for 'improving' public meetings. There were opportunities for healthy recreation like swimming or cycling or for spectating at football matches and race meetings. Yet, in spite of all of these attractions, the public house remained central to the social life of the mass of the population. In 1852 G. R. Porter declared that 'no person above the rank of a labouring man or artisan, would venture to go into a public house to purchase anything to drink', but in this at any rate the example of the middle class was rejected by the working class.

The Drink Trade

For a quarter of a century after 1850 consumption of beer rose, to an incredible 34·4 gallons per head per annum in 1876. A decrease in the next decade, perhaps due to temperance pressure, perhaps to economic pressure, was followed by fluctuating growth. What caused the fluctuations is not entirely clear. Some have suggested that there was a political factor which created 'psychological' pressures. In 1915 D. H. Robertson suggested that perhaps 'the consumption of alcohol is more subject than that of other things to the psychological influences of hope and excitement, and is a better index of mental temperature than (as Mr. Beveridge, for instance, is inclined to treat it) of genuine prosperity'.[1] There does seem to be a connection between the election of a Conservative Goverment (the drinking Party) and rising consumption from 1886 to 1892 and from 1895 to 1905, and the election of a Liberal Government (the temperance Party) and falling consumption from 1892 to 1895, and after 1906.[2]

Beer was sold in licensed beer houses, the creations of the Beer Act of 1830, in public houses along with wines and spirits, in many music halls and, increasingly, in working men's clubs. In spite of a near orgy following the Beerhouse Act of 1830, which took the tax off beer and allowed any ratepayer to purchase a licence from the local exciseman for the price of two guineas and to sell beer, free from magisterial control, the experiment was allowed to continue. Sydney Smith, as the Act came in, wrote of its deleterious effects: 'Everyone is drunk. Those who are not singing are sprawling. The sovereign people are in a beastly state.' None the less the beer house flourished, and by 1869 there were no fewer than 49,130 of them. In that year new beer–house licences were brought under the control of the magistrates. However, special protection was given to the pre-1869 beer houses and they continued to thrive, though their number had fallen to 30,311 by 1896.[3]

The Beerhouse Act had the effect, in some areas, of encouraging local J. Ps. to increase the number of public-house licenses, so that they could have some control over who ran them and what went on. As a result the number of fully licensed houses rose from around 50,000 in 1830 to about 70,000 in 1872. The Licensing Act of that year reflected Liberal, if not popular, concern with alcoholic consumption, and the number of licensed public houses remained fairly static from then until the turn of the century, when the activities of magistrates helped to reduce numbers.

From the eighteenth century onwards public houses had increasingly become tied to particular brewers. Publicans tended to look to brewers for credit facilities, which were often granted on condition that the publican would only sell that brewer's beer. Indeed, one of the aims of the Beerhouse Act of 1830 was to free beer from the tyranny of the brewers. Tied houses were probably more common in London than in the provinces, because of the cost of London property, but even in 1892 brewers owned only 2,100 out of over 7,000 London public houses.[4]

The 'brewers' wars' of the 1880s and 1890s transformed the public houses. As competition increased brewers took over more and more licensed property and the pub was revolutionised. Pubs were rebuilt and remodelled with a lavishness of gilding, decorated glass, painted tiles, mosaic floors, wrought metal lamps and elaborate mahogany fittings that immediately made the pubs of the previous twenty years, let alone the early Victorian gin palaces, seem dowdy and second rate.[5]

As one company bought tied houses, so others followed to ensure their share of the market. The price of licensed property doubled and trebled in a crazy spiral to peak in 1898. Legislation to limit licenses only encouraged the trend.

It was the growth in size of a number of brewing companies that helped to trigger off the 'brewers' wars'. Although, even at the end of the nineteenth century, there were few counties without their breweries offering something with a special local refinement, the trend towards size was marked throughout the nineteenth century, and even in 1800 much of the London trade was concentrated in the hands of a dozen great enterprises. The process of concentration was also taking place in the other major brewing centres of Dublin, Bristol, Burton upon Trent, Norwich and Edinburgh. The growth of national as opposed to regional markets encouraged further amalgamation particularly from the middle of the nineteenth century, when the lighter Burton ales broke into the London market. From the 1880s onwards technical and scientific improvements favoured larger units.[6]

Undoubtedly, a major turning point came in 1886 when Arthur Guinness, Son & Company of Dublin, who were and remained the largest brewers, went public with a £6 million issue, oversubscribed many times. Ind Coope of Burton followed almost immediately, as did Allsopp's of Burton in February 1887, and over the next ten years many breweries went public. Small companies disappeared as the larger firms bought them out. Other firms amalgamated: Watney & Company Ltd, Combe & Company Ltd and Reid's Brewery Company Ltd, all major companies, were amalgamated in 1898. Four local family breweries in Newcastle were amalgamated as Newcastle Breweries Ltd in 1890. The scramble for tied houses (which was a factor behind many of the takeovers and amalgamations) and excessive speculation rebounded on many major firms when profits began to fall after the Boer War. Some important firms such as Allsopp's and Meux's made quite severe losses through over-commitment and had to be rescued by major reorganisation or amalgamation. Many others, including famous names like Bass, Whitbread, Worthington and Watney, Combe and Reid, had to write down their shares in the tighter situation during the years just before the First World War.

Guinness, with an annual output of 2·5 million barrels, dominated the market and the other leading firms were each producing around 0.5 million barrels. In spite of all the amalgamations, local loyalties ensured that many small breweries still survived to add to the total of 35 million barrels per annum. But whereas in 1839 there had been 48,636 licenced brewers, in 1914 there were only 3692.

Music halls were another important distribution point for alcohol, much condemned by the temperance reformers. In the 1860s half the takings of London's thirty odd music halls came from drink.[8] As the century progressed, however, drinking played a smaller and more discreet part in their proceedings. Working men's clubs, such as those of the Club and Institute Union, formed by Henry Solly in 1862, had been intended originally to offer an alternative to the public house for the working man in search of 'social enjoyment and the love of excitement', offering, with non-alcoholic beverages, music 'to purify and refine' instead of music 'used as a temptation to drinking and other vices'.[9] By the 1890s, however, most clubs were selling beer and, particularly in the industrial north, they offered a powerful rivalry to public houses.

The attachment to beer was, of course, largely English and mostly among the working class. Among the better-off in the south there was a taste for gin, preferably imported from Holland rather than the often noxious, London distilled varieties, though Messrs Burnett & Company of Vauxhall combined the production of reasonable gin with their trade in vinegar and bitters. Brandy, with or without soda, was also enjoyed by the well-to-do, the former imported from France, the latter made at any of scores of aerated and mineral water firms, like Messrs Beaufoy's & Company in south London, or by Schweppes, Perrier or Idris & Company. North of the border the siren vapours of whisky (still spelt whiskey) beckoned all classes, but it made little impact outside Scotland before the 1880s.

The problems of the French wine industry gave Scotch whisky its opportunity in England. First mildew and then phylloxera devastated French vineyards in the mid-nineteenth century. Wine and brandy prices soared as French wine production was halved. Sherry proved an inadequate substitute and whisky had its chance. The product itself was being altered: traditonal single malts from a confusing proliferation of small distilleries were giving way to the bland uniformity of blended whisky. The advantage of this was not only in taste but in quantity, since the more easily produced grain whisky could be mixed with the restricted malt whisky. Thomas Dewar in Perth and Alexander Walker in Kilmarnock had both been producing blended whisky, mainly for export, for decades, but it was the Canadian-born Scot, James Buchanan, who really broke into the London market with standardised blends in the 1880s. With shrewd marketing it made its way into the houses of the well-to-do and into the music-hall bars, replacing what someone recalled as 'the dreadful brass-cleaning concoctions' which masqueraded as whisky before the arrival of Buchanan's blends.[10] Others shared Buchanan's effective ability to publicise his own products like Thomas Dewar who moved from Perth High Street to London in 1887, and pioneered lavish advertising displays and sponsored sports. Later, in 1908, Tom Brown's Johnnie Walker advertisement was to show that others had learned the tricks of publicity, and Walker's, which had started in Kilmarnock in 1820 became the best-selling blend.

Like all alcohol, whisky consumption was vulnerable to price changes, and Lloyd George's 11s per gallon duty on spirit in his budget of 1908 contributed to a sharp fall in consumption. The fall was already under way before 1908, and altogether between 1900 and 1914 spirit consumption fell by 69 per cent. As in other areas of British industry the response of the whisky firms was the eradication of competition by price fixing and amalgamation. The industry was effectively dominated by three amalgamations, the Distillers' Company, the Buchanan–Dewar combine and Walker's, though the extent of oligopoly was effectively hidden from the public by a great variety of brand names.

Tea and Tobacco

The anti-drink movement had actively offered alternatives to the public house, but there were others. Street-sellers with their home-made ginger beer at 1d or ½d per glass were everywhere in Mayhew's time. At the Great Exhibition a major supplier was the firm that the Swiss, Jacob Schweppe, had established in London in the 1790s to manufacture soda water as a 'medicine' available through apothecaries. Generally the ginger-beer firms were small and local, and subject to the fluctuations of weather. They made little attempt to build wider markets, though Charles Booth reported that soda water and lemonade travellers, who were largely paid by commission, could earn 40s–50s per week over the year and one of whom in a hot summer week might 'make as much as £10 on his sales'.[11]

Tea and coffee were the favourite alternatives to public houses offered by teetotallers, though the temperance hotels and restaurants, such as those of Thomas Lamb in Scotland in the 1850s, were of a drabness that did not seriously pose a threat. More direct attempts at competition, such as workmen's coffee houses with bread, coffee and snacks which were tried in Dundee in 1853, or the 'dry pubs' which appeared in Leeds in 1867, had a limited success. However, throughout the 1860s, 1870s and 1880s the number of coffee houses and eating houses provided by both philanthropic and commercial interests grew. At the time of the Moody and Sankey evangelical crusades, Robert Lockhart opened shops in Liverpool and then in London, first to provide cocoa and then tea, all in the cause of temperance. Whenever possible Lockhart's coffee houses opened next door to a public house. In 1884 the Aerated Bread Company first offered tea to its bread customers. By the 1890s the A. B. C. was the commuter's oasis throughout central London. Pearce Refreshment Rooms ('Pearce and Plenty') followed for the poorer class of Londoner, and later the Express Dairy Company opened some tea shops. Later still, in 1894, the firm of Salmon & Gluckstein who had been supplying the exhibition trade with tea since 1887, opened the first Lyons' tea shop at No. 213 Piccadilly.[12] By 1910 there were ninety-eight Lyons' tea shops in London.

It is doubtful if smoking was approved of by everyone in the new tea-rooms, but such was its popularity that there would have been no way of stopping it. Yet, as late as the 1840s, smoking was still generally frowned upon. A change of attitude came in the next decade when tobacco attained a growing popularity. By the 1860s the complaint was that men were smoking everywhere 'whilst they are occupied in working or hunting, riding in carriages, or otherwise employed'.[13] The 'cutties' and 'churchwardens' were likely to be of clay, selling for maybe 6d each. There were numerous clay-pipe manufacturers. Milo in the Strand and Inderwick & Company in Leicester Square were well known in London. Some of the largest firms were the Glasgow ones of W. White & Son and D. MacDougall & Company. The problem with the clay pipe was that it was so easily broken, so the coming of the briar pipe in the 1860s increased the pipe's popularity. Most briars came from Europe, and British firms generally did no more than mount and fit the imported bowls.[14] The cigar also increased in popularity in the 1860s, and there were numerous small cigar-making workshops in the East End of London, though the best were imported from Cuba. With the growth of demand for tobacco, major firms, fomerly catering for a local market, began to expand to cover the wole country. By 1860, for example, the firm of Wills based its sales policy on a national market, and others, like John Player & Sons of Nottingham followed suit.

The real potential for expansion proved to be in cigarettes. Ten or a dozen firms, such as Wills, Player, Lambert & Butler (London) Ogden, Hignett Bros, Cope Bros (Liverpool), Stephen Mitchell & Son (Glasgow) produced between a quarter and a third of the industry's output by the 1870s. Wills pulled ahead in the 1880s, when they obtained monopoly rights to the Bonsack cigarette machine in 1883. In 1890 cigarettes made up only 0·5 per cent of U.K. tobacco sales, but a decade later this had grown to over 12 per cent.[15]

A new element entered the industry in September 1901, when James Buchanan Duke bought Ogden's. Duke, the 'Napoleon of American Tobacco', having conquered the American tobacco industry, now turned to the United Kingdom. He hardly endeared himself to the British companies by the brash manner in which he approached his 'victims'. They responded by setting up the Imperial Tobacco Company, linking Wills, Players, Lambert & Butler, Stephen Mitchell & Company, Hignett Bros and a dozen lesser firms. A bitter advertising war between Imperial and the American Tobacco Company was launched. It was Duke's Moscow, if not his Waterloo, and in 1902 he sold off Ogden's to Imperial and withdrew from the United Kingdom, leaving the field to the British firms. But the two 'rivals' combined in the British American Tobacco Company to control the export trade. With Duke gone, the Imperial Tobacco Company in 1903 controlled about 47 per cent of the British market. Independents like Cope, Hill, Carreras and Phillips survived, but by a fairly generous policy of bonus on sales Imperial steadily increased its share of the market, though it generally avoided the public hostility which the trust tactics of its American associate attracted.

Sport

The changes in work patterns that came with the advance of industri-alisation brought with them a massive transformation of leisure activi-ties. Only with the coming of regular hours of work, particularly with the discipline of the factory, could the idea of regular hours of leisure and specific leisure activities emerge. With this came a view of leisure as not just a rest from work, but as an activity that could be pursued for its own sake. As a result, free-time activities broke their connec-tions with work and traditional communities. The village festival mostly disappeared. The works outing, while still carried on by those who valued paternalism, was secondary to the family outing or the mixed excursion, whether by train or charabanc. Just as the pub had changed and the Masons Arms or the Bricklayers Arms had no more significance for the mason and the bricklayer than had the Cat and Fiddle or the Duke of Wellington, where men from all kinds of manual labour could socialise, so leisure activities were open to all professions or communities. As a result commercial interests became involved in providing opportunities for leisure activities.

Initially there had been little to fill this 'lump of concentrated nothingness' as Sebastian de Grazia has called the leisure time that industrial workers found themselves faced with in the second half of the nineteenth century.[16] Traditional rural pursuits like cock-fighting, badger-baiting, or hunting had either been curbed or had little relevance to urban dwellers. Only boxing or unregulated fighting relieved the monotony between public-house visits. There were few open spaces in the growing cities and sabbatarianism ensured that there was little light relief. The Archbishop of Canterbury had effectively blocked band concerts in London's parks in the 1860s. Change came in the 1870s as a result of middle-class concern at the dangers of an idle, drunken working class at leisure.

There was particular concern about the position of the adolescent, who was being identified by the second half of the nineteenth century as part of a specific group. For a long time Churches had been the most important providers of free-time activities, second only to the pub. With their bible classes, institutes, social evenings and such, they took a lead in seeking to cater for adolescents. Church organisations began to form football teams, like Villa Cross Wesleyan Chapel's 'Aston Villa', Christ Church Bolton's 'Bolton Wanderers', St Domingo's Church Sunday School's 'Everton' and St Andrew's Sunday School, West Kensington's 'Fulham'. Public school men and graduates carried an enthusiasm for football to the working class and found a response. By the 1880s industrial teams like 'Royal Arsenal', from among the Woolwich Munitions workers, were making an appearance.[17] Initially football was seen as a participatory sport for working men, but the organisers soon found that games were also attractive to spectators. The success of many of the clubs produced its own problems. Intense competitiveness, with the growth of league competition, meant that clubs sought to attract and hold the best players, which encouraged thoughts of payment. Good matches attracted spectators and any club required playing grounds. Wealthy philanthropists were less willing to provide the funds for such activities, especially when it was difficult to exert control over their membership and their activities. Stephen Yeo has documented the pattern in Reading Football Club, which after a number of poor seasons first discussed professionalism in 1894, when the committee recommended some payment to players for their 'loss of time'. After a struggle and a breakaway by those who, for a variety of reasons, wished to cling to amateur sport, Reading Football Club turned professional. Once that decision had been taken the club needed a new ground which could attract sufficient spectators to meet the new costs. Although Elm Park was acquired by private philanthropy, the cost of maintaining and running it brought pressure for the setting up of a limited liability company, a step taken in 1897. Once this happened the main concern was with getting as many people as possible through the turnstiles. On the other hand, it was not an investment from which shareholders could expect either large or certain returns, and there was still a belief in the moral and social value of the game.[18]

As Yeo has shown, similar financial problems were to force other voluntary organisations, such as athletic, cycling and cricket clubs, to seek new approaches and methods, particularly to attract paying spectators. Working men could spend small regular sums to attend games and sports much more easily than they could expend a substantial lump sum for the increasing high membership fees of a club.

Although almost three-quarters of a million amateur players participated in the game, by the 1890s football was well established as a spectator sport. The first cup final at Crystal Palace in 1895 attracted 45,000 spectators: by 1913 the number had risen to 120,000.[19] Average attendance at the matches of leading clubs rose from around 7000 in 1891 to 30,000 by 1911.[20] Commercial interests now realised that the most energy people wanted to expend in their leisure time was a hoarse shout from the terracing or enclosures, and so developed football stadiums in response.

A new consciousness of the spectator also arose in the sport that had long linked the upper and lower classes – horse-racing. Traditional race meetings up and down the country began to attract crowds from beyond their locality, especially when the railways simplified and cheapened travel. The first enclosed racecourse to charge fees to everyone was Sandown Park in 1875. From the 1880s onwards companies began to build enclosed courses at centres throughout the country: one was opened at Derby in 1880, at Leicester in 1884, at Hamilton in 1887, at Nottingham in 1892, at Haydock in 1898 and at Newbury in 1906. More meetings switched from mid-week holidays to Saturday afternoons to catch the largest possible working-class crowd, though entry charges of half-a-crown, as at Sandown, must have limited the numbers.[21]

Music Halls

For those who wanted their leisure time to be even more effortless there was the music hall. Between the 1850s and 1880s many public houses were converted into music halls. There was an earlier tradition of public-house musical and theatrical entertainment at places like the Eagle Tavern (of nursery-rhyme fame) in the City Road which was operating in the late 1830s, but after the Theatre Act of 1843 such places were forced to make a choice between becoming legitimate theatres under the power of the Lord Chamberlain and without a drink licence in the auditorium, or becoming tavern concert rooms, without the right to stage plays.

The first custom-built hall in London was the Canterbury built by Charles Morton in Lambeth Marsh in 1852. He had been influenced by Evans's Music Hall in Covent Garden and earlier had run 'sing-songs' and 'free and easys' at various public houses. To 'men only' nights on Saturdays and Mondays were added 'ladies' Thursdays' and such was their popularity that Morton had a hall built which could accommodate 1700 people at 3*d* a head for admission, and 6*d* for a refreshment ticket for drink. He opened a second hall in 1856, and in 1861 built and opened the first 'Oxford' in Oxford Street, which was burned down some seven years later.[22] Halls had already appeared in provincial towns, such as the Surrey Music Hall in Sheffield in 1851, the People's Hall in Manchester in 1853, and the Casino in Leeds sometime during the 1850s. Such halls offered something different from the freak shows of two-headed cows and Tom Thumb, which had pulled thousands into places like the Egyptian Hall in Piccadilly in the 1840s. Some, like the Parthenon in Liverpool which was one of the earliest, grew from Bianchi's Waxworks. Morton even built an art gallery next to the Canterbury which offered not only paintings by Maclise, Frith and others, but also made available newspapers and periodicals. He had, however, to pick his way through a minefield of legislation relating to stage plays, and not until 1912 was the issue of sketches and one-act plays in music halls finally settled.

From the 1870s onwards building regulations took their toll of many of the older pubs-*cum*-halls, and the traditional music hall became much more theatre-like in appearance. As early historians of the halls wrote of the West End:

Hitherto the halls had been almost exclusively patronised by a class composed mainly, if not exclusively, of the lower and middle grade of society, that huge section of the public comprehensively summed up in the term 'the people'. Now, however, wealth, fashion and *ton* became attracted to these handsome 'Palaces' of amusement.[23]

The coming of the London County Council in 1889 brought regulation of the shows' content, with a purging of offensive 'gags' and indecent songs, so that by 1895 working men could 'take their wives and daughters to places which, six years ago, they would have hesitated to enter with their own family'.

During the 1890s music halls began to fall into the hands of combines, though these generally were centred on some old-established family businesses. H. E. Moss started in his father's hall in Greenock, and ran another hall in Edinburgh after 1875. In 1892 he built the first of many halls called the Empire in Edinburgh. Richard Thornton of South Shields had started a pub music-room in 1884. He built a full music hall in 1885 and in 1898 linked up with Moss to develop a chain of Empires throughout Scotland and England. In 1899 they reached London, and the various companies were amalgamated into Moss Empires Ltd with a share capital of around £1 million. Oswald Stoll, who inherited Liverpool's Parthenon Music Hall, took over other halls in the 1890s. He moved to London in 1901, and three years later opened the Coliseum in rivalry to Moss Empires' Hippodrome. He eventually linked up with his rivals and was for a time managing director of Moss Empires. Other lesser chains, like Barrasford's and MacNaghton's, spread in different parts of the country.[24]

The first stars of mass entertainment, complete with agents on 10 per cent, made their appearance with the Great Macdermott, whose rendering of G. W. Hunt's 'We don't want to fight' gave the word 'jingoism' to the language in 1878; with James Fawn's satire which probably only the 'unrespectable' working class fully appreciated, 'If you want to know the time ask a policeman'; with the universal sentimentality of 'My Old Dutch' from Albert Chevalier. In the Edwardian era new names, like Lauder, Robey and Formby joined older ones like Marie Lloyd and Dan Leno. Many of them welcomed the regular employment which the chains offered them, but resisted the increasing attempt to tie them to particular groups of halls.

Also during the 1880s Barnum's innovations in the circus began to be felt in the music hall, and music-hall proprietors and circus showmen, always on the look out for novelty to retain the interests of a fickle public, developed the new moving picture show. The first public presentation of moving pictures was in February 1896 by the Lumière Brothers at the Regent Street Polytechnic, and they caught on rapidly. The Alhambra Music Hall commissioned Robert Paul to film the 1896 Derby,[25] and in the following year a Mr Cheetham was offering holiday makers in Rhyl a 'living picture' show including the latest Blackburn Rovers versus West Bromwich football match.[26] For a time travelling showmen and circus groups were the main people to show films, then music halls took them up and films were added to the end of music hall shows. An increasing number of films were imported from the United States, making the problems of distribution more complex. Companies began to appear which imported the films and showed them on a regular basis in halls hired in different towns. In the north of England in the first years of the twentieth century, there were companies like Pringle's North American Pictures, which combined the know-how of a Huddersfield variety artist with the expertise of a representative of Edison's Electric Pictures, and New Century Pictures, which was run by a Bradford music hall proprietor and a Birmingham showman. The first custom-built cinema appeared in Colne in Lancashire in 1908, and the number grew when, following some disastrous fires, the Cinematographic Act of 1910 insisted on separate fire-proof projection rooms.[27] These required much more capital and brought in new investors. An important distribution company, the Provincial Cinematograph Theatres Ltd, linked the old leisure industry with the new under the chairmanship of Sir William Bass,[28] but in other cases pioneering showmen were able to adapt. Albany Ward, who owned twenty-nine cinemas in England in 1914 and George Green, who controlled a substantial part of the Scottish distribution network, both came from fairground backgrounds. In other cases music halls were converted to cinemas, and, although a lively music-hall tradition persisted beyond 1914, the cuckoo in the music–hall nest was already beginning to do its nasty work.

Cycling

The cinemas were to open up broader vistas for many of Britain's population, but before then a wider world beyond the city's boundaries had been opened up by the bicycle. In 1868 Rowley B. Turner had persuaded the Coventry Sewing Machine Company to build some 'boneshakers', which he had seen while acting as the company's agent in Paris. In 1869 the Coventry Machinists' Company was formed and under the foreman James Starley, many improvements were made to the primitive pedal-less 'boneshaker'. Starley was later to set up in business on his own and then in partnership with William Hillman, producing the light all-metal 'Ariel' ordinary, as the 'penny farthing' was known. In 1874 twenty firms were making these far from ordinary, 'ordinaries' and five years later, Henry Sturmey, an important publicist of the bicycle, identified about sixty firms. Coventry, with its early start, became an important centre. George Singer opened his successful firm there in 1874, and in 1878 James Starley's nephew, J. K. Starley, started the firm which was to develop into the Rover Cycle Company. Most of the firms were small, back-shed affairs – only about a thousand people in the whole of the United Kingdom were engaged in cycle manufacture in 1881. Within three or four years the situation had changed completely and between three and five thousand people were employed in the industry in Coventry alone.

An important breakthrough came when H. J. Lawson developed the 'safety' cycle in Brighton in the late 1870s. This model was initially promoted by George Singer, but it was J. K. Starley's 'Rover which established the safety cycle commercially in the mid-1880s, by way of Starley & Sutton of Coventry. Many cycle firms remained small, but a few market leaders began to emerge, principally in the Midlands, where in 1891 71 per cent of the 8300 workers in the industry were employed. The Coventry Machinists' Company, which became the 'Swift' Cycle Company in 1891, was producing 35,000 machines per annum in 1896. The New Premier Cycle Company employed 600 people and had an output of 20,000 cycles per annum between 1893 and 1895. These firms were both in Coventry, where another future market leader, Thomas Humber & Company of Beeston in Nottinghamshire, opened a factory in 1886. There were at least thirty-five cycle-makers in Coventry by 1892.[29] In Birmingham, William Brown, who in 1877 had been the first to use ball bearings in cycles, was employing between six and seven hundred workers by 1889 and twice as many at the height of the 'safety' boom five years later. By then there were over 150 makers of complete cycles in Birmingham, and the number doubled over the next three years.[30] Frank Bowden opened his factory in Raleigh Street, Nottingham in 1887, and expanded rapidly, as did about fifty other companies in the boom of 1896. The firm which claimed to be the largest in the world was in Barton, near Hull – F. Hopper & Company was producing 1000 bicycles a week in 1907, having started with two a week in 1881.[31] As they did so often with new ideas, American firms moved quickly into the market, but wooden rims which warped, mud-guards that were too short, and poor quality tyres all created suspicion of the American product, and British firms, in contrast, achieved a reputation for quality. None the less foreign competition plus over-production did bring an end to the boom from 1897–8 onwards, and by 1912 only about 30 per cent of the firms listed in 1896 still survived. The first effect was a sharp reduction in prices. Rudge-Whitworth led the way, by reducing the 'Standard' from £20 to twelve guineas in July 1897.[32] Eventually other companies followed their lead; by 1908 Rudge-Whitworth were offering a £5 15s machine. Many perceptive firms had responded to falling sales by moving into motor-car production. Humber, Triumph, Rudge, Swift and Riley to name but a few, combined cycle and car production. Early in the century Rover abandoned cycle production entirely.[33]

The motor industry had appeared in Britain in 1896 when the British Motor Syndicate, a group led by H. J. Lawson of the 'safety' bicycle, decided to take up some well-established French developments. Between 1901 and 1905, 221 car-building firms were founded. Many had a brief and transitory existence and only twenty-two of these firms still survived by 1914. Humber was the largest in 1906, producing 1000 cars in that year; only the Argyll Company in Scotland. formed in 1899 but forced into liquidation in 1907, came near this with 800 cars. Of the others only Rover and Daimler produced more than 500 cars in 1906. Mass production methods came when the Ford Motor Company of the United States opened an assembly plant in Trafford Park, Manchester in 1911, selling cars at £135–£200. In 1913 Ford was the market leader, producing over 6000 cars, twice as many as Wolseley and Humber, four times as many as Austin or Singer. By 1914 100,000 people were employed in the industry.[34]

Excursions

It was, however, the train, and particularly the excursion train, that introduced most workers to a world beyond their own. Thomas Cook's successfully organised excursion for temperance supporters from Leicester to Loughborough in 1841 publicised the commercial value of excursions, and Cook and others branched out in the following years. Rowland Hill offered the first seaside excursion on the Brighton line in 1843. Most railway companies saw the advantage of mass travel. Small, fashionable resorts, formerly confined to the upper and middle classes, now were opened up to the masses. By the mid 1840s thousands of third-class travellers were making their way from Fleetwood station to the beaches of Blackpool a few miles away.[35] Naturally, the sedate and the respectable protested, but commercial interests, – the shopkeepers, the publicans and the potential landladies – all saw the railway as a necessary prerequisite for the development of their resort.

The Great Exhibition brought a dramatic expansion of cheap outings when the railways carried three-quarters of a million trippers from the north of England to view the wonders of the Crystal Palace, with Thomas Cook alone organising 165,000 excursionists from Yorkshire. By the time of the Paris Exposition of 1867 it was possible to buy a package-tour week in Paris for 30s. Even ordinary rail travel became cheaper when after 1871, the Midland Railway Company provided third-class travel at 1d per mile on all trains, abolished second class and made first class the former second-class price. Cheap package holidays were well established by the 1880s and 1890s through organisations such as the Cyclists' Touring Club, the Co-op Holiday Association, or through agents like Frame's and Sir Henry Lunn's. By the 1890s football supporters' trains were being run on a Saturday afternoon.

Seaside resorts gained most from the arrival of cheap travel. Surprisingly, the same resorts generally succeeded in catering for the well-to-do as well as for the excursionists, though their views of what a holiday at the seaside was about differed dramatically. Brighton, the most popular of the South Coast resorts, by the 1850s had fine new hotels along the sea front, as well as a proliferation of cheap lodging houses. Since working-class holidays were confined to a short period in July or August, so there was plenty of opportunity for the better off to avoid the crowds. It is not always clear whose were the financial interests which provided the capital for rapid expansion. It seems likely that much of it was local and small scale. The 'rags to riches' story of progress from whelk stall to restaurant to guest house to hotel was certainly not unknown, but in the majority of cases accommodation was provided largely in response to demand, and people recognised that extra money could be made by moving the whole family into the kitchen and letting out the bedrooms.

Further encouragement to the expansion of holidays was given by Sir John Lubbock's 'Bank Holiday' Act of 1871. Millions took to road, rail and river upon 'St Lubbock's Day', when if the evidence is to be believed the sun always shone in the years before 1914. It is during the 1870s that the working-class season began to spread beyond a few summer week-ends. By the 1890s the holiday pattern had been adopted much beyond the 'respectable' artisan class. Even among the poorer subjects of the surveys of Booth and Rowntree, a holiday by cheap rail excursions was not unknown, and increasingly there were complaints of disorder and rowdiness among the excursionists.

Once at the seaside, entertainment was needed after the novelty of sand and sea had turned to discomfort. Piers, pioneered early in the century at Margate, Brighton and Southend to catch the steamers, were being transformed by the 1860s into places of fun, entertainment, and shelter from the rain, and attractions in their own right. By the start of this century few leading resorts were without a pier, and they competed with one another in their ornateness. Theatres, music halls, winter gardens, zoos, skating rinks and ballrooms followed. Special seaside entertainments developed with nigger-minstrel shows growing into pierrot troupes. Concert groups which had formerly entertained on the sands began to build permanent accommodation. Members of Catlin's White-Faced Pierrots, a well-known northern group, opened halls in Whitley Bay, Scarborough, Colwyn Bay and Llandudno early in the twentieth century. At the same time the stage-struck son of a Bradford stockbroker, Ben Popplewell, rejected 'respectability' for the delights of pierrot pavilions. By the turn of the century the seaside concert party could attract music-hall 'stars' for the summer season.

The provision of entertainment at the seaside gave endless scope for the enterprising. Alderman William Broadhead, a Manchester builder who had started organising 'swimming entertainments' in Blackpool in 1889, built up a theatre chain in the north west precisely for such entertaiment. He was responsible for the South Pier at Blackpool in 1893 and for the Tower in 1894. Other nameless men of enterprise brought the novelties of Coney Island to the English foreshore, with big wheels, electric buses, film shows and electric bulb displays, The need for entertainment meant that smaller enterprises flourished: the man with the donkey on the beach, the travelling Punch and Judy show, the photographer on the promenade, the sellers of doubtful concoctions masquerading as ice cream (nothing about ice-cream making seems to have been learnt from the United States), and chiropodists who took advantage of bare feet.[36] Until local authorities began to exercise some control, stalls and booths proliferated, not only on the beach but in any strategically placed front garden. One day on Blackpool beach in 1895, 316 standings were counted, including 62 fruit vendors, 52 ice-cream stalls, 21 oyster and prawn dealers and 36 photographers. Some of these would be local entrepreneurs, others were likely to be travelling showmen, dealers and stall holders.[37] Large and small commercial enterprises and, in a few cases, the whole community through municipal enterprises combined to separate the working man from his holiday pennies.

Even the Post Office recognised a market when, on 1 September 1894, they allowed private postcards to be printed and sent with a half-penny stamp. By the turn of the century well-known firms like Messrs Tuck & Sons, Valentine's of Dundee and Corkett's of Leicester were producing picture postcards. These firms had been producers of Christmas, birthday and Valentine cards for many decades and brought a wide range of skills to the art of the postcard; so much so that the decade before 1914 saw a postcard collecting 'craze'. It was by no means confined to holiday cards – one of the largest markets was in patriotic cards – but by early in the century the postcard with a view was a *sine qua non* of a holiday trip. Interestingly, the *risqué* quality, somehow associated with a seaside holiday, was perpetuated in the comic postcard by such masters of poster and advertising art as Phil May and John Hassall. Donald McGill, who was to epitomise the art of the vulgar postcard for half a century, was designing for the Pictorial Postcard Company among others from about 1904 onwards; the Mrs Grundys of this world were concerned about a proliferation of 'vulgar and semi-indecent postcards'.[38]

Another holiday feature that was *de rigueur* by 1914 was the snapshot. Since 1888, when George Eastman of New York marketed his simple Kodak camera, photography had become an increasingly popular hobby, especially among skilled artisans. Until then a real public desire to be immortalised first on plate and then on celluloid film had to be met by the professionals, but now clasping his Brownie the enthusiastic amateur could capture family moments on the beach.[39]

Reading Matter

Both for those who travelled and for those who stayed at home, in spite of the inadequacies of popular education, reading offered a measure of relaxation. Indeed, the first 'mass market' was recognised among the reading public, with song sheets, pamphlets, magazines and newspapers. Long before the Education Acts, enterprising publishers catered for a distinctly macabre public taste. James Catnach of Seven Dials was merely the best known of a variety of back-street publishers, who gave the public the details of the 'Red Barn Murders' and other sensational cases, to be followed by accounts of the trial, the hanging, the last dying speech and confession of the murderer. In the 1830s and 1840s publishers like John Clements, J. Cunningham, John Cleave and Edward Lloyd, based around Salisbury Square in London, were exploiting an obvious taste for the lurid and macabre with their production of neo-Gothic, penny-a-week novels such as *The Black Monk, The Ranger of the Tomb* and *The Feast of Blood*, alternatively entitled *Varney the Vampire*. The last was by one of the most productive of the Salisbury Square authors, James Malcolm Rymer. The complete mechanisation of bookbinding in the 1840s allowed such books to be produced inexpensively and rapidly.[40]

Gothic works gave way to crime fiction, and that in turn gave way to the highly sentimentalised domestic novel, epitomised by such titles as *Fatherless Fanny or the Mysterious Orphan*. 'Respectable' novels coming out in weekly parts had their parallels in the 'penny dreadfuls', like *Oliver Twiss, Nichelas Nicklebery* and *Martin Guzzlewit*. Like Catnach's publications of an earlier decade these were mainly hawked in the streets, particularly at week-ends, when after his Sunday morning shave the working man might have time to sit and read. The Salisbury Square publishers applied the same formula to the Sunday newspapers. *Bell's Weekly Dispatch* spiced strong, radical political comment with ample accounts of rapes, murders and seductions. It had first appeared soon after 1815, and was the model for most succeeding Sunday papers aimed at the working class. From the 1840s ownwards these increased in number with the appearance of *The News of the World* in 1843, published by J. B. Bell. It was sold for 3*d* , compared with *Bell's* 8½*d*, and the lower price met strong resistance from the newsagents, so that, like the penny dreadfuls, most Sunday papers were sold by street hawkers. Edward Lloyd, who had achieved notoriety with his parodies of Dickens, such as *The Penny Pickwick* edited by 'Bos', was another who turned to newspapers with his *Penny Sunday Times*, later *Lloyd's Weekly News*. G. W. M. Reynolds's *Weekly Newspaper* came in 1850, though it was more radical than pornographic.[41]

There was a number of other short-lived ventures. They had in common an attempt to cater for the better-off sections of the working class: the Chartist craftsmen who were anti-establishment, whether in state or church, and who wanted thier politics mixed with titillation to brighten an increasingly dull Sunday. The presentation of the papers was lively, with bold headlines and with fewer of the endless columns of print that characterised the daily papers. It was nearly half a century before the daily newspapers adopted these techiques.

The decreasing cost of production helped the more serious

publisher, catering for a slightly more educated market than the Salisbury Square school. The one and a half guinea three-decker novel was hardly suitable to carry around on a long train journey, and it was kept going largely by the circulating libraries, like C. E. Mudie's, which dated from 1842. It was for a travelling public that George Routledge started his Railway Library in 1848. He was not the first, by any means, to feel that the potentially profitable cheap end of the market should not be left to the penny dreadfuls. Archibald Constable, in the 1820s, had spoken of the possibilities of 'literature for the millions', and the Society for the Diffusion of Useful Knowledge had backed the improving publications of Charles Knight in the 1830s. With a studied indifference to the rights of authors, a number of publishers had issued cheap abridgements or reprints of all the most popular respectable authors. In 1847 Simms and McIntyre began their Parlour Library, with shilling volumes published each month, and it was this example that Routledge was following.

The Railway Library started with Fenimore Cooper's *The Pilot*, pirated from the United States, and included among its early volumes Jane Austen's *Sense and Sensibility* and *Pride and Prejudice*.[42] All this was in marked contrast to the typical offering of existing railway bookstalls, and arrived just in time to stock the shelves of W. H. Smith's new bookstalls, the first of which was opened at Euston towards the end of 1848. Before that time the main offerings were 'cheap French novels of the shadiest class, and mischievous trash of every description which no respectable bookseller would offer'.[43] Some of the volumes reached huge circulations. James Grant's *Romance of War* sold 100,000 copies, and when in 1852 Harriet Beecher Stowe's *Uncle Tom's Cabin* reached the market more than a score of publishers started producing it. Routledge sold more than half-a-million copies, and for a time in 1853 Routledge was sending out 10,000 copies a day to booksellers.[44]

In the fifty years after 1848 the Railway Library published 1300 titles. There were numerous competitors, such as the Travellers Library and the Run and Read Library, at prices ranging from 1s 6d to 6d. These were the 'yellowbacks', as they came to be called from about 1855 after Simms & MacIntyre's particularly eye-catching volumes. Smith's themselves embarked on a short-lived publishing venture in this area with Chapman & Hall. The main market was for novels, but cookery books like *Shilling Cookery for the Millions,* by Alexis Soyer of the Reform Club which was published in 1855, sold nearly a million copies in half a century. John Cassell tapped the market among self-improvers with his *Cassell's Popular Educator*, which came out in penny numbers from 1852 onwards. But, much to the chagrin of scores of Mrs Grundys, the 'dreadful' sensational or sporting novel or the thriller and detective stories that became as popular from the late 1870s onwards continued to flourish. Reputedly, by 1887, as many as two million copies per week of sensational novels in serial form were being sold, with individual titles selling from ten thousand to sixty thousand copies.[48] Little wonder that H. M. Inspector of Schools. Matthew Arnold, bemoaned the cheap literature, hideous and ignoble of aspect, like the tawdry novels which flare in the bookshelves of our railway stations'.

By no means all publishers either catered for or approved of the market in cheap books. More conservative publishers like Blackwoods and Longman's had their main market in the circulating libraries, with three-decker novels at 10s 6d a volume. For an annual subscription of a guinea, middle-class readers could obtain the latest Ouida, Charlotte Yonge or Marie Corelli novel from Mudie's or one of a number of other great circulating libraries. The libraries tyrannised publishers and sought to control taste and price. They successfully resisted numerous attacks until the 1890s, when Mudie's and Smith's, the two largest, overplayed their hand in setting prices and discount. The new six-shilling novel now became the norm with greater sales than were ever achieved when libraries dominated the market.[46] Marie Corelli's best-selling novel, *The Master Christian*, had a pre-publication printing of 75,000 in 1900.

The trend of prices was steadily downwards. Even the most respectable firms offered some of their copyright works in paperback. Macmillan issued Kingsley's works at 6d a volume in 1889 and distributed a million copies. Threepenny reprints of Bulwer-Lytton, Victor Hugo or Captain Marryat's works still loaded the railway bookstalls. In 1896 the enterprising George Newnes introduced his Penny Library of Famous Books, which in the first year sold an average of more than 96,000 copies per week.[47] There was no sign that the market was in any way saturated, though apparently the taste for fiction declined during the Boer War years.[48]

Although book publishers showed an awareness of a vast and ever-growing reading public, surprisingly the publishers of daily newspapers were much slower to tap it. Stamp duty and paper duty had, of course, kept the price of newspapers artificially high at 5d a copy, and circulations were minute. *The Times*, with an issue of 25,878 copies in 1845 was far ahead of any of its rivals, while the *Morning Chronicle* and the *Morning Herald* printed 5000 copies or less. Elsewhere a paper like the twice-weekly *Glasgow Herald* had an issue of 3654,

while *The Scotsman* in Edinburgh paid stamps for 2385 on its Monday
and Saturday issue days. Distribution of such papers was very limited.
Half the *Glasgow Herald*'s circulation was posted, while elderly
'runners' delivered to subscribers in the city and suburbs. Less than a
dozen booksellers took 210 copies altogether. These they either sold
or lent out at 1*d* per hour. There were only two street-sellers, one at
the station and one at the harbour.[49] In contrast, there were constant
complaints about the way in which 'irreligious and immoral literature'
circulated easily. It was claimed that one such periodical in Glasgow
had a circulation of 25,000 per week, while another had 12,500 and
that these were available from over 200 shops in the city.[50]

Change came in the early 1850s. The 1*s* 6*d* tax on advertisements
was abolished in 1853; as were the compulsory penny newspaper
stamp in 1855 and the paper duty in 1861. The coming of the telegraph
had resulted in the first news agency, the Electric Telegraph Company
of 1846 to collect and supply news as well as to transmit it. Julius
Reuter set up his foreign news agency in London in 1858; and when
the Government took over the telegraphs the Press Association was
formed by leading newspapers. There were also other major technological changes of great importance. The *Daily News*, for example,
started in 1846 with steam presses that produced between 5000 and
6000 copies an hour. When it was reduced in price to 1*d* in 1868 new
machines from the American Hoe Company produced 7500 copies an
hour. In 1873 six 'Walker' web presses gave production of 100,000
copies an hour.[51]

Fears that the end of the newspaper stamp would result in 'a swarm
of low-class papers . . . which would be filled with sedition, lewdness,
scandal and other forms of wickedness' were hardly realised with the
appearance in June 1855 of the *Daily Telegraph and Courier*, which
cost 1*d* in September of that year. At first a conscious effort was made
to do something new and to learn from the American example of bold
and attractive headlines. Door-to-door selling of the new cheaper
papers flourished briefly until the Hawkers' Act of 1859 put restrictions on this. Street selling did, however expand. But, although other
papers eventually followed the *Telegraph* in price, presumably hoping
thereby to capture a wider market, newspaper proprietors and editors
showed what can only have been a blind pomposity. All the morning
papers, in London and the provinces, set out to compete with *The
Times* in dullness. As Stanley Morison has written,

In 1860, 1870 and 1880 it was still assumed that the papers were
taken by earnest-minded seekers after news to whom search was

part of the discipline which they readily exacted from themselves. And the assumption was that the readers were interested above all in political news, political speeches and political leading articles.[52]

Even Cassell's evening paper, *The Echo*, which came out in December 1868 at the astonishing price of ½d, had all the respectability and the dullness of the morning dailies.

Attempts to produce something more popular came in 1881 with the halfpenny *Evening News*, and later with T. P. O'Connor's *Star*, launched in 1888. These, like most provincial presses in the 1880s, realised that for most readers sports news was more important than city news. Saturday football editions had become popular with provincial evening papers during the 1880s. Although the content lightened, the presentation remained fairly cautious, until W. T. Stead, taking over the *Pall Mall Gazette*, a staid London evening paper, hitherto edited with little imagination by John Morley, began to apply American techniques, with interviews, gossip columns and clear headlines.

At long last in the 1890s the 'new journalism', as Matthew Arnold called it, came to the morning papers. The *Morning* of 1892 had the 'sensational' innovation of news on the front page and display headlines, reflecting the American influence of its editor, Charles Ives. In all these experiments Alfred Harmsworth found the ideas for and the confidence with which to launch the *Daily Mail* in 1896, though even then, the early issues had advertisements, not news, on the front page. (Morning papers had to 'look' like *The Times* it was felt.)[53] None the less, in 1900, the *Mail's* circulation crossed the million mark. It was Arthur Pearson's *Daily Express* which brought the more dramatic presentation of news on the front page, and a blandness which gave the impression of being specially packaged for a stereotyped consumer. 'It will be the organ of no political party', wrote Pearson in the first leader, 'Nor the instrument of any social clique . . . Its editorial policy will be that of an honest Cabinet Minister . . . Our policy is patriotic; our policy is the British Empire.' From the start the optimism that was to become the hallmark of the *Express* was there: 'We will tell you the comedy of life, putting its minor tragedies in the background', it announced.[54] Like the *Mail*, the *Express*, when it did take a political stance, tended to offer a crude chauvinism.

Magazines and periodicals also saw a steady growth of circulation in the second half of the nineteenth century. A large number of religious magazines were published (253 out of 630 magazines listed in 1873). But there were also women's magazines, like *Bow Bells* with its serialised romantic novels and dressmaking patterns, produced by the extensive paperback publisher, John Dicks. Juvenile magazines came initially from the 'penny dreadful' producers, but gradually moved towards respectability. Edwin J. Brett started issuing the highly suc- cesful *Boys of England* in 1866, while W. L. Emmett followed with his *Young Gentleman's Journal.* There were many others like *Boys' Standard, Boys' Own Journal* and *Boys' World* and so forth, full of often gory adventures. For many, such magazines were as pernicious as the 'penny dreadfuls' themselves and Christian groups sought to combat them with their own magazines. The Rev. J. Erskine Clark launched *Chatterbox* in 1866, and the Religious Tract Society offered the *Boys' Own Paper* from 1879. Those which succeeded, however, were those which, while plugging some simple Christian message, none the less retained a sufficient quantity of the blood, gore and ex- citement of non-Christian competitors. Alfred Harmsworth made his own distinctive contribution in this field with *Chips* and *Comic Cuts* in the 1890s, and many others followed, including the classic *Gem* and *Magnet* in 1907 and 1908.[55]

The greater circulations and the greater competitiveness both for readers and for the ever-vital advertising had a crucial effect on ownership. In the 1880s most newspapers had been owned by indi- vidual proprietors or small partnerships, and profit was generally a secondary consideration to principle or enthusiasm. In the twenty years after 1890 this changed and the proprietorial system gave way to corporations. By 1913 nine-tenths of the leading daily and evening newspapers belonged to limited companies and twelve such large companies were quoted on the Stock Exchange. It meant, on the whole, that principle was sacrificed to profit, although it did not mean that major shareholders abandoned a proprietorial role.[56]

Slight as the time available for leisure pursuits was for many of the work- ing class, compared with the standards of the present day, none the less it had grown in the last half of the nineteenth century. Just as the manu- facturers saw profits in the accumulated pennies and halfpennies of the poor, so enterprising people saw the profits that could be made by filling just a few hours of the working man's leisure. Traditional pur- suits were adapted and refined when outside interests moved in to organise and to exploit them, and gradually leisure pursuits ceased to be a response to a genuine demand, but instead shaped and created that demand. Thus the pub, the race meeting, the seaside trip, the music hall and the football match lost much of their earlier character. For- mality replaced spontaneity, pressures for respectability and modera- tion intensified. While the new opportunities of more leisure time undoubtedly had broadened the perspectives of masses of people, as they experienced new worlds at the end of their cycle or train trip, or from the pages of their papers and comics, the new worlds offered increasingly became the bland, 'safe' worlds of the lower middle class.

To a large extent, the world of working class leisure was brought under the control of the middle class by a mixture of commercial ownership and direct regulation. Undoubtedly many of the middle classes had feared what the workers might do with their leisure time, and as a result pubs were controlled by licensing, music halls were censored, beaches were cleaned up, (bathers were clothed), sports and games were formalised and moderated. In other ways, however, the process was a self-imposed one, as perspectives broadened through travel and reading 'educated' working-class families into generally 'acceptable' behaviour.

Caveats and Conclusions

England ... shows traces of American enterprise and German order, but the enterprise is faded and the order muddled. They combine to a curious travesty in which activity and perseverance assumes the expression of ease and indolence. The once enterprising manufacturer has grown slack, he has let the business take care of itself, while he is shooting grouse or yachting in the Mediterranean.

A. Shadwell, *Industrial Efficiency* (1909).

It is easy to exaggerate the extent to which social improvement took place in the years after 1851. One can too readily be caught up in the optimism of late Victorian Britain or in the nostalgia for a lost world which influences views of Edwardian Britain. Amid the confidence and the prosperity, the squalor was there. Charles Booth's studies revealed the reality of life for many in London's East End. Seebohm Rowntree confirmed that even in an elegant cathedral town, a gracious façade hid a world where 10 per cent of the people belonged to families in which, no matter how frugally their money was spent, earnings were not adequate to provide a diet good enough for proper physical development. Yet another 18 per cent, with higher earnings, still existed in conditions of acute poverty.

None the less, it would be equally dangerous to assume that Rowntree's labourers are somehow more typical than the slightly better off. Neither London nor York was a city central to the industrial revolution. Both lacked the factories and large workshops which for many other areas, like Lancashire, provided adequate, steady wages. The smoke, the grime, the noise of industry may have been polluting the environment, but the Yorkshire dictum that 'where there's muck there's brass' was a sound observation. One needs also to be aware of the cyclical pattern in the lives of many. For periods in the lives of most families grinding poverty was relieved by a windfall, by the process of a family growing up, by a little overtime, by the wife finding an extra job, by an ability to improvise. Likewise, there were periods when comfort was undermined by accident, by an unwanted child, by business collapse, by unemployment, by sickness or by fecklessness. By no means everyone was prospering, and for 30 to 40 per cent of the population there was little surplus left to purchase anything beyond a few basics that were inadequate to maintain a healthy existence. Large numbers of men, women and children sometimes went hungry, were frequently inadequately clothed and lived in cold, bare, filthy surrounds. Many were dependent upon the handouts of private charity and on the even meaner offerings of the Poor Law. However, if generalisations about the standard of living are ever of value, it is probably fair to say that in the period from 1850 to 1914 more people had more to spend for a longer part of their lives than they had ever had before. Improvement had been slow at first, and in the first decade of the twentieth century there was a setback to the growth of real incomes, but over the period as a whole there is a clear pattern of real gains for both wage-earners and the growing middle class.

Some of these gains were spent on rising rents, but the rest was spent on consumption: first on food – more and with greater variety – then on clothing, household goods and leisure. The order of priority after food had been bought varied, and was influenced by such things as social class, the expenditure patterns of peer groups, and the extent to which an individual family sought to emulate those it regarded as its social superiors. How money was spent depended upon intangibles like 'fashion', but how fashion was shaped is not at all easy to assess. It was by no means all social emulation: not all upper-class fads caught on with the middle class or the working class. Advertising clearly played some part, but whether that part was to stimulate total demand for particular kinds of goods or merely to guide the consumer to a specific brand of an item he had already decided to buy is difficult to say.

A growth in domestic demand created by rising standards presented important opportunities to British industrialists, but how successfully they responded to this has been the subject of long debate. Many contemporaries were concerned about the challenge to British industry from overseas. Since at least the Napoleonic Wars, Britain had always imported a great deal more than she exported, mainly foodstuffs and raw materials. Many of the gains of the late nineteenth century stemmed from the opening up of new areas of supply which, in spite of a rising world demand, made food and raw materials available relatively cheaply. Sir Edward Arnold illustrated this in a speech which he gave at the Midland Institute in Birmingham in 1893, entitled 'The Artisan's Dinner-Table'.

Without being luxurious, the whole globe has played him serving man to spread it. Russia gave the hemp, or India or South Carolina the cotton, for that cloth which his wife lays upon it. The Eastern islands placed there those condiments and spices which were once the secret relish of the wealthy. Australian downs sent him frozen mutton or canned beef; the prairies of America meal for his biscuit and pudding; and if he will eat fruit, the orchards of Tasmania and the palm woods of the West Indies proffer delicious gifts, while the orange groves of Florida and of the Hesperides cheapen for his use those 'golden apples' which dragons used to guard. His coffee comes from where jewelled humming birds hang in the bowers of Brazil, or purple butterflies flutter amid the Javan mangroves. Great clipper ships, racing by night and day under clouds of canvas, convey to him his tea from China and Assam, or from the green Singhalese hills. The sugar that sweetens it was crushed from the canes that waved by the Nile or the Orinoco; and the plating of the spoon with which he stirs it was dug for him from Mexican or Nevadan mines. The currants in his dumpling are a tribute from classic Greece and his tinned salmon or kippered herring are taken from the seas and rivers of Canada or Norway. He may partake, if he will, of rice that ripened under the hot skies of Patna or Rangoon; of cocoa, that 'food of the gods', plucked under the burning blue of the Equator. For his rasher of bacon, the hog-express runs daily with 10,000 grunting victims into Chicago; Dutch or Brittany hens have laid him his eggs, and Danish cows grazed the daisies of Elsinore to produce his cheese and butter. If he drinks beer, it is odds that Belgium and Bavaria have contributed to it the barley and the hops; and when he has finished eating, it will be the Mississippi flats or the gardens of the Antilles that fill for him his pipe of comforting tobacco.[1]

Britain was at the centre of an increasingly elaborate international trading system which allowed her to gain the advantages of the opening of new areas of production and to finance imports from them by exports of coal and cotton textiles. While many gained from this pattern, there were those who were conscious of the increasing number of manufactured goods that were being drawn in unhindered by tariff barriers. For some this seemed to be a major cause for concern, and F. A. Mackenzie in 1901 warned of *The American Inva-*

ders, who were taking over everywhere:

> In the domestic life we have got to this: the average man rises in the morning from his New England sheets, he shaves with 'Wilhams' soap and a Yankee safety razor, pulls on his Boston boots over his socks from North Carolina, fastens his Connecticut braces, slips his Waltham or Waterbury watch in his pocket, and sits down to breakfast. There he congratulates his wife on the way her Illinois straight-front corset sets off her Massachusetts blouse, and he tackles his breakfast, where he eats bread made from prairie flour (possibly doctored at the special establishments of the Lakes), turned oysters from Baltimore, and a little Kansas City bacon, while his wife plays with a slice of Chicago ox-tongue. The children are given 'Quaker' oats. At the same time he reads his morning paper printed by American machines, on American paper with American ink and, possibly, edited by a smart journalist from New York City . . .[2]

Having made the journey to the office by way of the American-built underground and by American escalators, he observes his secretary at her American typewriter and,

> At lunch time he hastily swallows some cold roast beef that comes from the Mid-West cow, and flavours it with Pittsburgh pickles, followed by a few Delaware tinned peaches, and then soothes his mind with a couple of Virginia cigarettes.

A few years before the main threat to certain industries seemed to come from Germany, which was accused of flooding the market with pots, pans, dishes, clocks and pianos, while farmers complained of competition (almost always 'unfair competition') from Denmark, Holland, France and Spain.[3] Undoubtedly this invasion of the home market disturbed people even more than did the decline in Britain's share of overseas trade, and it led to a revival of the demand for protectionism and an end to free trade.

Historians have accepted the validity of at least some of these squeals of pain from British farmers and manufacturers, but increasingly with qualifications. There is agreement that both in home and export markets British manufacturers were facing competition from more recently industrialised countries, and there is also general agreement that some deceleration in the rate of growth of British industrial production took place in the last quarter of the nineteenth century. While a number of factors contributed to this – such as the end of the railway building boom (emphasised by Rostow); a decline in the application of power, transport and machinery (emphasised by Phelps Brown and Handfield-Jones); the end of the general application of steam and iron machinery to the staple industries (as emphasised by Coppock) – historians seem to be emphasising social factors increasingly, such as the lack of an educational system at all levels to meet the needs of industry, and the persistence of a class system which stifled initiative.[4] Much has been made of the signs of a falling off in enterprise among businessmen. D. H. Aldcroft put it most bluntly: 'The British entrepreneur had lost much of the drive and dynamism possessed by his predecessors of the classical industrial revolution.'[5] What is meant by such words as 'drive' and 'dynamism' can never be fully agreed. What is clear, however, is that the sweeping generalisation does not get us very far in this argument, and, following Charles Wilson's important article on 'Economy and Society in Late Victorian Britain', historians have looked beyond the traditional industries, on which most earlier generalisations were made, to the expanding sectors of retailing, foodstuff production and consumer goods industries. Wilson noted that the 'Armstrongs, the Whitworths and Brassays were giving way to (or being joined by) the Levers, Boots, Harrods, Whiteleys and Lewises'.[6] While most work has tended to focus on the changes in retailing, such changes were generally closely related to changes taking place in production methods. The expansion of retailing outlets helped to stimulate demand, but to satisfy that demand output had to be increased. In many cases this involved a process of vertical integration, with retailers gaining control of their supplies, as was the case with Lipton, Lever, Boot and the Co-operative Societies. In other cases formerly small firms already in existence grew very much larger and greatly increased their output. This was the pattern with the cocoa and chocolate firms, such as Rowntree and Cadbury, with biscuit firms, like Huntley & Palmer and McVitie, with a soap firm like Crosfield, a tobacco firm like Wills and a clothes firm like Barron or Corah. There was no lack of innovation or of managerial expertise in firms such as these.

It is, however, all too easy to focus excessive attention on these large firms. The typical shop was not the multiple, with its clean, clearly priced, well-laid-out goods, but the small corner shop where the odour of paraffin added a certain something to the appeal of a few ounces of cheese or a child's candy. The typical firm was not the industrial giant supplying a national or international market, but the small enterprise selling still to a largely regional market. Because of their size and because they were, in most cases, still run by families, many of these firms probably did display a conservatism in their approach to new economic conditions. The impression remains of many small firms still producing quality goods for a limited market. There was a tendency to aim for the top end of the market, with emphasis on a variety of individual specifications, rather than for the standardisation of the mass market. The striking feature even in 1914 is the survival of small firms in most of the consumer goods industries and the organisation of their products through factors and warehousemen. While the factory system was clearly developed for a whole variety of consumer goods, at least elements still persisted of what was basically a domestic system with outwork at home or in small workshops. This was true in many of the hardware firms, in the various clothing firms and in the furniture and fittings business. Small-scale businesses persisted alongside the large firms and it was still possible at the end of the century, with very little capital, for new people to break into these industries. The large firms which did exist were often dependent upon small sub-contractors. Even the large firms tended to remain family dominated until the need for extensive capital investment, particularly during the 1890s, forced them to look to the wider public for backing and to convert to limited liability.

Not that size on its own necessarily brings greater dynamism. Many of the larger firms that were aiming at a mass market and were developing the techniques of mass production were hostile to competition. The response of many such firms to competitiveness was not to improve efficiency, or increase productivity, but to seek to eliminate competition by means of price-fixing and market-sharing agreements and amalgamations. Competitors were bought up so growth could be accomplished with the minimum of entrepreneurial effort.

With these reservations in mind, however, it is doubtful if there is much evidence that in supplying goods to the mass domestic market Britain was suffering from so-called 'entrepreneurial fatigue'. In soap, cycles, cigarettes and the leisure industries there were investors and risk takers. On the whole, in these new growth areas it is very doubtful if there was as much conservatism among British businessmen as has sometimes been suggested. Management was ready to innovate, and in most of these industries trade unionism was not powerful enough to offer any real resistance to change. In many cases, however, these were new men taking advantage of the new opportunities. It may have been less true in older firms in older established industries. What does stand out is the continuing importance of the entrepreneur. Thus, one decision by Wills – to buy the patent rights of the Bonsack machine – was an immensely important entrepreneurial decision for them which allowed the firm to expand rapidly. John Barron's innovations with the bandsaw allowed his firm to pull ahead of other tailors. Elsewhere, however, there seemed to be a lack of inventiveness and of innovation. So many of the new patents came from the United States: sewing machines, cigarette-making machines, linotype printing machines, corned beef, 'big wheels' from Coney Island, advertising techniques. There is a wealth of evidence that the Americans were producing and using new machines more rapidly and more extensively than were British businessmen. A good example of this comes in the match industry, long dominated by Bryant & May. Until the 1890s they had more or less a British monopoly and paid their shareholders dividends of 20 per cent. In 1896, however, the American Diamond Match Company set up a factory in Liverpool and began producing cheaper matches. When Bryant & May belatedly sought to modernise their production in order to compete, they found that the key patents were all controlled by the Americans and they were forced to sell out to them. The president of the American company spelled out the realities of the situation to the Bryant & May shareholders:

The machinery now being used in Bryant and May's factory ... was the invention of men who had been in the employ of the Diamond company since its inception, but that machinery was discarded by the American company fifteen or sixteen years ago, and we have been gradually improving upon it. I do not think there has been a year when the Diamond company of America has not expended at least 50,000 dollars in experiments in improving their machinery. We have good inventive talent, and we have quite a large number of people working continuously with the sole object of improving our machinery. Then again we have representatives always travelling in different parts of the world for the purpose of acquiring any new invention which would be of assistance to our business.[7]

While this slowness to innovate had probably something to do with the quality of British education and with the social *mores* within which British industry operated, it was also a product of the very different economic conditions that existed in Britain compared with the United States. A rapidly growing and very large market, coupled with a scarcity of skilled labour in the United States, forced American businessmen to look for labour-saving inventions and for ways in which goods could be produced in greater quantities – hence the search for patents and the development of standardisation and interchangeability in American industry. In Britain the home market was not as large, and neither population nor income was growing at the American rate. Demand in Britain grew at a much slower rate and, therefore, British industry's adjustment to the needs of a mass market could be a great deal slower than in the United States. Gradual expansion in existing firms and growth in the number of small firms could cope with the demand. The long-term result was that mass-produced goods could make their way from the United States to Britain more cheaply than some British goods could be produced, which forced British firms to look for economies of scale, and to develop new approaches.

It is important to emphasise the patchiness of developments and lack of uniformity in the experience of different areas of British industry. Precisely because so many firms remained small there was a variety of patterns and responses. In most cases British industrialists did succeed in adapting to the constantly changing conditions of the market, of supplies and of resources. Many did grasp the new economic opportunities which existed. The result was that, for most of the people, industry was able to offer an ever-widening range of choices for their food, their clothing, their domestic furnishings and for their entertainment. In all these areas future growth was to come in the direction of a continuing stimulation and satisfaction of the needs of the masses. By 1914 it was clearly recognised that a mass market had arrived and had to be catered for.

Acknowledgements

The author and publishers wish to thank the following for permission to reproduce photographs: The Mansell Collection, Plates 1(a), 2, 7(b), 14; The Hamilton Museum, Plates 1(b), 8(a); The Illustrated London News, Plate 3; The Benjamin Stone Collection, Birmingham Public Libraries, Plate 4; Allied Suppliers, Plates 5, 6(b); The Victoria and Albert Museum, Plate 6(a); Graham Collection, Mitchell Library, Glasgow, Plate 9(a); The George Washington Wilson Collection, Aberdeen University Library, Plates 7(a), 13; W. H. Smith and Son Ltd, Plate 8(b); UML Ltd, Plate 10(a); The British Library, Plates 11(a), 15; Newark Houses Museum, Leicester, Plate 11(b); BBC Hulton Picture Library, Plate 12(a); Mary Evans Picture Library, Plates 12(b), 16; North Yorkshire County Library, Plate 9(b); Coventry Reference Library, Plate 10(b).

Notes and References

Note: for books the place of publication is London unless otherwise stated.

1. Numbers

1. D. J. Oddy, 'The Working Class Diet, 1886–1914', unpublished Ph.D. thesis, University of London, 1970, p. 289.

2. J. A. Banks, *Prosperity and Parenthood* (1954) *passim*.

3. Helen Bosanquet, *The Family* (1906) p. 201

4. M. V. Hughes, *A London Child of the Seventies* (1934) pp. 38–9

5. C. Trent, *Greater London: Its Growth and Development Through Two Thousand Years* (1965) p. 202

6. C. F. G. Masterman, *The Heart of the Empire* (1901) p. 13.

7. H. Pollins, 'Transport Lines and Social Divisions', in R. Glass (ed.), *Aspects of Change* (1964).

8. A. K. Cairncross, 'Internal Migration in Victorian England', *The Manchester School*, xvii (1949) 78.

9. J. Saville, *Rural Depopulation in England and Wales* (1957) pp. 12–13.

10. Ibid., p. 74.

11. Cairncross, 'Internal Migration', p. 70.

12. J. H. Clapham, *An Economic History of Modern Britain* (Cambridge, 1963) vol. iii, p. 454.

13. *Report of Royal Commission on Housing of the Industrial Population of Scotland* (1917) Q. 27, 745, cited in Clapham, *An Economic History*, vol iii, p. 462.

2. Incomes

1. J. R. Bellerby, 'Distribution of Farm Income in the U.K., 1867–1938', *Journal of the Proceedings of the Agricultural Economics Society*, x (1953).

2. The main sources for wages and prices are A. L. Bowley, *Wages and Income in the United Kingdom since 1860* (Cambridge, 1937), E. H. Phelps Brown and M. Browne, *A Century of Pay* (1968), G. H. Wood, 'Real Wages and the Standard of Comfort since 1850', *Journal of the Royal Statistical Society*, lxxiii (1909) and W. T. Layton and G. Crowther, *History of Prices*

241

(1937). The various indexes cited are most readily available in B. R. Mitchell and P. Deane, *Abstract of British Historical Statistics* (Cambridge, 1962).

3. G. Barnsby, 'The Standard of Living in the Black Country during the Nineteenth Century', *Economic History Review*, XXIV (1971) 220–39; E. Hopkins, 'Small Town Aristocrats and Their Standard of Living, 1840–1914', *Economic History Review*, XXVIII (1975) 222–42.

4. S. Pollard, *History of Labour in Sheffield* (Liverpool, 1959) pp. 105–9.

5. E. H. Hunt, *Regional Wage Variations in Britain, 1850–1914* (Oxford, 1973) pp. 58–63.

6. H. Bosanquet, *Social Conditions in Provincial Towns* (1912) p. 18.

7. *Report of the Select Committee on Pawnbrokers, P.P.* 1870 VIII, Q. 2102.

8. A. Morrison, *A Child of the Jago*, ed. P. J. Keating (1897, reprinted 1969) pp. 164–5.

9. O. C. Malvery, *The Soul Market*, 6th edn (n.d.) p. 73.

10. Ibid., pp. 87,100.

11. T. A. B. Corley, *Quaker Enterprise in Biscuits* (1972) p. 304.

12. *Daily Mail Year Book* (1901).

13. A. L. Bowley, 'Earners and Dependents in English Towns in 1911', *Economica*, I (1921) 101–12.

14. R. Boyson, *The Ashworth Cotton Enterprise* (1970) pp. 105–6.

15. E. Roberts, 'Working-Class Standards of Living in Barrow and Lancaster, 1890–1914', *Economic History Review*, XXX (1977) 306–21; S. Rowntree, *Poverty: A Study of Town Life* (1901).

16. Hunt, *Regional Wage Variations*, ch.1.

17. J. C. Stamp, *British Incomes and Property* (1916) p. 448.

18. A. L. Bowley, *The Change in the Distribution of National Income, 1880–1913* (Oxford, 1920) p. 21.

19. B. Webb, *My Apprenticeship* (1926) pp. 20–2.

20. Phelps Brown and Browne, *A Century of Pay*, pp. 132–46.

21. Earl of Birkenhead, *F. E. Life of the First Lord Birkenhead* (1933) p. 90.

22. Mrs C. S. Peel, *Marriage on Small Means* (1914).

23. T. R. Gourvish, 'The Standard of Living, 1890–1914' in A. O'Day (ed.), *The Edwardian Age: Conflict and Stability* (1979) pp. 23–4.

3. Patterns of Consumption: Food

1. D. J. Oddy, 'The Working Class Diet, 1886–1914', unpublished Ph.D. thesis, University of London, 1970, p. 20.

2. Ibid., p. 30.

3. Ibid., p. 34.

4. Flora Thompson, *Lark Rise to Candleford* (1945) p. 13.

5. Oddy, 'The Working Class Diet', p. 85.

6. R. L. Cohen, *A History of Milk Prices* (1936) pp. 4–5.

7. Oddy, 'The Working Class Diet', p. 152.

8. Ibid., p. 34.

9. *The Times* (16 December 1876), cited in J. C. Drummond and

A. Wilbraham, *The Englishman's Food* (1957) p. 306.

10. *Report of the Select Committee on the Butter Substitute Bill, P.P.* 1887 IX.

11. G. M. Wilson, *Alcohol and the Nation* (1940) p. 14.

12. A. Torode, 'Trends in Fruit Consumption' in T. C. Barker, J. C. McKenzie and John Yudkin (eds), *Our Changing Fare* (1966) p. 127.

13. Thompson, *Lark Rise*, p. 111.

14. S. G. Hanson, *Commercial Egg Farming from Practical Experience gained over a period of years* (1916) p. 9.

15. W. A. Mackenzie, 'Changes in the Standard of Living in the U.K., 1860–1914', *Economica*, no. 3 (1921).

16. Smith's Report with an introduction by Sir John Simon is in *Sixth Report of the Medical Officer of the Privy Council, 1863 P.P.* 1864 XXVIII.

17. *Labour Statistics: Returns of Expenditure by Working Men, P.P.* 1889 LXXXIV.

18. *Cornhill Magazine*, n.s., x (1901) 446–56.

19. B. S. Rowntree and M. Kendall, *How the Labourer Lives: A Study of the Rural Labour Problem* (1913) p. 44.

20. Ibid., p. 75.

21. M. Davies, *Life in an English Village* (1909) p. 194.

22. Mrs Pember Reeves, *Round About a Pound a Week* (1913) p. 45.

23. R. G. D. Allen and A. L. Bowley, *Family Expenditure: A Study of its Variation* (1935) p. 5.

24. F. T. Bullen, *Confessions of a Tradesman* (1908) p. 161.

25. O. C. Malvery, *The Soul Market*, 6th edn (n.d.) p. 48.

26. 'The Cost of Living', *Cornhill Magazine*, xxxi (1875) 412–21.

27. Mrs C. S. Peel, *How to Keep House* (1902) p. 14.

28. *The Listener* (28 December 1961).

29. G. B. Shaw, *The Commonsense of Municipal Trading* (n.d.) pp. 69–70.

30. *Report of the Select Committee on the Marketing of Frozen Meat, P.P.* (1893–94), quoted in Oddy, 'The Working Class Diet', p. 91.

31. R. E. Dingle, 'Drink and Working-Class Living Standards in Britain 1870–1914', *Economic History Review*, xxv (1972) 608–22.

32. E. Roberts, 'Working-Class Standards of Living in Barrow and Lancaster, 1890–1914', *Economic History Review*, xxx (1977) 313–19.

33. D. J. Oddy, 'A Nutritional Analysis of Historical Evidence in the Working-Class Diet, 1880–1914', in D. J. Oddy and D. S. Miller (eds), *The Making of the Modern British Diet* (1976) p. 229.

4. *Patterns of Consumption: Shelter*

1. E. Gauldie, *Cruel Habitations* (1974) p. 47.

2. F. M. Lupton, *Housing Improvement* (1906) p. 2, quoted in S. D. Chapman (ed.), *The History of Working-Class Housing* (Newton Abbot, 1971) p. 115.

3. Helen Bosanquet, *The Family* (1906) p. 64.

4. 'The Journeyman Engineer' (Thomas Wright), *The Great Unwashed* (1868) p. 43.

5. Ibid., p. 136.

6. E. Gwyn in *Public Health*, XIII 4 (January 1901), quoted by A. S. Wohl in Chapman (ed.), *The History of Working-Class Housing*, p. 35.

7. Mrs Pember Reeves, *Round About a Pound a Week* (1913) p. 76.

8. *Board of Trade Inquiry into Working-Class Rents, Housing, and Retail Prices, 1905*, P.P. 1908 CVII.

9. Lady Florence Bell, *At the Works* (1911) p. 107.

10. B. S. Rowntree and M. Kendall, *How the Labourer Lives: A Study of the Rural Labour Problem* (1913) pp. 44–60.

11. Bell, *At the Works* (1911) p. 171–2.

12. O. C. Malvery, *The Soul Market*, 6th edn (n.d.) p. 76.

13. Flora Thompson, *Lark Rise to Candleford* (1945) p. 6.

14. P. Razzell and R. W. Wainwright (eds), *The Victorian Working Class: Selections from Letters to the 'Morning Chronicle'* (1973) p. 167.

15. T. Wright, *Our New Masters* (1873) p. 48.

16. Malvery, *The Soul Market*, p. 17.

17. Wright, *Our New Masters*, pp. 49–50.

18. Liverpool Economic and Statistical Society, *How the Casual Labourer Lives* (Liverpool, 1909) p. 311.

19. M. Loane, *The Queen's Poor* (1910) p. 160, c.f. Reeves, *Round About a Pound a Week*, p. 205.

20. S. Reynolds, *Seems So!* (1913) pp. 48–9.

21. R. Roberts, *The Classic Slum* (Harmondsworth, 1973) p. 33.

22. Reynolds, *Seems So!*, pp. 35–6.

23. Razzell and Wainwright (eds), *The Victorian Working Class*, p. 167.

24. Thompson, *Lark Rise*, pp. 163–4.

25. Razzell and Wainwright (eds), *The Victorian Working Class*, p. 226.

26. Ibid., p. 227.

27. Roberts, *The Classic Slum*, p. 35.

28. Razzell and Wainwright (eds), *The Victorian Working Class*, pp. 168, 227.

29. C. Wilson, *The History of Unilever*, vol. I (1954) p. 38.

30. Mrs. C. S. Peel, *The New Home* (1898) pp. 8–10.

31. M. V. Hughes, *A London Child of the Seventies* (1934) p. 39.

32. *London's Latest Suburbs: An Illustrated Guide to the Residential District reached by the Hampstead Tube.* (1910) *passim*.

33. Mrs C. S. Peel, *Marriage on Small Means* (1914) pp. 21–2.

34. *Cornhill Magazine*, n.s. x (1901) 790–800.

35. Mrs C. S. Peel, *How to Keep House* (1902) p. 3.

36. P. Thompson, *The Edwardians* (1975) p. 99.

37. J. H. Walsh, *Manual of Domestic Economy* (1898) pp. 40–1.

38. Mrs C. S. Peel, *The New Home* (1898) pp. 40–1.

39. Ibid., p. 56.

40. Marghanita Laski, 'Domestic Life', ch. 4 of S. Nowell-Smith (ed.), *Edwardian England, 1901–1914* (1964) p. 163.

5.   Patterns of Consumption: Clothing

1. Asa Briggs, *Friends of the People* (1956) p. 128.

2. *Labour Statistics: Returns of Expenditure by Working Men*, P.P. 1889 LXXXIV, p. 30.

3. *Accounts of Expenditure of Wage-Earning Women and Girls*, P.P. 1911 LXXXIX, p. 10.

4. Elias Moses and Son, *The Growth of an Important Branch of British Industry* (1860), quoted in P. G. Hall, *The Industries of London* (1962) p. 53.

5. Flora Thompson, *Lark Rise to Candleford* (1945) p. 92.

6. B. S. Rowntree and M. Kendall, *How the Labourer Lives: A Study of the Rural Labour Problem* (1953) p. 40.

7. S. Reynolds, *A Poor Man's House* (1908) pp. 66–7.

8. H. Mayhew, *London Labour and the London Poor* (1861–2, reprinted 1967) vol. I, *passim*.

9. Thompson, *Lark Rise*, p. 18.

10. R. Roberts, *The Classic Slum* (1973) p. 38.

11. Lady Florence Bell, *At the Works* (1911) p. 113.

12. *Accounts of Expenditure of Wage-Earning Women and Girls*. P.P. 1911 LXXXIX, *passim*.

13. *Cornhill Magazine*, n.s. x (1901) p. 660.

14. Mrs C. S. Peel, *How to Keep House* (1902) pp. 25–6, *Marriage on Small Means* (1914) pp. 21–2.

15. A. Adburgham, *Shops and Shopping* (1964) p. 93.

16. Ibid., p. 188.

17. Ibid., p. 64.

18. Bell, *At the Works*, pp. 118–19.

19. M. Loane, *The Queen's Poor* (1910) pp. 120–1.

20. N. McCord, 'Ratepayers and Social Policy' in Pat Thane (ed.). *The Origins of Social Policy in Britain* (1978).

6. Patterns of Consumption: Luxuries

1. S. Rowntree and A. Sherwell, *The Temperance Problem and Social Reform* (1900).

2. Flora Thompson, *Lark Rise to Candleford* (1945) p. 53.

3. T. Wright, *Some Habits and Customs of the Working Classes* (1867) p. 125.

4. Thompson, *Lark Rise*, p. 53; *Cornhill Magazine*, n.s. x (1901) 454–5.

5. John Burnett, *Plenty and Want* (1968) p. 199.

6. Ibid., p. 226.

7. S. Reynolds, *A Poor Man's House* (1908) p. 68.

8. B. Harrison, 'Pubs' in H. J. Dyos and M. Wolff (eds). *The Victorian City: Images and Reality* (1973) p. 161.

9. Ibid., p. 167.

10. J. B. Jefferys, *Retail Trading in Britain, 1850–1950* (Cambridge, 1954) p. 268.

11. Wright, *Some Habits and Customs*, p. 92.

12. G. L. Apperson, *The Social History of Smoking* (1914) p. 167.

13. B. W. E. Alford, *W. D. & H. O. Wills and the Development of the U.K. Tobacco Industry, 1786–1965* (1973) p. 225.

14. Quoted in S. Alexander, *St. Giles's Fair, 1830–1914* (1970) p. 24.

15. Alford, *W. D. & H. O. Wills*, p. 169.
16. Compton Mackenzie, *Sublime Tobacco* (1957) pp. 34–4.
17. *Capital and Labour* (24 January 1877).
18. R. D. Altick, *The English Common Reader* (Chicago, 1957) p. 287.
19. Ibid., p. 345.
20. Circulation figures are from Altick, *The English Common Reader, passim,* and from H. Herd, *The March of Journalism,* (1952) *passim.*
21. P. Razzell and R. W. Wainwright, *The Victorian Working Class: Selections from Letters to the 'Morning Chronicle'* (1973) p. 175.
22. *Answers* (16 February 1889).
23. Lady Florence Bell, *At the Works* (1911) p. 236.
24. R. Pound and G. Harmsworth, *Northcliffe* (1959) pp. 277–8.
25. Altick, *The English Common Reader,* p. 25.
26. Wright, *Some Habits and Customs,* p. 198.
27. Bell, *At the Works,* p. 185.
28. P. Redfern, *The Story of the C. W. S.* (1913) p. 52.
29. Wright, *Some Habits and Customs,* pp. 120–3.
30. G. B. Wilson, 'Variations in the Consumption of Intoxicating Drinks in the U.K.', *Journal of the Royal Statistical Society,* LXXV (1912) 205.
31. Wray Vamplew, *The Turf* (1976) p. 38.
32. *Jackson's Oxford Journal* (9 September 1854) quoted in S. Alexander, *St. Giles's Fair,* p. 12.
33. Flora Thompson, *Lark Rise to Candleford,* pp. 228–9.
34. *Jackson's Oxford Journal* (8 September 1908), quoted in Alexander, *St. Giles's Fair,* p. 12.
35. *Report of the Royal Commission on Holidays with Pay, P.P.* 1837–38 XII, pp. 275–81.
36. A. Hern, *The Seaside Holiday* (1967) p. 60. J. A. R. Pimlott, *The Englishman's Holiday* (1947) pp. 161–4.
37. Pimlott, *The Englishman's Holiday,* p. 174.
38. F. Alderson, *Bicycling: A History* (Newton Abbot, 1972) p. 116. See also S. McConagle, *The Bicycle in Life, Love, War and Literature* (1968).
39. D. Rubinstein, 'Cycling in the 1890s', *Victorian Studies,* XXI 1 (1977) 62.
40. *Motor Guide to London* (1909).
41. Ibid.
42. W. J. Reader, *Victorian England* (1964) p. 200.
43. S. B. Saul, 'The Motor Industry in Britain to 1914', *Business History,* V (1962) 24.
44. Rubinstein, 'Cycling in the 1890s', p. 62.

7.   The Credit System

1. R. Roberts, *The Classic Slum* (1973) p. 81.
2. B. S. Rowntree and M. Kendall, *How the Labourer Lives: A Study of the Rural Labour Problem* (1913) p. 44.
3. J. Foster, *Class Struggle and the Industrial Revolution* (1974) p. 238.
4. *Report of the Select Committee on Manufactures and Trade, P.P.* 1833 VI Q. 10,572ff.

5. W. B. Robertson (ed.), *Encyclopaedia of Retail Trading* (1911) p. 133.

6. Flora Thompson, *Lark Rise to Candleford* (1945) pp. 116–17.

7. In some parts tallymen were actually called 'Scotchmen' and, like the term 'Scotch Draper', this may have derived from the keeping of accounts by a series of notches or scotches on a tally stick. Miss Malvery, however, specifically makes the point that they tended to be either Jews or Scots. See O. C. Malvery, *The Soul Market*, 6th edn (n.d.) p. 255.

8. 'The Journeyman Engineer' (Thomas Wright), *The Great Unwashed* (1868) pp. 143–6.

9. Malvery, *The Soul Market*, pp. 252–3.

10. Lady Florence Bell, *At the Works* (1911) pp. 110–11.

11. Malvery, *The Soul Market*, p. 143.

12. *How the Casual Labourer Lives: Report of the Liverpool Joint Committee on the Domestic Condition and Expenditure of the Families of Certain Liverpool Labourers read before and published by the Liverpool Economic and Statistical Society* (Liverpool, 1909) pp. xv–xvi.

13. *Report of the Select Committee on Pawnbrokers P.P.* 1870 viii Q. 15.

14. Malvery, *The Soul Market*, p. 259.

15. *Report of Select Committee on Pawnbrokers*, Appendix 9, p. 645.

16. Ibid., Q. 2102.

17. *How the Casual Labourer Lives*, pp. xvii–xix.

18. Roberts, *The Classic Slum*, p. 82.

19. Malvery, *The Soul Market*, p. 170.

8. Pack, Stall and Shop

1. Henry Mayhew, *London Labour and the London Poor*, i (1967 edn) p. 9.

2. O. C. Malvery, *The Soul Market*, 6th edn (n.d.) p. 143; Mayhew, *London Labour*, p. 30.

3. Mayhew, *London Labour,* pp. 54–5.

4. Ibid., p. 159.

5. Ibid., p. 196.

6. Ibid., p. 198.

7. 'Lord' George Sanger, *Seventy Years a Showman* (1926) pp. 144–5.

8. Mayhew, *London Labour*, p. 185.

9. Ibid., p. 194.

10. Ibid., p. 367.

11. *Victoria County History, Essex*, ii (1907) p. 488.

12. Mayhew, *London Labour*, p. 60.

13. S. Alexander, *St. Giles's Fair, 1830–1914* (1970) pp. 10–11.

14. In Flora Thompson's *Lark Rise* the 'year of the cheap-jack' was long remembered.

15. G. Rees, *St Michael: A History of Marks and Spencer* (1969) p. 6.

16. *Jackson's Oxford Journal* (10 September 1892), quoted in Alexander, *St. Giles's Fair*, p. 13.

17. C. Booth, *Life and Labour of the People in London: Industry* iii,

2nd ser. (1903) pp. 262–3.

18. Ibid., p. 270; Malvery, *The Soul Market*, p. 269.
19. R. Roberts, *The Classic Slum* (1973) pp. 105–6.
20. Booth, *Life and Labour: Industry*, III, p. 254.
21. L. Lee, *Cider with Rosie* (Penguin edn, 1962) p. 16.
22. P. Mathias, *Retailing Revolution* (1967) p. 17.
23. Malvery, *The Soul Market*, p. 103.
24. *Baker and Confectioner* (25 March 1904), quoted in D. J. Oddy, 'The Working-Class Diet, 1886–1914', unpublished Ph.D. thesis, University of London, 1970, p. 71.
25. Oddy, 'The Working-Class Diet', p. 97.
26. J. C. Drummond and A. Wilbraham, *The Englishman's Food* (1957) p. 308.
27. R. A. Clemen, *The American Livestock and Meat Industry* (New York, 1923) p. 271; *Report of the Select Committee on Marketing Foreign Meat etc.*, *P.P.* 1893–94 XII.
28. J. T. Critchell and J. Raymond, *A History of the Frozen Food Trade* (1912) *passim*.
29. Malvery, *The Soul Market*, p. 97.
30. *Glasgow Herald* (24 January 1880); Charles Booth made a similar point in the 1890s, see Booth, *Life and Labour: Industry*, III, p. 204.
31. Critchell and Raymond, *A History of the Frozen Food Trade*, pp. 200–25.
32. Oddy, 'The Working-Class Diet', p. 91.
33. Drummond and Wilbraham, *The Englishman's Food*, p. 322.
34. S. Chapman, *Jesse Boot of Boots the Chemist* (1974) p. 58.
35. Malvery, *The Soul Market*, p. 162.
36. R. S. Lambert, *The Universal Provider: The Story of Whiteley's* (1938) p. 71.

9.   The Transformation of the Shop

1. J. B. Jefferys, *Retail Trading in Britain, 1850–1950* (Cambridge, 1954) p. 137.
2. P. Mathias, *Retailing Revolution* (1967) p. 98.
3. Ibid.
4. Jefferys, *Retail Trading*, p. 139.
5. Mathias, *Retailing Revolution*, p. 98.
6. Ibid., pp. 59–60.
7. Ibid., p. 46.
8. Ibid., *Retailing Revolution*, pp. 103–16.
9. R. A. Clemen, *The American Livestock and Meat Industry* (New York, 1923) p. 271.
10. J. T. Critchell and J. Raymond, *A History of the Frozen Food Trade* (1912) p. 423.
11. Ibid., p. 170.
12. Tables 9.1 and 9.2 are both based on figures in Jefferys, *Retail Trading*, *passim*.
13. Ibid., p. 363.
14. Ibid., p. 324.

15. S. Chapman, *Jesse Boot of Boots the Chemist* (1974) p. 23.

16. Jefferys, *Retail Trading*, p. 385.

17. Chapman, *Jesse Boot*, p. 85.

18. G. D. H. Cole, *A History of Co-operation* (1944) p. 14.

19. E. P. Thompson, 'The Moral Economy of the English Crowd in the Eighteenth Century', *Past and Present*, 50 (1971) 76–136.

20. Cole, *A History of Co-operation*, pp. 25–6.

21. Ibid., pp. 63–4.

22. P. Redfern, *The History of the C. W. S., 1863–1913* (1913) p. 28.

23. Ibid., p. 29.

24. W. Maxwell, *History of Co-operation in Scotland* (1910).

25. Redfern, *The History of the C. W. S.*, p. 34.

26. Ibid., p. 74.

27. Jefferys, *Retail Trading*, p. 16.

28. Redfern, *The History of the C. W. S.*, p. 95–169.

29. Cole, *A History of Co-operation*, p. 371.

30. Ibid., p. 213.

31. B. Webb, *My Apprenticeship* (1926) pp. 368–9.

32. R. Roberts, *The Classic Slum* (1973) p. 83.

33. W. Maxwell, *First Fifty Years of St Cuthbert's Co-operative Association Ltd, 1859–1909* (Edinburgh, 1909) pp. 89–90.

34. Molly Weir, *Shoes Were for Sunday* (1970) p. 46.

35. Maxwell, *History of Co-operation*, p. 148.

36. Ibid., pp. 148–9.

37. Redfern, *The History of the C. W. S.*, p. 43.

38. Maxwell, *History of Co-operation*, pp. 292–3.

39. Redfern, *The History of the C. W. S.*, p. 98.

40. Jefferys, *Retail Trading*, p. 423.

41. Ibid., p. 19.

42. Most of the information in the above paragraphs is taken from J. Hood and B. S. Yamey, 'The Middle-Class Co-operative retailing Societies in London, 1864–1900', *Oxford Economic Papers*, IX (1957) 309.

43. A. Adburgham, *Shops and Shopping* (1964) pp. 33–78.

44. Most of this section draws on Adburgham, *Shops and Shopping, passim*.

45. Ibid., pp. 137–59.

46. R. S. Lambert, *The Universal Provider: The Story of Whiteley's* (1938) p. 72; Adburgham, *Shops and Shopping*, pp. 149–59.

47. A. Briggs, *Friends of the People: The Centenary History of Lewis's* (1956) p. 39.

48. Quoted in Adburgham, *Shops and Shopping*, p. 238.

10. *Advertising*

1. B. W. E. Alford, *W. D. & H. O. Wills and the Development of the U.K. Tobacco Industry, 1786–1965* (1973) p. 167.

2. Cyril Sheldon, *A History of Poster Advertising* (1937) pp. 3–20.

3. C. Moran, *The Business of Advertising* (1905) pp. 17–18.

4. P. Hadley, *The History of Bovril Advertising* (1971), *passim*; M. Rickards, *Posters at the Turn of the Century* (1968) *passim*.

5. C. Wilson, *History of Unilever*, vol. I (1954) p. 50.

6. H. F. Hutchison, *The Poster, an Illustrated History from 1860* (1968) *passim*.

7. Moran, *The Business of Advertising*, p. 117.

8. E. S. Turner, *The Shocking History of Advertising* (1952) pp. 112–19.

9. Sheldon, *A History of Poster Advertising, passim*.

10. Moran, *The Business of Advertising*, p. 6.

11. Most of the paragraph is based on D. and G. Hindley, *Advertising in Victorian England, 1837–1901* (1972).

12. Hadley, *The History of Bovril Advertising*, p. 12; Moran, *The Business of Advertising*, p. 66; Wareham Smith, *Spilt Ink* (1932) p. 51.

13. *Illustrated London News* (17 August 1889).

14. *Illustrated Sporting and Dramatic News* (25 February 1896).

15. *Report of the Select Committee on Patent Medicines, P.P.* 1914 IX, p. xviii.

16. Ibid., p. xix.

17. H. G. Wells, *Tono-Bungay* (1933) pp. 94–9.

18. *Report of the Select Committee on Patent Medicines*, pp. xviii–xix.

19. *Cigar and Tobacco World* (12 November 1892), quoted in R. J. Richardson, 'The History of the Catering Industry, with special reference to the Development of J. Lyons & Co. Ltd to 1939', unpublished Ph.D. thesis, University of Kent at Canterbury, 1970, pp. 182–3.

20. Turner, *The Shocking History of Advertising*, p. 136.

21. Hadley, *The History of Bovril Advertising*, p. 18.

22. *Langham Hotel Guide to London* (1905).

23. Wilson, *History of Unilever*, vol. I, p. 38.

24. R. Pound and G. Harmsworth, *Northcliffe* (1954) pp. 98–106.

25. B. N. Reckitt, *The History of Reckitt & Sons Ltd.*, (1951) p. 57.

26. Anon., *The Food Makers: A History of General Foods Ltd* (1972) p. 14.

27. T. A. B. Corley, *Quaker Enterprise in Biscuits* (1972) p. 66.

28. Wilson, *History of Unilever*, vol. I, p. 23; Corley, *Quaker Enterprise*, p. 63.

29. Alford, *W. D. & H. O. Wills*, p. 287.

30. *Progress*, I (1900) 160.

31. A. Warren, *Commercial Travelling: Its Features Past and Present* (1904) p. 45.

32. Corley, *Quaker Enterprise*, p. 162.

33. Alford, *W. D. & H. O. Wills*, pp. 261–9.

34. Earl of Birkenhead, *Frederick Edwin, Earl of Birkenhead, the First Phase* (1933) pp. 101–6.

11. The Nation Fed

1. J. H. Clapham, *An Economic History of Modern Britain* (Cambridge, 1963) vol. II, p. 277.

2. Quoted in G. E. Mingay, *Rural Life in Victorian England* (1976) p. 21.

3. Clapham, *Economic History of Modern Britain*, p. 278.

4. B. R. Mitchell and P. Deane, *Abstract of British Historical Statistics* (Cambridge, 1962) p. 224.

5. S. Smith M.P., quoted in E. E. Williams, *The Foreigner in the Farmyard* (1897) p. 123.

6. *Daily Mail Year Book* (1906); W. E. Bear, 'The Food Supply of Manchester – Part III. *Journal of the Royal Agricultural Statistical Society of England*, 3rd ser. x (1899) 32–3.

7. W. E. Bear, 'The Food Supply of Manchester – Part I, *Journal of the Royal Agricultural Statistical Society of England*, 3rd ser. VIII (1897) 223.

8. *Report of the Departmental Committee on the Fruit Industry* (1905) p. 5.

9. Bear, 'The Food Supply of Manchester – Part I, p. 208.

10. Ibid., pp. 212–13.

11. Ibid., Part II, p. 491.

12. *Report of the Departmental Committee on Poultry Breeding in Scotland* (1909) p. 409.

13. E. Brown, 'The Marketing of Poultry', *Journal of the Royal Agricultural Statistical Society of England*, 3rd ser., IX (1898) p. 276.

14. Clapham, *Economic History of Modern Britain*, vol. III, pp. 84–5.

15. S. G. Hanson, *Argentine Meat and the British Market* (Stanford, 1938) p. 18.

16. J. T. Critchell and J. Raymond, *A History of the Frozen Food Trade* (1912) p. 423.

17. *Report of the Departmental Committee on Combinations in the Meat Trade* (1909) p. 13.

18. Ibid., p. 5.

19. D. Taylor, 'The English Dairy Industry, 1860–1930', *Economic History Review*, 2nd ser. XXIX (1976) 591.

20. Ibid., pp. 589–90.

21. G. E. Fussell, *The English Dairy Farmer* (1966) pp. 290–4.

22, E. H. Whetham, 'The London Milk Trade, 1860–1900', *Economic History Review*, XVII (1964) 369–80.

23. Fussell, *The English Dairy Farmer*, pp. 312–3; E. H. Whetham, 'The London Milk Trade, 1900–1930' in D. J. Oddy and D. S. Miller (eds), *The Making of the Modern British Diet* (1976) p. 67.

24. H. A. MacEwan, *The Public Milk Supply* (Glasgow, 1910) p. 39.

25. Whetham, 'The London Milk Trade 1860–1900', p. 376.

26. *Fabian Tract*, no. 90. *The Municipalization of the Milk Trade* (July 1899).

27. Quoted in *Fabian Tract*, no. 122, *Municipal Milk and Public Health* (June 1905).

28. MacEwan, *The Public Milk Supply*, pp. 70–2.

29. Ibid., p. 66.

30. J. C. Drummond and A. Wilbraham, *The Englishman's Food* (1957), p. 303.

31. W. H. Beable, *The Romance of Great Businesses* (1926) pp. 209–10; A. Jenkins, *Drink a Pinta* (1970) p. 58.

32. Fussell, *The English Dairy Farmer*, pp. 290–1.

33. E. E. Williams, *Made in Germany* (1896) p. 65.

34. J. H. Van Stuyvenburg, *Margarine: An Economic Social and Scientific History* (Liverpool, 1959).

35. Williams, *The Foreigner in the Farmyard*, pp. 77–9.

36. Bear, 'The Food Supply of Manchester – Part II, *Journal of the Royal Agricultural Statistical Society of England*, 3rd, ser. VIII (1897) 512.

37. J. Dyson, *Business in Great Waters* (1977) pp. 58–9.

38. C. L. Cutting, *Fish Saving: A History of Fish Processing from Ancient to Modern Times* (1955) pp. 233–4.

39. Cutting, *Fish Saving*, p. 299; J. Blackman, 'The Food Supply of an Industrial Town: A Study of Sheffield's Public Markets, 1780–1900', *Business History*, v (1962–3) 94.

40. Cutting, *Fish Saving*, p. 241.

41. I am grateful to my colleague, Dr Gordon Jackson, for letting me use a typescript of his on the history of the Humber ports, and a great deal of my information on fishing is taken from this and from conversations with him.

42. F. G. Aflalo, *The Sea–Fishing Industry of England and Wales* (1904) p. 341.

43. J. J. Manley, 'Preservation of Food', in G. P. Bevan (ed.), *British Manufacturing Industries*, vol II (1876) p. 59.

44. Henry Mayhew, *Shops and Companies of London* (1865) p. 59.

45. E. H. Taylor, *The Story of Preserved Foods* (Newcastle-upon-Tyne, 1921).

46. Manley, 'Preservation of Food', p. 60.

47. O. C. Malvery, *The Soul Market*, 6th edn (n.d.) p. 99.

48. J. Burnett, *Plenty and Want* (1968) p. 160.

49. J. J. Manley, 'Bread and Biscuits' in Bevan (ed.), *British Manufacturing Industries*, p. 87.

50. G. Dodd, *The Food of London* (1856) p. 195.

51. J. Burnett, 'The Baking Industry in the Nineteenth Century', *Business History*, v (1962) 101.

52. Manley, 'Bread and Biscuits', p. 98.

53. C. Booth, *Life and Labour of the People in London: Industry*, III, 2nd ser. (1903) p. 155.

54. *Fabian Tract*, no. 94 (1894), *Municipal Bakeries* (December 1900).

55. R. Q. Gray, *The Labour Aristocracy in Victorian Edinburgh* (1976) p. 28.

56. P. Mathias, *Retailing Revolution* (1967) pp. 312–16.

57. J. T. Collins, 'The "Consumer Revolution" and the Growth of Factory Foods', in Oddy and Miller (eds), *The Making of the Modern British Diet*, pp. 29–30.

58. T. A. B. Corley, *Quaker Enterprise in Biscuits* (1972) p. 66.

59. J. S. Adams, *A Fell Fine Baker: The Story of United Biscuits* (1974) p. 12.

60. Corley, *Quaker Enterprise, passim*.

61. P. Redfern, *The History of the C. W. S., 1863–1913* (1913) pp. 169, 208.

62. F. Lewis, *Essex and Sugar* (1976).

63. Ibid., pp. 86–7.

64. N. Deer, *The History of Sugar* (1950).

65. D. Forrest, *Tea for the British: The Social and Economic History*

of a Famous Trade (1973) p. 189.

66. Mathias, *Retailing Revolution*, p. 102.

67. Beable, *The Romance of Great Businesses*, p. 38.

68. J. Othick, 'The Cocoa and Chocoate Industry in the Nineteenth Century', in Oddy and Miller (eds), *The Making of the Modern British Diet*, p. 79.

69. Ibid., p. 81.

70. Henry Mayhew, *Shops and Companies of London* (1865) pp. 174–6.

71. F. A. Mackenzie, *The American Invaders* (1902) p. 57.

72. C. B. Hawkins, *Norwich, a Social Study* (1910) p. 17.

73. Anon., *The Food Makers: A History of General Foods* (1972).

74. M. F. Davies, *Life in an English Village* (1909) p. 197; B. S. Rowntree and M. Kendall, *How the Labourer Lives: A Study of the Rural Labour Problem* (1913) p. 44.

75. P. Thompson, *The Edwardians* (1975) p. 180.

12. The Nation Clothed

1. Charles Kingsley, 'Cheap Clothes and Nasty', preface to *Alton Locke* (1849).

2. E. P. Thompson and E. Yeo, *The Unknown Mayhew* (1971) p. 236.

3. *Victoria County History: Essex*, II (1907) pp. 483–4.

4. C. Booth, *Life and Labour of the People in London: Industry*, IV, 2nd ser. (1903) p. 45.

5. Ibid., p. 55.

6. Joan Thomas. *A History of the Leeds Clothing Industry* Yorkshire Bulletin of Economic and Social Research, Occasional Paper, No. 1, Hull, 1955; D. Ryott, *John Barron's of Leeds* (Leeds, 1951).

7. *Men's Wear* (6 September 1902), quoted in Thomas, *Leeds Clothing Industry*, p. 44.

8. Thomas, *Leeds Clothing Industry*, p. 11.

9. R. B. Davies, '"Peacefully Working to Conquer the World": The Singer Manufacturing Company in Foreign Markets', *Business History Review*, XLIII, 3 (1969) 366–8.

10. J. H. Clapham, *An Economic History of Modern Britain*, vol. I (Cambridge, 1963) p. 181.

11. Thompson and Yeo, *The Unknown Mayhew*, p. 287.

12. H. Cox, *British Industries under Free Trade* (1903) p. 237.

13. F. W. Wheldon, *A Norvic Century* (Norwich, 1946) p. 145.

14. A. Fox, *A History of the National Union of Boot and Shoe Operatives* (Oxford, 1958) pp. 14–16.

15. *Shoe and Leather Record* (4 February 1888), quoted in Fox, *National Union of Boot and Shoe Operatives*, p. 26.

16. Booth, *Life and Labour of the People in London: Industry*, IV, 2nd ser. (1903) p. 74.

17. Fox, *National Union of Boot and Shoe Operatives*, p. 230–46.

18. *Victoria County History; Leicester*, III (1955) p. 28.

19. Fox, *National Union of Boot and Shoe Operatives*, p. 418.

20. K. Hudson, *Towards Precision Shoemaking: C. & J. Clark Limited and the Development of the British Shoemaking Industry* (Newton Abbot, 1968) *passim*.

21. P. Head, 'Boots and Shoes' in D. Aldcroft (ed.), *The Development of British Industry and Foreign Competition* (1968) pp. 161–2.

22. *Ibid.*, p. 170.

23. J. B. Jefferys, *Retail Trading in Britain, 1850–1950* (Cambridge, 1954) p. 268.

24. W. H. G. Armytage, *A. J. Mundella 1825–1897: The Liberal Background to the Labour Movement* (1951).

25. K. Jopp, *Corah of Leicester, 1815–1965* (Leicester, 1965) p. 11.

26. F. A. Wells, *The British Hosiery and Knitwear Industry* (Newton Abbot, 1972).

27. Booth, *Life and Labour: Industry*, III, p. 31.

28. *Victoria County History: Bedfordshire*, II (1908) pp. 120–1.

29. R. E. Tyson, 'Cotton Industry', in Aldcroft, *The Development of British Industry*, p. 103.

30. S. J. Chapman, *The Lancashire Cotton Industry* (Manchester, 1904).

31. J. D. Clapham, *An Economic History of Modern Britain*, vol. III (Cambridge, 1963) p. 176.

32. E. M. Sigsworth and J. M. Blackman, 'The Woollen and Worsted Industries' in Aldcroft (ed.), *The Development of British Industry*, ch. 5.

33. G. C. Allen, *The Industrial Development of Birmingham and the Black Country* (1966 edn) p. 312.

34. R. A. Church, *Economic and Social Change in a Midland Town: Victorian Nottingham, 1815–1900* (1966) pp. 290–1.

35. *Victoria County History: Warwickshire*, VII (1969) p. 128.

36. Allen, *The Industrial Development of Birmingham*, p. 164. 2d a gross was the price paid for this task in 1862; *Victoria County History: Warwickshire*, VII, p. 131.

37. *Victoria County History: Warwickshire*, VII, p. 162.

38. Allen, *The Industrial Development of Birmingham*, p. 258; W. C. Aitken, 'Needles' in G. P. Bevan (ed.), *British Manufacturing Industries*, vol. III (1876) p. 107.

39. M. Blair, *Paisley Thread* (Paisley, 1907) p. 49.

40. *Ibid.*, p. 62.

41. *Glasgow Herald* (11 November 1905).

42. *Report into Alleged Existence of a Combine among the Manufacturers of Sewing Cotton* (1920).

43. *Victoria County History: Warwickshire*, VII, p. 144.

44. Bevan (ed.), *British Manufacturing Industries*, vol. III, p. 73.

45. R. A. Church, 'Nineteenth-Century Clock Technology in Britain, the United States and Switzerland', *Economic History Review*, 2nd ser., XXVIII 4 (1975) 621.

46. *Victoria County History: Lancaster*, II (1908) p. 367; F. J. Britten, 'Watches and Clocks' in Bevan (ed.), *British Manufacturing Industries*. pp. 73–103.

47. Booth, *Life and Labour: Industry*, II, pp. 26–9; Church, 'Nineteenth-Century Clock Technology', p. 626.

13. The Nation Furnished

1. D. Yarwood, *The English Home* (1956) pp. 336–7.
2. J. E. Panton, *From Kitchen to Garret: Hints for Young Householders* (1890) pp. 51–71.
3. Ibid., p. 30.
4. I have been unable to find anything except the barest of information on the important paint industry – see Yarwood, *The English Home*; G. D. Holley, *Analysis of Mixed Paints, Colour Pigment and Varnishes* (1908).
5. H. J. Schonfield, *The Book of British Industries* (1933) p. 365.
6. For the carpet industry see J. Neville Bartlett, *Carpeting the Millions* (Edinburgh, 1978).
7. Yarwood, *The English Home*, p. 347.
8. Augustus Muir, *Nairn's of Kirkcaldy: A Short History of the Company* (Cambridge, 1956).
9. Mrs. C. S. Peel, *The New Home* (1898) p. 59.
10. E. P. Thompson and E. Yeo, *The Unknown Mayhew* (1971) pp. 469–71.
11. C. Booth, *Life and Labour of the People in London: Industry* I (1903) pp. 180–3.
12. This section draws on I. G. Sparkes, *The English Country Chair* (Bourne End, 1973) pp. 24–35.
13. *Victoria County History: Buckingham*, II (1908) p. 110; J. L. Oliver, 'A Study of the Location and Migration of the Furniture Industry in Metropolitan England', unpublished Ph.D. Thesis, University of London, 1962.
14. *Victoria County History: Warwickshire*, VII (1969) p. 131, G. C. Allen, *The Industrial Development of Birmingham and the Black Country* (1966 edn) pp. 60, 217.
15. Muir, *Nairn's of Kirkcaldy*, p. 61; G. Christie, *Storey's of Lancaster, 1848–1964* (1964) p. 123.
16. *Victoria County History: Staffordshire*, II (1967) pp. 28–32.
17. Ibid.
18. Yarwood, *The English Home*, pp. 352–4.
19. Allen, *The Industrial Development of Birmingham*, p. 270.
20. *Victoria County History: Warwickshire*, VIII, p. 147.
21. H. Nockolds, *Lucas: The First Hundred Years* (Newton Abbot, 1976) pp. 30–1.
22. *Victoria County History: Surrey*, II (1905) p. 397.
23. W. Minchinton, *The British Tinplate Industry: A History* (Oxford, 1957) pp. 26, 35.
24. *Victoria County History: Staffordshire*, II (1967) pp. 174–9.
25. Allen, *The Industrial Development of Birmingham*, p. 152.
26. R. A. Church, *Kenricks in Hardware: A Family Business* (Newton Abbot, 1968).
27. G. I. H. Lloyd, *The Cutlery Trades* (1913) p. 182.
28. Ibid., p. 41.

29. Ibid., p. 347.
30. Peel, *The New Home*, p. 71.
31. For developments in the soap industry I have relied on C. Wilson, *History of Unilever*, vol I (1954) and A. E. Musson, *Enterprise in Soap and Chemicals: Joseph Crosfield and Sons Ltd* (Manchester, 1965).
32. B. N. Reckitt, *The History of Reckitt and Sons Ltd* (1951) p. 23.
33. Ibid., p. 50.
34. Ibid., p. 18.

14.   The Nation Entertained

1. D. H. Robertson, *A Study of Industrial Fluctuations* (1915) p. 197.
2. M. Girouard, *The Victorian Pub* (1975) p. 181.
3. G. M. Wilson, *Alcohol and the Nation* (1940) p. 101.
4. Girouard, *The Victorian Pub*, p. 77.
5. Ibid., p. 75.
6. J. Vaizey, *The Brewing Industry, 1886–1951* (1960) pp. 5–6.
7. Wilson, *Alcohol and the Nation*, p. 48.
8. B. Harrison, *Drink and the Victorians* (1971) p. 325.
9. Original prospectus of the Club and Institute Union, quoted in Wilson, *Alcohol and the Nation*, p. 136.
10. A. Andrews, *The Whisky Barons* (1977) p. 39.
11. C. Booth, *Life and Labour of the People in London: Industry*, III, 2nd ser. (1903) pp. 130–1.
12. J. Bone, *The London Perambulator* (1925) *passim*.
13. Quoted in G. L. Apperson, *The Social History of Smoking* (1914) p. 167.
14. Booth, *Life and Labour: Industry*, II, p. 67.
15. B. W. E. Alford, *W. D. & H. O. Wills and the Development of the U.K. Tobacco Industry, 1786–1965* (1973) p. 171.
16. 'Of Time, Work and Leisure', in M. R. Marrus (ed.), *The Emergence of Leisure* (New York, 1974) pp. 70–100.
17. James Walvin, *The People's Game: A Social History of British Football* (1975) pp. 56–7.
18. S. Yeo, *Religion and Voluntary Organisations in Crisis* (1976) pp. 189–96.
19. Walvin, *The People's Game*, p. 75.
20. G. B. Wilson, 'Variations in the Consumption of Intoxicating Drinks in the U.K.', *Journal of the Royal Statistical Society*, LXXV (1912) 205.
21. Wray Vamplew, *The Turf* (1976) p. 41.
22. R. Mander and J. Mitcheson, *British Music Hall* (1974) pp. 21–9.
23. Quoted in Ibid., p. 49.
24. G. J. Mellor, *The Northern Music Hall* (1970) *passim*.
25. A. Delgado, *Victorian Entertainment* (Newton Abbot, 1972) p. 79.
26. J. Walvin, *Beside the Seaside* (1978) p. 82.
27. R. J. Cruickshank, *The Roaring Century, 1846–1946*, pp. 142–3; Asa Briggs, *Mass Entertainment: The Origins of a Modern Industry* (Adelaide, 1960) p. 15; G. J. Mellor, *Picture Pioneers* (Newcastle, 1971).
28. Briggs, *Mass Entertainment*, pp. 15–16.

29. A. E. Harrison, 'The Competetiveness of the British Cycle Industry, 1890–1914', *Economic History Review*, 2nd ser., xxii 2 (1969) 287.

30. Ibid., p. 289.

31. L. J. Franks and H. E. C. Newham (eds), *The Port of Hull and its Facilities for Trade* (Hull, 1907) p. 204.

32. Harrison, 'The Competetiveness of the British Cycle Industry', p. 297.

33. *Victoria County History: Warwickshire*, viii (1969) pp. 172–4.

34. S. B. Saul, 'The Motor Industry in Britain to 1914', *Business History*, v (1962–63) 22–44.

35. James Walvin, *Beside the Seaside* (1978) p. 38.

36. G. J. Mellor, *Pom-Poms and Ruffles: The Story of Northern Seaside Entertainment* (Clapham (via Lancaster) Yorkshire, 1966).

37. J. K. Walton, 'The Pursuit of Happiness at the Seaside', paper given to the Anglo-American Historical Conference, London, 1979.

38. Tonie and Valmai Holt, *Picture Postcards of the Golden Age* (1971).

39. H. and A. Gernsheim, *A Concise History of Photography* (1965).

40. R. D. Altick, *The English Common Reader* (Chicago, 1957) pp. 286–7.

41. S. Morison, *The English Newspaper* (Cambridge 1932) p. 251.

42. F. A. Munby, *The House of Routledge, 1834–1934* (1934) pp. 41ff.

43. H. Maxwell, *Life of W. H. Smith*, quoted in Munby, *The House of Routledge*, p. 40.

44. Munby, *The House of Routledge*, p. 51.

45. *Edinburgh Review*, clxv (1887), 'The Literature of the Street'. pp. 43, 47, quoted in Altick, *The English Common Reader*, p. 308.

46. G. L. Griest, *Mudie's Circulating Library and the Victorian Novel* (Newton Abbot, 1970) pp. 176–212.

47. Altick, *The English Common Reader*, p. 315.

48. F. A. Mackenzie, *The American Invaders*, p. 71.

49. A. Sinclair, *Fifty Years of Newspaper Life, 1845–1895* (privately printed, n.d.) p. 87.

50. John Knox, *The Masses Without*, quoted in John McCaffrey (ed.), *Shadow's Midnight Scenes* (Glasgow, 1858; reprinted 1976).

51. Cruickshank, *The Roaring Century*, p. 66.

52. Morison, *The English Newspaper*, p. 270.

53. Ibid., p. 296.

54. S. Dark, *The Life of Sir Arthur Pearson* (n.d.) p. 88

55. E. S. Turner, *Boys Will Be Boys* (1957).

56. *Address of Robert Donald to the Institute of Journalists* (18 August 1913).

Caveats and Conclusions

1. H. Dyer, *The Evolution of Industry* (1895) pp. 81–2.

2. F. A. Mackenzie, *The American Invaders* (1902) pp. 59–61.

3. E. E. Williams, *Made in Germany* (1896), *The Foreigner in the Farmyard* (1897).

4. For a discussion of the literature see S. B. Saul, *The Myth of the Great Depression, 1876–96* (1972).

5. Quoted in C. M. Wilson, 'Economy and Society in Late Victorian Britain', *Economic History Review*, 2nd ser., xviii (1965) 184.

6. Ibid, pp. 189–90.

7. Mackenzie, *The American Invaders*, pp. 19–20.

Suggestions for Further Reading

Part I   The Growth of Demand

The most useful summary of population change can be found in R. Mitchison, *British Population Change Since 1860* (1979), which contains a full bibliography. On incomes and expenditure there is a variety of important works: J. A. Banks, *Prosperity and Parenthood* (1954) is about the middle classes and J. H. Treble, *Urban Poverty in Britain* (1979) for the other end of the social spectrum. J. Burnett, *A History of the Cost of Living* (1969) seeks to provide a national picture, but E. H Hunt, *Regional Wage Variations in Britain, 1850–1914* (Oxford, 1973), G. Barnsby, 'The Standard of Living in the Black Country during the Nineteenth Century', *Economic History Review*, xxiv (1971) 220–39, E. Hopkins, 'Small Town Aristocrats of Labour and their Standard of Living, 1840–1914', *Economic History Review*, xxviii (1975) 222–42, and E. Roberts, 'Working-Class Standards of Living in Barrow and Lancaster, 1890–1914', *Economic History Review*, xxx (1977) 306–21, all reveal the significance of regional variations.

Rather variable collections of essays on diet can be found in T. C. Barker, J. C. Mckenzie and J. Yudkin (eds), *Our Changing Fare: Two Hundred Years of British Food Habits* (1966) and in D. J. Oddy and D. S. Miller (eds), *The Making of the Modern British Diet* (1976). There is also J. Burnett's *Plenty and Want: A Social History of Diet in England from 1815 to the Present* (1966). For housing and rent see E. Gauldie, *Cruel Habitations* (1974).

There are a number of delightful contemporary studies from which important insights can be gained, such as S. Reynolds, *A Poor Man's House* (1908) and *Seems So!* (1913), O. C. Malvery, *The Soul Market* (n.d.), Mrs Pember Reeves, *Round About a Pound a Week* (1913), Thomas Wright ('The Journeyman Engineer'), *Some Habits and Customs of the Working Class* (1868) and *Our New Masters* (1873), and Lady Florence Bell, *At the Works* (1911). The incomparable Henry Mayhew's *London Labour and the London Poor* (1851) available in a variety of editions should not be missed, together with the collection of additional material in E. P. Thompson and E. Yeo, *The Unknown Mayhew* (1971). There are also reminiscences such as Flora Thompson, *Lark Rise to Candleford* (Oxford, 1945), M. V. Hughes, *A London Family, 1870–1900* and Robert Roberts, *The Classic Slum, Salford Life in the First Quarter of the Century* (1971). Paul Thompson's *The Edwardians* (1975) is based on interviews.

Part II   The Stimulation of Demand

For changes in retailing the starting point is the comprehensive and pioneering study by J. B. Jefferys, *Retail Trading in Britain, 1850–1950* (Cambridge, 1954). For a study of one particular group of shops which includes some of the main multiples see Peter Mathias, *Retailing Revolution* (1967). Other works dealing with aspects of retailing are Alison Aldburgham, *Shops and Shopping* (1967), Asa Briggs, *Friends of the People: The Centenary History of Lewis's* (1956) and S. Chapman, *Jesse Boot of Boots the Chemist* (1974).

D. and G. Hindley, *Advertising in Victorian England, 1837–1901* (1972) is the best recent account of developments in this area, but E. S. Turner, *The Shocking History of Advertising* (1952) is still a useful little work.

Part III   Demand Satisfied

Business histories vary tremendously in quality. Many have been written with the uncritical glorification of a particular company as their purpose, while others are largely anecdotal. However, an increasing number of important academic works is now being published. Some of the recent ones include, B. W. E. Alford, *W. D. & H. O. Wills and the Development of the U.K. Tobacco Industry, 1786–1965* (1973), T. A. B. Corley, *Quaker Enterprise in Biscuits: Huntley and Palmers of Reading, 1822–1972* (1972), Charles Wilson, *The History of Unilever* (1954), A. E. Musson, *Enterprise in Soap and Chemicals, Joseph Crosfield & Sons Ltd, 1815–1965* (Manchester, 1965).

A valuable start to a study of the clothing industry has been made by Joan Thomas, *A History of the Leeds Clothing Industry, Yorkshire Bulletin of Economic and Social Research*, Occasional Paper, No. 1, (Hull, 1955) but much still remains to be done in this area.

Leisure activities have recently attracted the attention of a number of historians. Works include James Walvin's *Beside the Seaside* (1978) and *The People's Game: A Social History of British Football* (1975). M. Girouard, *The Victorian Pub* (1975), which is largely about London's public houses, should be read along with B. Harrison's essay, 'Pubs', in J. Dyos and S. Wolff (eds), *The Victorian City: Images and Realities*, Wray Vamplew, *The Turf* (1976) focuses on another key area of working-class leisure, and more respectable pursuits are studied in S. Yeo, *Religion and Voluntary Organisations in Crisis* (1976), which deals mainly with Reading. P. Bailey, *Leisure and Class in Victorian England* (1978) draws its examples mainly from Lancashire. Asa Briggs's short piece, *Mass Entertainment, the Origins of a Modern Industry* (Adelaide, 1960) pointed historians in new directions, but is only gradually being followed up. There is surprisingly little on book publishing and on newspapers and Stanley Morison, *The English Newspaper* (1932) is still a key source.

Index

261